Research and Education

This core text, now in its second edition, provides an easy-to-read, comprehensive introduction to educational research that will develop your understanding of research strategies, theories and methods, giving you the confidence and enthusiasm to discuss and write about your research effectively.

Specifically written for undergraduate education studies students, the book guides you through the process of planning a research project, the different research methods available and how to carry out your research and write it up successfully. Highlighting the theoretical and methodological debates and discussing important ethical and practical considerations, the book is structured to help you tackle all the different aspects of your project from writing your literature review, designing a questionnaire and analysing your data to the final writing up. This new edition is updated throughout with activities, case studies and further reading lists.

New chapters include:

- Mixed-methods research.
- Narrative inquiry.
- Creative and visual research methods.
- Extended chapter on research with children and vulnerable groups.

Part of the *Foundations of Education Studies* series, this timely new edition is essential reading for students undertaking a research methods course or a piece of educational research.

Sam Shields is Senior Lecturer in Education at Newcastle University, UK.

Alina Schartner is Senior Lecturer in Applied Linguistics at Newcastle University, UK.

Will Curtis is Professor and Deputy Pro-Vice Chancellor (Education, Quality and Standards) at the University of Warwick, UK.

Mark Murphy is Reader in Educational Leadership and Policy at the University of Glasgow, UK.

Foundations of Education Studies Series

This is a series of books written specifically to support undergraduate education studies students. Each book provides a broad overview to a fundamental area of study exploring the key themes and ideas to show how these relate to education. Accessibly written with chapter objectives, individual and group tasks, case studies and suggestions for further reading, the books will give students an essential understanding of the key disciplines in education studies, forming the foundations for future study.

Policy and Education
Paul Adams

Philosophy and Education: An Introduction to Key Questions and Themes
Joanna Haynes, Ken Gale and Mel Parker

Psychology and Education
Diahann Gallard and Katherine M. Cartmell

Placements and Work-based Learning in Education Studies: An Introduction For Students
Edited by Jim Hordern and Catherine Simon

Research and Education: An Introduction to Methods, Approaches and Processes (2nd edition)
Sam Shields, Alina Schartner, Will Curtis and Mark Murphy

Forthcoming titles

Sociology and Education
Richard Waller and Tamsin Bowers-Brown

Research and Education

An Introduction to Methods, Approaches and Processes

Second Edition

Sam Shields, Alina Schartner,
Will Curtis and Mark Murphy

LONDON AND NEW YORK

Designed cover image: © Thinkstock

Second edition published 2025
by Routledge
4 Park Square, Milton Park, Abingdon, Oxon, OX14 4RN

and by Routledge
605 Third Avenue, New York, NY 10158

Routledge is an imprint of the Taylor & Francis Group, an informa business

© 2025 Sam Shields, Alina Schartner, Will Curtis and Mark Murphy

The right of Sam Shields, Alina Schartner, Will Curtis and Mark Murphy to be identified as authors of this work has been asserted in accordance with sections 77 and 78 of the Copyright, Designs and Patents Act 1988.

All rights reserved. No part of this book may be reprinted or reproduced or utilised in any form or by any electronic, mechanical, or other means, now known or hereafter invented, including photocopying and recording, or in any information storage or retrieval system, without permission in writing from the publishers.

Trademark notice: Product or corporate names may be trademarks or registered trademarks, and are used only for identification and explanation without intent to infringe.

First edition published by Routledge 2014

British Library Cataloguing-in-Publication Data
A catalogue record for this book is available from the British Library

Library of Congress Cataloging-in-Publication Data
Names: Shields, Sam, 1979- author. | Schartner, Alina, author. | Curtis, Will, Dr., author. | Murphy, Mark, 1969 June 17- author.
Title: Research and education : an introduction to methods, approaches and processes / Sam Shields, Alina Schartner, Will Curtis, Mark Murphy.
Description: Second edition. | Abingdon, Oxon ; New York, NY : Routledge, 2025. | Series: Foundations of education studies | Includes bibliographical references and index. | Identifiers: LCCN 2024035995 (print) | LCCN 2024035996 (ebook) | ISBN 9781032944470 (hardback) | ISBN 9781032942100 (paperback) | ISBN 9781003569428 (ebook)
Classification: LCC LB1028 .C87 2025 (print) | LCC LB1028 (ebook) | DDC 370.72--dc23/eng/20240810
LC record available at https://lccn.loc.gov/2024035995
LC ebook record available at https://lccn.loc.gov/2024035996

ISBN: 978-1-032-94447-0 (hbk)
ISBN: 978-1-032-94210-0 (pbk)
ISBN: 978-1-003-56942-8 (ebk)

DOI: 10.4324/9781003569428

Typeset in Bembo
by KnowledgeWorks Global Ltd.

Contents

1 Introduction: Approaches to educational research   1

PART I
Planning an education research project   7

2 Choosing a topic and writing a proposal   9

3 Reviewing the literature   18

4 Sampling   28

5 Data analysis   37

6 Writing up your research project   48

PART II
Research strategies   59

7 Surveys   61

8 Mixed-methods research   69

9 Case studies   80

10 Ethnography   87

11 Action research   97

12 Narrative inquiry   104

PART III
Methods of data collection 111

13 Questionnaires 113

14 Interviews and focus groups 125

15 Observations 135

16 Documents 145

17 Creative and visual research methods 153

PART IV
Theorising research 161

18 Using theories and concepts in educational research 163

19 Evaluating methods 169

20 Ethical issues in educational research 178

21 Research with children and vulnerable groups 186

Glossary 200
Index 203

CHAPTER 1

Introduction: Approaches to educational research

Introduction

This chapter introduces students to the nature of research, considering in particular the meaning of 'research' and approaches to educational research. The chapter also looks at key research paradigms, presenting the key differences between scientific (i.e positivist) and interpretivist perspectives. It will then explore some of the popular themes and topics within educational research. The chapter ends with useful recommendations for further reading in relation to qualitative and quantitative research.

What do we mean by educational research?

Mertler (2022) provides a good definition of educational research. 'Educational research requires the collection, analysis, and interpretation of data as a means of answering the inherent questions or problem under investigation' (Mertler, 2022: 7). This definition is a concise statement of the focus of this book. Collecting information in order to answer an educational research question is significant for many reasons – political, personal, social and cultural. Developments in education receive coverage in the media as understanding the implications of educational research findings is significant to many stakeholders: parents, pupils, educational professionals and policymakers.

ACTIVITY

Have a look at a media source, for example newspaper or news website:
- How many stories can you identify related to education?
- What sort of educational themes/topics are present in the news articles?

DOI: 10.4324/9781003569428-1

Educational researchers may ask questions related to:

- How do children learn?
- What are the most effective approaches to teaching in the classroom?
- Does social class matter in the classroom?
- What curriculum works best for primary school pupils?
- What subjects should pupils' study in secondary school?
- How do students experience study in higher education?

These are just some examples of popular questions asked in education research, but the list is endless, with more and more specialised questions engaging researchers. This vast field of research is also reflected in the ever-increasing number of academic journals devoted to the topic area, including journals devoted to specific subjects such as music education, mathematics education and physical education, as well as journals that focus on specific thematic areas such as special educational needs, teaching and learning in higher education and the sociology of education.

Approaches to educational research

Alongside this diversity of topics, there is also a wide variety of research *designs*.

Comparative

Comparative research designs are particularly popular when doing educational research across different countries, for example comparing the early years' provision in Italy and England. However, comparative research does not have to involve the use of different countries, it can also be used in thinking about rural and urban educational contexts, private and state educational provision, formal and informal learning contexts or comparisons based on demographic characteristics shaping experiences of education. The significance of comparative research is that it helps us to understand similarities and differences across contexts. Comparative research is generally descriptive.

Case study

A case study tends to be largely qualitative in approach and it is up to the researcher to decide what constitutes the 'case'. A 'case' might be a school or a classroom or a teacher. The researcher will want to present a deep and holistic descriptive portrayal of the 'case' using a variety of research methods, for example interviews, observations, policy document analysis and visual research methods. Case study research is often criticised for its lack of generalisability – indeed the purpose of case study research is to present a unique description. However, it can be argued that the depth of the portrayal of a 'case' can mean that this is transferable to another setting, for example we might be able to see similarities to another suburban primary school based on the analysis of the data.

Longitudinal design

Longitudinal research is likely to span many years. Longitudinal research can capture changes over time. A longitudinal piece of research might use a series of surveys to identify changes amongst a set of participants over time. A challenge with longitudinal research is that of attrition, as it may be that the participants do not continue to participate over time. A great example of educational research using this design is the Millennium Cohort Study (UCL, 2024: https://cls.ucl.ac.uk/cls-studies/millennium-cohort-study/) which follows children and their families over time. This type of research is extremely important for identifying trends and patterns amongst groups with different demographic characteristics. However, it is a very expensive type of research and is not typically available to students who often have a relatively limited time to complete a piece of research. Nevertheless, it is an important design to be aware of for its strengths and limitations.

Cross-sectional design

A cross-sectional design provides a snapshot of a population often on one day. The population should be demographically representative. This type of research has some similarities to longitudinal research, as a series of snapshots might be taken over a period of time. However, whilst the population is always deemed to be representative, it is not the same population (as you would see in a longitudinal design). In order for the population to be representative, it is likely that this is going to be a large study and quantitative approaches are likely to be used in order to make sense of patterns statistically, amongst and between the different participants, within the population sample.

Experimental design

A true experiment involves the manipulation of an independent variable with a dependent variable remaining the same. A classic example of this might be testing the efficacy of a new medicine. Participants would be randomly allocated into two groups: 'control' group and 'test' group. The difference in health outcomes between the 'control' group (who received a placebo) and the 'test' group (who received the new medicine) can be evaluated. In order to test the impact of the intervention, there is generally a pre-test to establish baseline data ahead of the intervention, and then a post-test to measure the impact/effectiveness of the intervention. In educational research, it can be very difficult to conduct a true experiment so it is more likely that a quasi-experimental design will be adopted. A quasi-experiment will not randomly assign participants, but instead use natural occurring groups, for example two classes at the same school, this means a number of variables can influence the effectiveness of interventions. A further challenge with 'post-tests' in educational settings is that children will naturally mature over time, making it difficult to ascertain the efficacy of the intervention. However, despite the challenges of experimental research within educational settings, Randomised Control Trials remain a gold standard form of research. The classic reading on experimental research is from Campbell and Stanley (1963).

Research paradigms in educational research

Research in the social sciences has classically been thought of as two opposing paradigms. Positivism is a 'scientific' approach using many principles of research from the natural sciences, for example:

- The researcher is viewed as neutral and value-free with an objective research approach being highly valued.
- Numerical data collection enabling statistical analysis of correlations between variables is a preferred approach to data analysis.

Interpretivism is an approach which focuses on understanding meaning, recognising the socially constructed nature of society and the different perceptions and experiences people may have:

- The researcher recognises their own positionality and recognises their own subjectivity in relation to the research
- Descriptive data enables rich and detailed accounts of the experiences and perceptions of research participants

As Curtis and Pettigrew point out, the positivistic approach, which held sway for so long across the social sciences in the first half of the twentieth century, became the focus of sustained criticism once the sheen of 'science' had worn off the study of the social world. An alternative framework was offered 'by those who saw research as an interpretive rather than scientific act' (Curtis and Pettigrew, 2010: 58). However, it was always bound to be thus since ideas, concepts and intellectual frameworks borrowed from another sector, in this case the natural sciences, can never be copied and transplanted wholesale into another sector (the social sciences) without a certain amount of disjuncture and dissonance. Thus a movement that Cohen, Manion and Morrison (2007: 19) labelled 'anti-positivism' developed in the latter half of the twentieth century, staking a claim for a more appropriate framework for social science research. Cohen, Manion and Morrison provide a useful summary of this position below.

> In rejecting the viewpoint of the detached, objective researcher – a mandatory feature of traditional research – anti-positivists would argue that individuals' behaviour can only be understood by the researcher sharing their frame of reference: understanding of individuals' interpretations of the world around them has to come from the inside, not the outside. Social science is thus seen as a subjective rather than an objective undertaking, as a means of dealing with the direct experience of people in specific contexts, and

where social scientists understand, explain and demystify social reality through the eyes of different participants; the participants themselves define the social reality.

(Cohen, Manion and Morrison, 2007: 19)

Increasingly, there has been a focus on 'paradigm peace' (Bryman, 2006) as researchers consider the compatibility of qualitative and quantitative research methods. However, suffice to say that these two broadly opposed positions result in different sets of assumptions regarding the nature and purpose of educational research, revolving around a value-free (positivist) versus a value-laden (interpretivist) notion of the researcher and their relationship to their research subjects. Furthermore, this distinction sometimes gets translated into the *quantitative* vs. *qualitative* debate, but whilst there are certainly parallels in that positivist research tends to favour quantitative approaches, these two dichotomies are not the same. The decision to use a quantitative approach (i.e. an approach that places emphasis on the analysis of numbers) as opposed to a qualitative approach (i.e. one that places emphasis on meaning) should be centred on whether or not the respective methodologies are fit for purpose. After all, any form of research has both a qualitative and a quantitative element; at some stage all research must unavoidably involve some form of observation and some kind of measurement, regardless of the phenomenon under investigation.

Educational research themes

Education research groups in universities are organised under a broad range of themes and may also be interdisciplinary. The following are some of the most popular areas of focus in educational research:

- Social justice: This theme considers the educational opportunities of marginalised and disadvantaged groups and experiences of social mobility.
- Curriculum, assessment and pedagogy: This theme explores curricula content decisions, as well as the different ways in which learning can be assessed. This theme asks questions about different pedagogic styles, as well as how different groups might learn and the impact of educational policies on teachers and learners.
- Comparative education: This theme examines education across the world, as well as understanding how communication and culture can shape experiences of learning.
- Educational selves and identities: This theme examines the identities of learners and teachers and how these understandings of ourselves can shape our sense of belonging, confidence and engagement in educational contexts.

Furthermore, research in education can also focus on specific age phases, for example 'early years' or 'higher education', 'adult learning' or 'professional learning'. It can also be related to a specific subject, such as 'Music education' and research may be underpinned by one of the core disciplines of education, such as sociology or psychology.

> **ACTIVITY**
>
> Have a look at education departments on university websites to get a sense of the type of educational topics that are researched by academics.

Chapter summary

In this chapter, educational research has been defined. Furthermore, different educational research designs have been considered, such as comparative and longitudinal approaches. The chapter has provided an account of positivism and interpretivism, as the two research paradigms frequently underpinning educational research. Finally, the chapter has outlined popular research themes within the field of education.

Further reading

Hilton, A. and Hilton, G. (2020) 'Introduction to education research and practitioner research: What is it and why do it?' in *Learning to research and researching to learn: An educator's guide*. Cambridge: Cambridge University Press, pp. 1–17. doi:10.1017/9781108678872.002.

- This book is aimed at educational practitioners, but it is very helpful as it does not presuppose any knowledge of educational research. Therefore, points are carefully explained and some of the approaches discussed are applicable to those wishing to conduct small-scale, individual pieces of research.

Wellington, J.J. (2020) *Educational research: Contemporary issues and practical approaches*. 2nd edn. London: Bloomsbury Academic.

- An accessible and engaging introduction to understanding educational research, including helpful definitions of methodology, paradigms and some of the research approaches that are popular to use in educational research.

References

Bryman, A. (2006) 'Paradigm peace and the implications for quality', *International Journal of Social Research Methodology*, 9(2), pp. 111–126. doi:10.1080/13645570600595280.

Campbell, D. and Stanley, J. (1963) 'Experimental and quasi-experimental designs for research on teaching', in Gage, N. (ed.) *Handbook of research on teaching*. Chicago: Rand McNally.

Cohen, L., Manion, L. and Morrison, K. (2007) *Research methods in education*. 6th edn. London: Routledge.

Curtis, W. and Pettigrew, A. (2010) *Education studies: Reflective reader*. Exeter: Learning Matters.

Mertler, C.A. (2022) *Introduction to educational research*. 3rd edn. London: SAGE.

UCL (2024) *Millennium cohort study*. Available at: https://cls.ucl.ac.uk/cls-studies/millennium-cohort-study/ (Accessed: 12 January 2024).

PART

I

Planning an education research project

CHAPTER 2

Choosing a topic and writing a proposal

Introduction

Planning a research project begins with choosing a topic to research, and then writing a research proposal that describes the aims, objectives and rationale of the research (including its key research questions), the theoretical framework, the literature in the field, and the methodology and data collection methods that will be adopted in order to carry out the research. This chapter looks at how to choose a worthwhile topic to research in the field of education. It then explores the key components of a research proposal. The final section provides some useful tips on the writing process.

Choosing a topic

As outlined in the introductory chapter (see Chapter 1), the following are some of the most popular areas of focus in educational research and studies related to these themes are provided as a springboard for ideas:

Social justice

- An exploration of how teachers incorporate their beliefs about social justice into their teaching (Gandolfi and Mills, 2023).
- A study into how schools can support inclusivity for students (Horrigmo and Midtsundstad, 2023).
- Research exploring the extent to which 'local' students feel that they belong in higher education institutions (Ahn and Davis, 2023).

Curriculum, assessment and pedagogy

- A study into how primary school teachers in Australia interpreted the curriculum in relation to their subject knowledge and their understanding of pupils (Ross, 2023).
- A study analysing conversations, discussing understandings of feedback between students and academics, demonstrating that feedback literacy has the potential to be further developed (Matthews et al., 2024).
- A case study exploring if secondary school pupils had the potential to make effective mentors to beginning teachers (Albert, Scott and Rincon, 2023).

Comparative education

- This study is a comparative co-constructed narrative inquiry of three graduate student researchers (Nam et al., 2023).
- This study compares the experiences of loneliness amongst Chinese international students and local students in Germany (Bilecen, Diekmann and Faist, 2023).
- This study compares the leadership experiences of Charter School Principals in the USA and Academy School leaders in England (Ritchie, 2023).

Educational selves and identities

- This study considers the identities of grandparents as they engage in outdoor play with their grandchildren (Duflos, Hussaina and Brussoni, 2023).
- This interview-based study focused on the teacher identity development of classroom volunteers (Ballantyne, 2022).
- This study explores the conflicting identities of LGBTQ+ students (Trinh and Faulkner, 2023).

ACTIVITY

1. Read one of the articles above as a starting point to explore possible topic ideas and research designs.
2. Jot down any areas of educational research that you are interested in. A good starting point might be a reading from modules/topics that you have studied, stories in the media or a library search.

What should go into a research proposal?

If there is one guiding principle when putting together a research proposal, it should be clarity. How clear is your research topic? How well-defined is your research design? How explicit is the rationale, and how convincing is the stated significance of your proposed research? Clarity of thought is a must at any stage of the research process, but it is particularly essential at the proposal stage because this document forms an intellectual and practical plan for the rest of your study. As a result, any lack of clarity will have consequences for the quality of your research outcomes.

A secondary principle would be to 'keep it real' – be realistic about what you can achieve, and don't set yourself impossible targets that you have no hope of meeting. Of course, this is common sense, but all too often new researchers may feel they have to aim high, making bold claims and setting out to achieve startling originality. However, a good start to a successful research career would be more about making a useful and relevant contribution to the educational research community via a well-managed and thought-through project. A proposal will usually have the following parts (with minor variations):

Background to the research question: This section of your proposal should aim to both introduce the research area and provide the context within which it is situated. You are explaining to the reader why your topic might be timely and appropriate, and pointing out where the research question 'fits' within the overall education community and its set of interests. This section effectively functions as a narrative 'frame' within which the importance of your own research topic is highlighted – you are making a claim for the usefulness of your proposed research. For example, take the debate over the relationship between diet and learning in primary school classrooms. Some argue that there is a strong link between the two: do pupils learn more effectively if they have had a proper breakfast, or does it matter what kind of breakfast they have? It might be the case that not many researchers have focused on the importance of *lunch*, and what kinds of foods are eaten at lunchtime. This gap in the established knowledge base could be used as background context for your own research. This section should include some references to the existing research on the topic, so you should include some of the relevant literature while also making reference to the policy context. This is a vital aspect of your proposal – while it is not expected that you will have read the literature in great detail, it is useful to indicate that you know what it includes and what kinds of general research results have been gathered.

Statement of research question: Based on the narrative you provided in Section 1, you should then go on to provide a statement of your own research question – for example, 'What impact do different types of lunch have on afternoon learning outcomes?', 'How are notions of teacher professionalism shaped by different forms of management?', 'What is the role of parental expectations in educational achievement?'. Whatever your focus, the statement of your research question must be as precise as possible.

Aims and objectives: The aims and objectives should follow logically from the statement of your research question. The aim refers to the general rationale for the project, while the objectives detail the steps by which you will achieve the aim. This part of the proposal can cause as much anxiety at the statement of the research problem, but any anxiety is usually worth it because the clarity of these aims and objectives is a significant indicator of whether or not the research project will be a success – that is, whether it will achieve its aims. Any ambiguity at this stage is a clear indicator of an ambiguous design, which will result in ambiguous findings. Therefore, it is recommended that conceptual and definitional vagueness should be avoided at this early stage.

The aims and objectives section should look something like this:

Aim: The aim of the study is to (e.g.) examine the relationship between parental expectations and pupils' educational outcomes in secondary schools.

Objectives:

- To examine the existing research base on the relationship between expectations and outcomes
- To collect data on parental expectations and student outcomes from the case study sample
- To analyse the findings from the data collection phase
- To draw some conclusions about the expectations/outcomes relationship

Research design: This is where you outline the methodology and research methods you are going to use to gather your data, that is, the evidence that will help you answer the question that you have posed. This section should also provide justification for why you have chosen a particular methodology – for example, why you will use a case study as opposed to ethnography, why you will employ questionnaires when interviews might be more feasible and so on. This section needs to be convincing, and it must also indicate the clarity of what you are trying to achieve.

Timeline: Depending on the length of your project, you should give some indication of the duration of each part of the study, estimating the length of time you will devote to reading the literature, gathering the evidence, analysing the results and writing up. Try to be realistic in this timeline, and try not to put too much pressure on yourself to achieve unrealistic targets.

Significance of the study: It is important to include a section in your proposal that makes the case for the significance of the research, because it allows you to reiterate the rationale for carrying out the research in the first place. Why is this research necessary? Why do we need it? What kind of contribution does it make to the existing knowledge base? Here you are effectively making an assertion about the future worth of your work. This might seem artificial on paper, but in practice, it 'sets the scene' while clarifying the kind of potential contribution that you can make.

The limitations of the study: It might seem counter-intuitive to include a section which details the shortcomings of the research (especially when you have devoted a lot of effort to 'bigging it up' earlier in the proposal), but it does your research no disservice to outline the limits of its reach and scope. No study can avoid such limits, and a built-in statement of intellectual and professional modesty does the proposal no harm. Examples of research limitations might include the lack of time for a more in-depth approach to the research question, or the fact that your study is questionnaire-based and therefore lacking a qualitative dimension (or vice-versa). Whatever these limits might be, a demonstration of your knowledge and awareness of their existence allows you to make reasonable claims on behalf of the evidence that you have gathered.

A note on the challenges of interdisciplinarity

Designing a research project based on a vague research question is an occupational hazard in any research discipline, but it has particular implications for fields such as education. Because it is a field of study and practice as much as it is a 'discipline', education tends to be grounded in the ideas and theories of other disciplines such as history, politics, psychology and sociology as much as its own. So while the education researcher must be answerable to the ongoing paradigmatic debates in education (e.g. continuous vs. final assessment, play vs. structured learning and so on) and must situate their research within these paradigms and debates, often they also need to be at least on nodding terms with the paradigms and debates of other disciplines as well. Research should add to the stock of knowledge in a specific way, by confirming or rebutting existing ideas or at least adding to the complexity of understanding on the topic at hand. Ensure that you have focused on *one* main research question, and also that there is a definable field of study to research and an academic debate within which to situate your findings and analysis.

Tips for getting started with writing

The process of writing itself is rarely discussed. Understanding the writing process is particularly important if you have a large piece of writing to complete, such as a dissertation. Dissertation data collection is often a very enjoyable and interesting process, but then the actual writing up of a piece of research for an assignment can feel very daunting. The next part of this chapter is going to demystify the writing process – so this is not about what you need to write, but more about how to get going with writing. Here are a number of tips to help you start the writing process:

- Planning: Writing say a whole dissertation of somewhere between 10,000 and 20,000 can seem very daunting. However, breaking down your writing into manageable sections makes this much more accessible. Go further than breaking down your assignment into chapters and consider each specific section that will need to be included in this chapter. For example, a Methodology chapter is likely to include: an introduction, research approach, research design, research questions, participants, sampling technique, research methods, ethics, validity, reliability, triangulation and data analysis. Suddenly when you have broken down your assignment into small sections – the idea of writing say 300 words on ethics becomes much more manageable than writing a whole chapter in one go.
- Getting started: If you are finding it difficult to be motivated to write your 300 words on ethics there are a number of tricks to get you started. The first is to set a timer on your phone say for 15 minutes (the argument being you can do anything for 15 minutes) Have a go at writing – knowing that you can stop shortly. Experiment with different mediums – try pen and paper, try the notes section on your phone (which you can email to yourself), and try using the voice function on your phone which turns your words into text.

Remember the aim here is not perfection — the aim is a first draft. The opportunity to edit and refine will come later — for now try and get some words on the page.

- Accountability: It can really help to form a study group or find a study partner. This provides accountability to another person to help you get the work completed. Try to find a time and day that works for you and your group. Agree to all work communally in a study space — tell each other what you are hoping to achieve, before agreeing a period of time for working in silence — anywhere between 30 mins and one hour works well before having a short break. Plan to do this over a 2 or 3 hour session — you will be amazed as to how much writing you get done in this designated writing time. If it is not practical for you to meet up in person, a similar 'writing group' technique can be achieved through the use of an online tool such as Zoom. Set up your agreed time each week to meet and log on at the correct time. Tell your group/study partner what you hope to achieve by the end of the session. You can designate a group member to keep time — so you all have a 5-minute break every 30 mins for example. The key is to keep your camera on for maximum accountability — even if you don't feel like staying at your computer screen knowing that others are working is a powerful motivator.

- Managing tiredness: If you are feeling tired you can pick an alternative task to writing, such as doing some reading and taking notes, starting some data analysis, tidying up your references — the key is that whatever the task is — it is contributing to helping you complete your assignment. Building in breaks is really important to give your brain a rest, move your body and to get yourself a drink or snack. Try to think about rewards that you might give to yourself after you have finished a particular section of your writing, for example watching an episode of a TV programme.

- Distractions: Cal Newport's (2016) book 'Deep Work' is excellent and inspirational and I would recommend this. However, here are my practical tried and tested methods that work for me personally and enable me to be a productive writer. We live in a very busy and 'connected' world with the price of multi-tasking being that you may find it difficult to concentrate. Realistically you are not going to be working for more than 30 mins to one hour at a time — so if you cannot manage the whole two or three hour session of not looking at your phone or social media - try to at least turn notifications on silent during your writing period. You will be amazed at how much you can get done by not constantly switching tasks and you get to give yourself the reward of looking at your phone etc. at the end of your writing group session. What if you are in a noisy environment? Noise cancelling headphones can be helpful. I find listening to music or the radio impossible when I am writing — but I do find listening to 'café sounds' (a soundtrack which recreates the noises you would hear in a café) very effective and I also find listening to 'white noise' very soothing and it helps to take away the background noise of voices that make it difficult for me to concentrate.

- Go back to the reading: Sometimes you just do not know what else to write and you are really struggling to add any more information or elaborate meaningfully on the point that you have already made. If you get to this stage it probably means that you have not read enough on the subject and/or that you simply need to read more. It is always really tempting to try and just finish the piece, but going back to the reading and making a few more notes can make a huge difference to the significance and level of analysis and critique that you are able to apply

- Editing: We often do not think about writing being in a series of stages. The information I have provided for you above is to really help you with the first draft stage. This stage is not about perfection, but it *is* about not procrastinating and finding solutions to when the circumstances for writing are not perfect (they rarely are). The later stage is about polishing your writing – editing and refining – for many people this is a really enjoyable stage that can be done in relatively small chunks of say an hour when you are re-writing a sentence and adding in references etc. Using text-to-speech software can be really helpful for checking for overly long sentences, the need for additional punctuation and any typos.

- Closing a document: It is time for a break and you may not return to your writing for a few days. There are a number of strategies which will help making re-opening your document easier. Write a list of 'to-do jobs' at the top of your document and do not be afraid to use highlighting on various sections of your draft – it can be much easier to 'add reference' or 'refine paragraph' or 'edit clunky sentence' or 'write section on triangulation' if you have highlighted where you need to do this. It saves you time in remembering the tasks that need to be completed and enables you to start working again quickly when you re-open your document.

- Perspective: It is also helpful to have some perspective – we could all make things a bit more perfect if we had a bit more time, but often deadlines drive us and we need to submit the dissertation/assignment to achieve a qualification. Therefore, whilst a mantra can be a bit 'cheesy', it is important to consider the bigger picture – so I often find writing something on the topic of my writing like 'done is better than perfect' – this means that I can keep some perspective on what I am writing and meet my deadlines.

Chapter summary

This chapter began by identifying four broad research themes in the education sector with examples of relevant research studies. The chapter then described some of the issues that should be considered when choosing a specific research topic (personal interest, feasibility, manageability). It went on to suggest what should be included in a research proposal, including some information on the background to the research question, a statement of the research question itself, the aims and objectives of the research, the research design, a timeline and an indication of the significance and limitations of the study. The chapter highlighted the challenge of interdisciplinarity in terms of conducting educational research in the context of ideas generated within other disciplines. The final section of the chapter provided some useful tips on the writing process.

Further reading

Denscombe, M. (2019) *Research proposals a practical guide*. 2nd edn. Oxford: Open University Press.

- This is a really helpful guide with a series of questions to help you shape your research proposal. The quality of research proposals from students who have read this book is always very high!

Terrell, S.R. (2022) *Writing a proposal for your dissertation: Guidelines and examples*. 2nd edn. New York: Guildford Press.

- This book is marketed at doctoral students, but its accessible style means that much of the advice and guidance is also relevant for those writing research proposals for undergraduate and postgraduate taught programmes. The examples are varied, and the book includes an education-specific example.

References

Ahn, M.Y. and Davis, H.H. (2023) 'Are local students disadvantaged? Understanding institutional, local and national sense of belonging in higher education', *British Educational Research Journal*, 49, 19–34. doi:10.1002/berj.3826.

Albert, M., Scott, C.E. and Rincon, M. (2023) 'Can even one adult please just listen to me? Rethinking the mentoring of beginning teachers by positioning secondary students as guides', *Teaching and Teacher Education*, 128. doi:10.1016/j.tate.2023.104111.

Ballantyne, C.A. (2022) 'A kaleidoscope of I-positions: Chinese Volunteers' enactment of teacher identity in Australian classrooms', *Journal of Language, Identity & Education*. doi:10.1080/15348458.2022.2057991.

Bilecen, B., Diekmann, I. and Faist, T. (2023) 'Loneliness among Chinese international and local students in Germany: The role of student status, gender, and emotional support', *European Journal of Higher Education*. doi:10.1080/21568235.2023.2215992.

Duflos, M., Hussaina, H. and Brussoni, M. (2023) '"When I'm playing with him, everything else in my life sort of falls away": Exploring grandparents' and grandchildren's learning through outdoor play', *Journal of Adventure Education and Outdoor Learning*. doi:10.1080/14729679.2023.2230503.

Gandolfi, H.E. and Mills, M. (2023) 'Teachers for social justice: Exploring the lives and work of teachers committed to social justice in education', *Oxford Review of Education*, 49(5), pp. 569–587. doi:10.1080/03054985.2022.2105314.

Horrigmo, K.J. and Midtsundstad, J.H. (2023) 'Schools' prerequisites for inclusion – The interplay between location, commuting, and social ties', *International Journal of Inclusive Education*, 27(4), pp. 493–506. doi:10.1080/13603116.2020.1853257.

Matthews, K.E. *et al.* (2024) 'What do students and teachers talk about when they talk together about feedback and assessment? Expanding notions of feedback literacy through pedagogical partnership', *Assessment & Evaluation in Higher Education*, 49(1), pp. 26–38. doi:10.1080/02602938.2023.2170977.

Nam, B.H. *et al.* (2023) 'Subjectivities and the future of comparative and international education: Teacher researchers and graduate student researchers as co-constructive narrative inquirers', *Educational Review*. doi:10.1080/00131911.2022.2159934.

Newport, C. (2016) *Deep work*. London: Piatkus.

Ritchie, M.M. (2023) 'Shared experiences of leadership transition: A cross comparative study of schools in England and the United States', *Leadership and Policy in Schools*, 22(2), pp. 527–544. doi: 10.1080/15700763.2021.1995878.

Ross, E. (2023) 'Teachers' interpretation of curriculum as a window into 'curriculum potential'', *The Curriculum Journal*, pp. 1–18. doi:10.1002/curj.239.

Trinh, V.D. and Faulkner, S.L. (2023) 'Using the communication theory of identity to examine identity negotiation among LGBTQ– college students with multiple conflicting salient identities', *Communication Quarterly*, 71(2), pp. 154–174. doi:10.1080/01463373.2022.2136009.

CHAPTER 3

Reviewing the literature

Introduction

This chapter offers guidance on the selection, use and presentation of the existing literature in a research project. It outlines different strategies for accessing material and identifies some of the most important journals in the study of education. Electronic literature searches are increasingly important, and the chapter identifies a number of useful databases and approaches for managing the process of electronic searching effectively. The chapter suggests strategies for managing and engaging critically with your selected literature. In the final section, it outlines effective approaches for writing up a literature review.

What is a literature review and what is it for?

A literature review is an essential component of any research project. Your project does not stand alone. It needs to be situated within the existing literature in your chosen field of study, allowing you to justify and contextualise your project and create a space for your work. The literature review surveys the body of existing scholarly articles in your chosen area of study. It is 'a written document that develops the case to establish a thesis. This case is based on a comprehensive understanding of the current knowledge of the topic. A literature review synthesizes current knowledge pertaining to the research question' (Machi and McEvoy, 2022: 1). In other words, your literature review will use scholarly articles to develop an argument about the research, concepts and theories that relate to your study. In doing so you are not simply listing relevant literature. Rather, you are critically engaging with it – analysing, organising, evaluating and synthesising. By reviewing existing work, you can increase your understanding of your topic and demonstrate this knowledge to your reader. You can also show your skills in selecting and interpreting relevant material. You can identify common themes, competing perspectives and approaches to gathering information, and different uses and meanings of the concepts you intend to use. Engagement with the literature can also help you to develop, consolidate and question your own developing perspectives. Most importantly, the evidence you gather here will prove invaluable when you analyse your own research findings.

Steps in a literature review

A literature review is not linear; it will evolve constantly as you identify new research and develop new concepts and arguments. Nevertheless, there are a number of useful steps in the process (and it should be noted that most of them take place before you start writing up!).

- Research focus: Identify your topic and develop clear aims and objectives.
- Gather relevant material: From a range of scholarly writing, collect and read a range of scholarly writing. Keep detailed reference notes or use a software package like *Endnote* to save a considerable amount of time later on: https://endnote.com/?language=en. Check information at your university to see if there is an online referencing system e.g. *Endnote* that your institution subscribes to and that you can access for free.
- Read, take notes and develop ideas: Begin by reading broadly on your topic. Then as you become more familiar with the literature, start to focus on your specific research aim.
- Organise, analyse and evaluate: Group your literature around concepts and approaches, identifying relationships, similarities and differences, strengths and weaknesses.
- Synthesise: Develop a table or concept map that organises the literature to form your own independent and coherent argument.
- Write it up!

ACTIVITY

Find a journal article that is relevant to your chosen topic of study. Skim it to identify important ideas. Now read key sections carefully, using different colours to highlight useful quotes, key points, ideas that support and challenge your own thoughts, and strengths and weaknesses. Write a brief summary of these points and make an accurate note of the reference details.

Accessing a range of literature

The literature review is generally the most substantial and time-consuming part of your project. There is simply so much information you could access. There is some good news though, today you can access tremendous amounts of material from your computer. Search engines and databases provide mechanisms by which you can narrow and refine your search, sifting out inappropriate material and giving you control over the search parameters. Because you are engaging in an academic enquiry, journal articles should be your main source for your literature review. Not only are journal publications often among the most contemporary of sources, but published articles also have the advantage of having undergone a peer review process. Authors submit their work for review by other academics, and only work that has passed through this gruelling process successfully will be published. Of course, there are thousands of journals in education today, however, among the most important education journals are:

- British Journal of Educational Studies
- British Educational Research Journal
- British Journal of Sociology of Education
- Gender and Education
- Journal of Philosophy of Education
- Assessment and Evaluation in Higher Education
- Computers and Education
- Studies in Higher Education
- Cambridge Journal of Education
- Journal of Comparative and International Higher Education

Alongside journal articles, other sources of scholarly writing include books, conference proceedings, reports, government publications, newspaper articles and other students' dissertations and theses. With access to so much academic writing, the search process can feel very daunting and it can be difficult to know where to start. One effective strategy is to begin with a landmark essay or piece of research – you might obtain this from notes from study modules, in a relevant textbook, or by asking your supervisor. After reading the seminal article you can use the reference list at the end of the paper to identify other relevant literature. You can also search the article and author names, identifying more recent scholarly work that has responded to or expanded the original ideas. These strategies mean your literature base 'snowballs' as you access more and more sources. Before long, the difficulty becomes knowing when to stop.

You cannot access all the literature in your topic. The relevant literature is not static, clearly defined or readily identifiable. You need to make choices about what is significant, and you must reach a point where you feel you have enough evidence to develop your argument. The literature is a continuously evolving network of scholarly writing, which interacts with itself to develop, challenge, expand and contradict an ever-growing body of knowledge. Your literature review needs to position your own work within this network.

Different sources

While journal articles should be your starting point in identifying scholarly writing, you should also try to use a range of other sources. Each source has strengths and limitations. For instance, academic books contain a lot of information and have the space to develop detailed arguments. However, books can be difficult and/or expensive to access, and due to publishers' lead-in times they are seldom up-to-the-minute or current. Newspaper articles are accessible and come in 'bite-sized' chunks, but journalistic writing is quite different from academic writing and newspapers are likely to present information in a partial, biased and sensationalised manner.

One of the most common ways of accessing relevant literature is via the internet. It is quick and easy to use a search engine to locate publications on your topic, and there is an enormous amount of freely accessible information. Most important is the emergence and rapid expansion of 'creative commons' licensing and open educational resources. Of course, you have to be especially careful when using scholarly writing from the web, since this material is less likely to have gone through an editorial or peer review process. Having said that, online 'web 2.0' communities increasingly self-regulate content – in many ways, Wikipedia has the most rigorous peer review system of all. The democratic nature of the web is both its strength and its weakness – multiple perspectives are readily available and anyone can publish anything.

Most importantly, whichever source you use, you need to develop what Postman and Weingartner famously termed 'crap-detecting skills' (Postman and Weingartner, 1971). As you read, question the credibility and accuracy of the source, distinguishing 'good' from 'bad' information. There are a number of university-based YouTube clips offering practical advice about 'how to evaluate internet sources'.

Using databases

A database is an organised collection of material. It is like an electronic filing system, helping you to access the resources you require. In general, you can define and narrow your search according to criteria such as keywords, titles, authors, dates, names and types of publication. Each database has distinct mechanisms for managing data, so it is crucial that you familiarise yourself with the processes.

Some databases provide access to a limited range of resources, for example peer-reviewed journal articles. Others list a wide range of materials, including books, policy documents, newspaper articles, blogs and so on. Some databases provide title and abstract information while others provide links to full articles, although many very recent articles will be embargoed for between six and eighteen months. While a growing number of databases are free to access, some require a personal or institutional subscription – check to see if you can access the latter via your university network or using your library login details.

There is a large number of databases which all provide excellent access to literature in education. Among these are:

- British Education Index: This database indexes education journals from 1975 onwards.
- Child Development and Adolescent Studies: A huge range of document types can be searched for and historical documents are included.

- Education Abstracts: This database covers a range of topics, such as adult education, multi-cultural education and teaching methods from 1983 onwards.
- ERIC (Educational Resources Information Center): This is a US-based database, with a helpful search mechanism by educational stage/level.

There are also some generic databases that may be useful:

- SCOPUS
- Web of Science
- Google Scholar

ACTIVITY

Try using a database to find scholarly writing in your chosen field of study. Access one of the online databases listed above. Start with a general keyword search. Now try to narrow your search – your database might allow you to refine your search parameters by:

- Date
- Type and title of publication
- Keywords in title or abstract only
- Peer reviewed only

Now try the same process with a different database. Do you get similar or different results?

Critically engaging with the literature

A literature review is certainly more than a list of books and studies that relate to your topic; it is not merely a series of annotated articles. The most important characteristic of a successful literature review is critical engagement. To help you to analyse and evaluate the literature, you might ask the following questions:

- How recently was the research undertaken?
- Do the local, social, historical, cultural, political and economic contexts match with your own study?
- Who is the intended audience?
- What evidence is used to justify the author's claims?
- Has the literature been scrutinised by peer review?
- How trustworthy is the source or the publication?

- If the paper is based on primary research, is the methodological approach sound? Consider, for example:
    - How large is the sample?
    - Is there any evidence of bias?
    - Are the findings based on small-scale qualitative research, large-scale survey, mixed methods…?
    - Can you challenge the research on grounds of reliability, validity, representativeness, generalisability, reflexivity…?

Your literature needs to identify scholarly work that is relevant to your project. Outline what you consider to be the important ideas in the literature and analyse and evaluate this literature using questions like the ones listed above. However, your review also needs to *synthesise* this literature, combining it to say something new. This is the most important characteristic of critical engagement – *using* the literature to help you develop your own argument. To do this, as you read you need to consider a number of further questions:

- How does it correspond with other scholarly writing I have read?
- How does it match and contradict my own thinking?
- What have I learnt?
- How can I use it?
- How does it fit into my developing arguments?

ACTIVITY

The following extract is taken from the literature review in a recent article on social class and access to higher education: Read the extract and consider the following:
  Identify where the author is:

- Describing existing literature
- Evaluating literature
- Using literature to define concepts
- Using ideas from literature to develop their own arguments
- Identifying relationships between different literatures
- Can you set out their argument as a list of short bullet points?
- How does this review of literature support the research?

Shields (2021)

The number of university entrants from working-class backgrounds has increased. The total number of entrants to higher education in the UK in 2017 was 533,890, and 82% of those were domiciled in the UK (437,789) according to the Universities and Colleges Admissions Service (UCAS, 2017).

The End of Cycle Report from UCAS for 2017 showed that the number of young people from areas with a low entry to higher education was 13.8%, up 0.2 percentage points from the previous year. However, when compared to the figures for entrants from backgrounds who were most likely to go to university, the gap had actually increased by 0.8 percentage points. 53.1% of entrants were from backgrounds most likely to go into higher education, which was a 1% increase on 2016. Thompson (2017, p. 751) contends that 'opportunity structures are to be understood dynamically and relationally ... educational expansion – including increased working-class participation – produces "social congestion" (Brown, 2013), ... and restricts opportunities for the most vulnerable'. Neves, Ferraz and Nata (2017) also note that those from socio-economically advantaged backgrounds have benefitted from the massification of higher education to a greater extent than those from poorer financial backgrounds. Hence, whilst the number of students from working-class backgrounds in universities has increased, they remain a minority group within the higher education sector.

In addition to being less likely to go to university, working-class students are also disproportionately concentrated in the lower ranking institutions according to the Higher Education Statistics Agency (HESA, 2018). This ranking of higher education institutions reflects a pattern of social stratification with lower ranking institutions typically being associated with those from widening participation backgrounds (Leathwood and O'Connell, 2003). Widening participation consists of practices which aim to remove barriers to university access. Such initiatives are not specific to the United Kingdom. In France, it is the public universities which offer non-selective programmes to enable the 'new bacheliers' (first-generation students) from underrepresented backgrounds the opportunity to pursue higher education (Bodin and Orange, 2018). Likewise, in the USA, working-class students and minority ethnic students are disproportionately participating in community college education, rather than becoming members of the elite Ivy League institutions (Espinoza, 2012).

Working-class women tend to have more interrupted educational histories than their middle-class counterparts (Reay, Ball and David, 2002) and are more likely to be mature students compared with men (UCAS, 2018). Female working-class experiences of university are also particularly likely to be combining studying with caring responsibilities (Fuller, 2018). It has been noted that when working-class female students attend university, there is often a focus on the financial stability that it will bring to their own families in the longer term (Reay, 2003). Working-class female undergraduates are therefore more likely to be mature students, attend less prestigious institutions, have caring responsibilities and have strong economic motivations for studying in comparison to their more advantaged counterparts.

Writing up your literature review

Your literature review is your own piece of original work and there are numerous ways in which you could write it. Nevertheless, there are some strategies that might help you write a good one:

- Link clearly to your overall project aims and objectives: Start by explaining how the selected literature relates explicitly to your project. You might choose to summarise the argument of your literature review here.

- Contested concepts: Define the key concepts at the heart of your study. During your reading you are likely to recognise that different authors use concepts in different ways. An excellent starting point is to consider different interpretations and uses of your key concepts before outlining the definition you intend to use.
- Building from landmark literature or classic studies: Another excellent way to begin is to outline one or two seminal pieces of work in your field. From this, you can discuss work that followed, considering how the original ideas have been challenged and refined over time.
- Inverted pyramid argument: You might follow a structure that starts with a broad exploration of the literature, before increasingly focusing on localised examples and narrowing definitions and uses.
- Structured around key themes or topics: Grouping your argument around key themes helps you to maintain clarity and structure in an extended piece of writing. These themes will also prove useful when analysing your own data.
- Maintain your voice: Because you are discussing other people's work, you can easily lose your own voice. Remember you are analysing their work rather than summarising it. By offering your interpretations of their arguments, you minimise the risk of plagiarism.
- Using evaluative language: Make sure you are not simply describing or listing existing scholarly work by using phrases like '….overstate the case', 'a problem with…', 'this is limited because…', 'others have argued…', 'while this is persuasive…', 'a convincing argument…'.
- Developing a coherent, integrated and sustained argument: The literature review should have a clear structure with an introduction and conclusion.
- Signpost – Tell the reader why you have selected specific literature and what you are using it for. Clearly indicate how your argument is developing.
- Finish: Oddly, it is much harder to finish than to start a literature review. New research is always being published and the enormous amount of scholarly work means you can never fully complete a review. Although you will need to revise and extend your literature review throughout the period of your study, you need to reach a point where you are happy with it.

Ten top tips for writing a successful literature review

1 Your best source of literature is the online database.
2 Read literature reviews that already exist in your topic of study.
3 Use a wide range of types of literature – theoretical, conceptual, empirical, contemporary, historical, statistical, landmark…
4 Ensure that you review some literature from the last two years.

5   Be prepared to modify and redefine your research topic as you identify new relevant literature.
6   Identify themes in the literature and group your discussion around these themes.
7   Keep a track of your references – you might use software like Endnote.
8   Don't list – always critically engage with the literature.
9   Use the language and 'signposts' you would normally use when writing a critical essay.
10 Use your literature to help you develop your own conceptual framework and argument.

Chapter summary

This chapter has outlined the main sources of literature, providing details of useful databases and key journals. It has encouraged you to reflect on the relative merits of different sources, most notably the increasing use of the internet as a gateway to a wide range of materials. It has helped you to develop strategies for critically engaging with literature and for writing your literature review as a discursive and coherent argument. To maximise your chances of producing an excellent literature review, remember the 'ten top tips'.

Further reading

Greetham, B. (2022) *How to write your literature review (macmillan study skills)*. London: Bloomsbury Academic.

- This is a detailed account of how to write your literature with details about different types of literature review and advice about how to manage your time and your reading of material. The book also supports you in citing your sources correctly and the editing process in terms of both structure and content. This is a well-structured book which supports the writer from start to finish with the literature review process with lots of handy tips.

Machi, L.A. and McEvoy, B.T. (2022) *The literature review: Six steps to success*. 4th edn. London: Corwin SAGE.

- A comprehensive account of the literature review process – starting with helping you to pick a research topic, guiding you through doing a literature search, helping you to critique the research literature and the practicalities of writing up your literature review. The book incorporates helpful diagrams and definitions of relevant terminology and is written in an accessible and clear way.

References

Bodin, R. and Orange, S. (2018) 'Access and retention in French higher education: Student drop-out as a form of regulation', *British Journal of Sociology of Education*, 39(1), pp. 126–143.

Brown, P. (2013) 'Education, opportunity and the prospects for social mobility', *British Journal of Sociology of Education*, 34(5–6), pp. 678–700.

Espinoza, R. (2012) *Working-class minority students' routes to higher education*. New York: Routledge

Fuller, C. (2018) 'The existential self: Challenging and renegotiating gender identity through higher education in England', *Gender and Education*, 30(1), pp. 92–104.

Leathwood, C. and O'Connell, P. (2003) "'It's a Struggle': The construction of the 'New Student' in Higher Education', *Journal of Education Policy*, 18(6), pp. 597–615.

Machi, L.A. and McEvoy, B.T. (2022) *The literature review: Six steps to success*. 4th edn. London: Corwin SAGE.

Neves, T., Ferraz, H. and Nata, G. (2017) 'Social inequality in access to higher education: Grade inflation in private schools and the ineffectiveness of compensatory education', *International Studies in the Sociology of Education*, 26(2), pp. 190–210.

Postman, N. and Weingartner, C. (1971) *Teaching as a subversive activity*. Harmondsworth: Penguin Books.

Reay, D. (2003) 'A risky business? Mature working-class women', *Gender and Education*, 15(3), pp. 301–317.

Reay, D., Ball, S. and David, M. (2002) "'It's Taking Me a Long Time but I'll Get There in the End': Mature students on access courses and higher education choice', *British Educational Research Journal*, 28(1), pp. 5–19.

Shields, S. (2021) 'Curiosity and careers: Female working-class students' experiences of university', *International Studies in Sociology of Education*. doi:10.1080/09620214.2021.1959378.

Thompson, R. (2017) 'Opportunity structures and educational marginality: The post-16 transitions of young people outside education and employment', *Oxford Review of Education*, 43(6), pp. 749–766.

CHAPTER 4

Sampling

Introduction

Sampling is the term used when picking participants to take part in a study derived from the population of interest. Population refers to the larger group from which individuals are selected to participate in a study. The description below of the sample used in Colombo, Rebughini and Domaneschi's (2022) study, tells us a great deal about the participants in their study. It also allows us to evaluate the findings about how young people in Italy from a range of backgrounds understand the 'individualization' process in relation to increasingly neoliberal policies.

> The research was conducted in Milan from 2017 to 2019 by carrying out 40 in-depth interviews with young people. We recruited participants in three main ways. First, we began with convenience sampling by contacting three secondary schools, which garnered 26 interviewees: 14 of them were lyceum students, and 12 of them attended vocational school. Ten other respondents were young people that we reached by spending time with a group of university students active in a squatted social centre. Finally, by means of snowball sampling, we located the final four interviewees among young adults engaged in political parties. Overall, the recruitment strategy, besides ensuring a basic socio-demographic distribution by gender (22 females, 18 males), age (from 18 to 31) and educational qualification, aimed at obtaining a variety of situations, resources and, in general, social positionings with respect to future expectations and the management of uncertainty by respondents.
>
> (Colombo, Rebughini and Domaneschi, 2022: 434)

Sampling techniques fall into two main categories – probability and non-probability sampling. Sampling is a way of 'picking' individuals from a population you want to find out more about. The way you choose your sample will depend on your research approach. This chapter helps you to choose your research sample, and it is organised under three sections: Why you should use a sample, different types of sampling and sampling bias.

DOI: 10.4324/9781003569428-5

Why use a sample?

In most cases it is unrealistic to expect to be able to work with a whole population. For example, it is not realistic to ask every teacher in England about their views on the possibility of all children in England being required to study mathematics up until eighteen years of age. However, it would be possible to pick a sample of teachers whose views are likely to be *representative* of *all* the teachers in England.

The use of a sample saves time and money! This statement may sound like an advertising gimmick, but there are important methodological reasons for using a sample. One of the key reasons is to be able to generalise your findings to a wider population. The key methodological reasons for using a sample are:

- It is not always feasible to survey every person in the population you wish to study.
- There is little evidence that asking every member of a population will increase the validity and reliability of your findings.
- A representative sample enables you to make generalisations about the wider population you are studying.
- A representative sample increases the confidence that you can have in generalising to the wider population you are studying.

As well as these advantages, there are also a number of obvious practical reasons for using a sample:

- It would take a long time to include every person in the population you wish to study.
- It is very expensive (e.g., in terms of the cost of researchers and travel) to ask every person in the population you wish to study.

However, you will need to explain the decisions you have made in regards to how you selected your sample of the population, because the participants you choose will influence the findings of your research.

ACTIVITY

You want to find out about Year 6 (aged 11 years old) pupils in transition from primary school to secondary school. Logistically you cannot ask every Year 6 pupil in the country, and they (or their parents and teachers) might not all agree to take part in your research anyway. This is where sampling comes in. You have already identified the population you wish to research – Year 6 pupils. Now you will select a smaller number from this population – this is your sample. You decide to select Year 6 pupils from schools in a small coastal town. Now there are a range of strategies you can use to choose the Year 6 pupils who will take part in your study.

- How would you pick the Year 6 pupils to be involved in the research?
- Why do you need to explain to the reader why you chose this sample?
- Could you generalise your findings to every Year 6 pupil in the country? Why? Why not?

Many of the factors which influence how you select your sample will be dependent on the type of research you are carrying out. In the next section we will discuss different sampling strategies based on conducting quantitative and qualitative research.

Different types of sampling

Probability sampling

The next part of this chapter explains how to pick a 'probability' sample for studies which are using large numbers of participants or researchers who believe that participants are likely to represent a cross-section of the population being researched. Probability sampling is based on the assumption that the people or events chosen as part of the sample are selected because, it is likely that they have characteristics which represent the wider population that the research is trying to find out about. The most popular types of probability sampling are random, systematic, stratified, quota and cluster sampling.

- Random sampling: It gives all the members of a population an equal chance of being selected. For example, if a number is given to each name on a list of Year 7 pupils, these numbers can then be picked at random to achieve a sample. Assume you have one hundred Year 7 pupils and they are all given a number from one to one hundred. You need to pick twenty out of your one hundred pupils. As in a tombola for a charity raffle, you could simply pick twenty numbers out of a hat to give you your sample. Alternatively, the same principle can be applied using a computerised random number generator, which will generate the twenty numbers you require.

- Systematic sampling: It is an alternative type of random sampling. For example, you may decide to pick every seventh name on a list. This is fine, but make sure that the list itself will not inadvertently influence the sample. A boy/girl/boy/girl list may mean that if you pick an even number, such as every fourth name, you will always get a girl. If you require a balance of male and female pupils, you need to ensure that your systematic sampling pattern will provide representativeness.

- Stratified sampling: This means that each member of a population has an equal chance of being selected based on the degree to which they represent part of the whole population. Stratified samples are more complicated than random samples since cases are selected in proportion to one or more characteristics in the population. For example, if socio-economic class is considered relevant to the study and this is determined by entitlement to free school meals, you need to select the appropriate proportion of participants who are entitled to free school meals. If the proportion entitled to free school meals is 20% of the overall population, then 20% of your sample needs to be selected on this basis. This becomes problematic because some schools may have a significantly higher proportion of children with entitlement to free school meals, while other schools may have a significantly lower proportion. Also, bear in mind that the assumptions you are making about a population will ultimately affect the results of your research. This is also problematic because you may want to select your sample based on sensitive issues such as age or sexual orientation, or very complex categories such as ethnicity or occupation.

- Quota sampling: This means that the members of the population who are targeted for inclusion in your sample are focused on because they meet the criteria of the predefined quota. For instance, the research may decide to interview ten newly qualified male teachers and ten newly qualified female teachers. This type of sampling is sometimes conducted on the high street by market researchers.

- Cluster sampling: Sometimes the population you are interested in naturally occurs in clusters, such as schools. In this way, rather than focusing on individuals, the population can be selected based on the cluster in which it occurs. An advantage of this technique is that if many of the individuals we wish to include in our study belong to a cluster, we can save travelling time because the individuals are often in the same location.

ACTIVITY

Read the following extract from Barg and Klein (2024):

> The study draws mainly on data from the UK Millennium Cohort Study (MCS). In addition, we use British Skills Surveys (BSS) data to generate mothers' occupation-specific skill variables. The MCS surveyed around 19,000 children born between September 2000 and January 2002. The sample was selected from all births in a random sample of electoral wards. It was disproportionately stratified, allowing for greater representation of all UK countries, deprived areas and areas with high concentrations of Black and Asian families in England. Owing to disproportionate sampling, we used sampling weights throughout the analysis (Plewis et al., 2004). For our analysis, we chose to sample families who responded to the third survey ($n=15,431$), considering outcome measures of expressive language, inductive reasoning and spatial awareness ability at the age of five. We used information from the first three waves (University of London, Institute of Education, Centre for Longitudinal Studies, 2020a, 2020b, 2020c) to derive family financial, human and social capital measures. Our analytical sample does not contain children living only with their grandparents or living in adoptive or foster families ($n=55$), that is, families in which no natural parent was present... Our analyses are based on children and their natural mothers (or natural fathers in single-father households), for whom we have complete data on all measures, leaving us with 13,543 observations... The BSS is a nationally representative survey conducted between 1997 and 2017 to gather information on the job skills of employed adults aged 20 to 60 (some surveys also include adults aged 61 to 65). We used data from the surveys in 2001 ($n=4470$), 2006 ($n=7787$) and 2012 ($n=3200$) to create several occupation-specific skills variables (Felstead et al., 2019), which we then assigned to mothers in the MCS using their Standard Occupational Classification-codes (SOC2000). The SOC2000 is the UK's official occupational classification system. Jobs are classified by work content and skill level.
>
> (Barg and Klein, 2024: 124–125)

- How would you define the type of sampling used? Why?
- How representative do you think the sample is for understanding the impact of maternal occupation-specific skills with children's cognitive development? Why?

Non-probability sampling

This section explains how to choose a 'non-probability' sample for studies which are using smaller numbers of participants, or where the researcher does not have enough information about the 'sample' to know if they are 'representative'. Non-probability sampling is more likely to be used in qualitative studies. Common types of non-probability sampling, such as purposive, snowball, convenience and theoretical sampling are outlined. In qualitative research this type of sampling is generally not seen to be problematic as small-scale research does not often attempt to generalise to a wider population; it is much more interested in providing an in-depth portrait of the experiences of those participants who are taking part in the research.

- Purposive: The sample is chosen specifically for the research because the researcher knows that these participants will be able to provide the best account of the phenomena that they wish to study. Purposive sampling is an approach which indicates that you know who the best participants for your research are, because they are the population who are most likely to know the most about your area of research. For example, if you are interested in Newly Qualified Teachers' (NQTs') experiences of teaching in their first few months, the NQTs themselves are much more likely to give an informative account of this experience than their mentor or the other teachers they work with. Interpretivist research approaches are not concerned with bias in the same way that positivist research is. The random selection used by positivists is undertaken to ensure that the researcher does not bias the research. However, the interpretivist stance is different because it acknowledges that researcher bias is inevitable – we are all shaped by the environment we live in, our life experiences and the views of those around us. Therefore, interpretivists argue that it is impossible not to bias the sample. After all, the very topic which is being researched will be based on the researchers' predisposition to an interest in this area. With purposive sampling the researcher acknowledges their bias and how it may affect the research process, and the choosing of research participants will be part of this. Crucially, a researcher using purposive sampling will not try to make broad generalisations to the wider population based on their findings. They may suggest that their findings are potentially indicative – for example, of the experiences of all NQTs within their first few months of teaching – and they may indicate that their findings correspond with other research in this area. However, they would not suggest that the findings are completely representative because there will be many other factors which have shaped the findings based on other factors related to the research process, the participants and the researcher. Consequently, it is important to remember the limitations of generalisability with purposive sampling, and to keep in mind the fact it is much more closely aligned with research within the interpretivist paradigm.
- Snowballing: This involves asking participants if they are aware of other individuals who would also be interested in participating in the research, and recruiting participants via other participants who act as gatekeepers. Perhaps the best example of the appropriate use of a non-probability sample is where a snowball technique is necessary. In some studies

of truancy, for example, it may be difficult to find people belonging to this population. In such a case we may start with a convenience sample of one or two pupils who agree to take part in the study. Then we can ask these participants to introduce us to or put us in contact with other pupils who also play truant. This approach should not be confused with convenience sampling.

- Convenience: This involves using the most easily available participants. By its very nature, this sampling technique can skew the findings of the research. Convenience sampling is not an approach that is generally considered within educational research because of its lack of methodological rigour. It is normally used by market researchers who have a quota to fill – for example, interviewing ten women and ten men. Generally, within educational research you will wish to be more specific about who your research participants are based on what you wish to find out – for example, teachers who have qualified in the last three years, or Year 6 teachers. However, to achieve a level of validity and reliability in your findings you may still have in mind the number of participants that you need to include in your research to have confidence in your findings (more information on evaluating research can be found in Chapter 19). Engaging enough participants in your research to reach a saturation of themes – which suggests that if you interviewed any more participants you would not find any new themes – is not the same principle as convenience sampling.

ACTIVITY

- Which types of sampling could you use to find out about teachers' views on the Curriculum and Assessment (Wales) Act 2021?
- How would the sampling approach influence the type of data collected?

Sampling bias

There will always be a chance that the particular sample selected will give inaccurate results, although it is possible to minimise the probability of this happening. Piaget's well-known research on children's developmental stages was derived from carrying out experiments with his own three children and his friends' children (Gallard and Garden, 2011). Like his own children, the children of his friends were from an advantaged socio-economic background and therefore his sample was not representative of the population, indicating a sampling bias. Advances in statistical techniques give us greater confidence in making generalisations from a sample to a whole population, but in truth, when using a sample, we cannot be completely sure about how representative it is of the population. There are several factors that influence sampling bias:

- The size of the sample influences both the representativeness of the sample and the statistical analysis of the data.

- Larger samples are more likely to detect a difference between groups.
- Smaller samples are less likely to be representative.
- Non-probability sampling increases the likelihood of sampling bias.
- Probability sampling is free of bias that might stem from choices made by the researcher.
- A problem in sampling arises due to bias from the use of 'volunteers'. Whether or not you provide an incentive for participants to take part in your research, the participants who choose to be involved in your study are likely to be different from those who do not.

ACTIVITY

Read the extract below from Mulvey (2022):

> The main research instrument was semi-structured interviews, which were conducted with 45 students and recent graduates of Chinese universities who hailed from 14 different African countries. While students from a wide range of countries are represented, a limitation is that potential interviewees were informed that the interview could be conducted in either English or Chinese, and this resulted in relatively few participants from outside Anglophone Africa participating in the study, as students (for example, those from francophone countries) who did not speak English or Chinese fluently were less willing to take part. As the focus is on planned trajectories rather than students' actual long-term post-graduation mobility, students and those who had graduated within the past six months were eligible to be interviewed. Most of the interviewees were male: This represents a second limitation of the study, as fewer female students or graduates indicated willingness to take part, meaning it was not possible to explore fully how experiences and migration intentions are differentiated along lines of gender (e.g., Holloway *et al.*, 2012). All of the interviewees were black. The participants studied various courses distributed throughout social sciences, arts and humanities and science, technology, engineering and mathematics (STEM) fields. Students studied at a range of universities in China. The universities are categorised according to the 'Double First-Class University Plan', a tertiary education development initiative introduced by the Chinese government in 2015 (Peters and Besley, 2018). 'Class A' universities are generally considered to be the most prestigious in China, whereas 'Class B' and 'double first-class disciplines' (DFCD) universities are less prestigious, but rank highly within China. Universities outside the Double First-Class University Plan are termed 'provincial' and are generally considered less prestigious than those within it. In the table, students' post-study mobility plans are indicated: A small number of students were unclear about their future plans. As the main aim of this article is to shed light on the relationship between students' decisions and structural inequalities, the focus is on those who had a clear trajectory in mind.
>
> (Mulvey, 2022: 418)

- What steps did the researcher take to minimise sampling bias?
- Are there any ways in which sampling bias may have crept into the research? Why?
- Drawing on your knowledge of sampling, is there anything that you would have done differently to minimise sampling bias?

Chapter summary

This chapter has highlighted the significance of sampling when carrying out research on a population of interest. A range of sampling techniques derived from non-probability and probability approaches have been discussed. Decisions about your method of choosing a sample need to be explained in your research, and any issues regarding sampling bias also need to be highlighted.

Further reading

Eichhorn, J. (2022) *Survey research and sampling (the SAGE quantitative research kit)*. London: SAGE.

- This is an accessible book aimed at students. This book enables the reader to develop a representative sample through research design with different types of sampling for quantitative research.

Tracy, S.J. (2020) *Qualitative research methods collecting evidence, crafting analysis, communicating impact*. 2nd edn. Hoboken, NJ: Wiley Blackwell.

- A detailed chapter in this book explains the different types of sampling approaches that can be used for qualitative research studies.

References

Barg, K. and Klein, M. (2024) 'Maternal occupation-specific skills and children's cognitive development', *Sociology*, 58(1), pp. 118–139. doi:10.1177/00380385231159005.

Colombo, E., Rebughini, P. and Domaneschi, L. (2022) 'Individualization and individualism: Facets and turning points of the entrepreneurial self among young people in Italy', *Sociology*, 56(3), pp. 430–446. doi:10.1177/00380385211037857.

Felstead, A. et al. (2019) 'Skills and employment surveys series dataset, 1986,1992, 1997, 2001, 2006, 2012 and 2017', [data collection]. UK Data Service. SN: 8589. doi:10.5255/UKDA-SN-8589-1

Gallard, D. and Garden, A. (2011) 'The psychology of education', in Dufour, B. and Curtis, W. (eds.) *Studying education: An introduction to the key disciplines in education studies*. Maidenhead: Open University Press, pp. 132–158.

Holloway, S.L., O'Hara, S.L. and Pimlott-Wilson, H. (2012) 'Educational mobility and the gendered geography of cultural capital: The case of international student flows between Central Asia and the UK', *Environment and Planning A*, 44(9), pp. 2278–2294.

Mulvey, B. (2022) 'Global inequality, mobility regimes and transnational capital: The post-graduation plans of African student migrants', *Sociology*, 56(3), pp. 413–429. doi:10.1177/00380385211037574.

Peters, M.A. and Besley, T. (2018) 'China's double first-class university strategy: 双一流', *Educational Philosophy and Theory*, 50(12), pp. 1075–1079.

Plewis, I. et al. (2004) 'Millennium cohort study', Technical report on sampling. London: Institute of Education, Centre for Longitudinal Studies.

University of London, Institute of Education, Centre for Longitudinal Studies (2020a) 'Millenniumcohort study: First survey, 2001–2003', [data collection]. 13th edn. UK Data Service. SN:4683. doi:10.5255/UKDA-SN-4683-5.

University of London, Institute of Education, Centre for Longitudinal Studies (2020b) 'Millenniumcohort study: Second survey, 2003–2005', [data collection]. 10th edn. UK Data Service. SN:5350. doi:10.5255/UKDA-SN-5350-5.

University of London, Institute of Education, Centre for Longitudinal Studies (2020c) 'Millenniumcohort study: Third survey, 2006', [data collection]. 8th edn. UK Data Service. SN: 5795. doi:10.5255/UKDA-SN-5795-5.

CHAPTER 5

Data analysis

Introduction

Analysis in educational research involves discovering the layers of meaning in your data, which means finding the patterns in 'what' and 'how' participants describe or explain educational experiences. However, the *type* of data analysis will depend on the kind of data you have collected. For the purposes of this chapter, we will broadly describe data as either *qualitative* or *quantitative*.

Qualitative data is in word-form – for example, interview transcripts or field notes from classroom observations. Qualitative data analysis can be daunting because there is no set way to interpret the data. The qualitative data analysis section is split into five sections: Beginning qualitative data analysis, computer-assisted qualitative data analysis, analysis techniques derived from grounded theory, language devices for analysis and absences in the data. Quantitative data is numeric. The section on quantitative data analysis is also divided into five sections: Frequency, descriptive statistics, measures of central tendency, chi-square tests and computer-assisted data quantitative analysis.

Beginning qualitative data analysis

First, read through all of your data and become familiar with its content. This is often easier if you have transcribed your own interview data because you will already (consciously or subconsciously) have started to think about what is being said. As you read through the data, jot down any points that seem significant and stand out to you – for example, particular words or phrases. As you can see from this initial process, qualitative data lends itself to the interpretivist paradigm since you are the one interpreting the data. A key way to analyse your data is through coding. The process of coding means putting labels on your data

DOI: 10.4324/9781003569428-6

There are various ways you can start to identify your codes. For many people, a range of coloured highlighters and a large empty space where pieces of paper can be spread out and shuffled is one way of starting to think about the codes for a qualitative data analysis. Alternatively, you can use a simple Word document and put the appropriate interview quotes under the codes you have created with judicious use of bold text and highlighting. The key to qualitative data analysis is recognising that you are required to do the thinking about what codes and themes are in your data and how these fit together. Miles and Huberman (1994: 9) recommend that your focus should be to identify 'patterns and processes, commonalities and differences'. This can take time and you need to think deeply to identify the layers in your data. You may also find it helpful to talk to other people about your interpretation of the data, or let others look at your data and see if their interpretations are similar to your own.

Computer-assisted qualitative data analysis software

For the more technically-minded, qualitative data analysis software such as NVivo can be used. Check with your university about what qualitative data analysis software may be available to you if you are a student. The principle of qualitative data analysis software is that as you develop codes, you can attach appropriate examples to each code. With qualitative data analysis software, such as NVivo you can start a 'new project' and set reminders for the programme to save and update your progress. After importing your interview transcripts (also often other formats, such as video), you can then take each transcript and highlight the relevant part and create a 'code'. A good starting point for coding is thinking about your research question. You can add new codes or add new highlighted parts of the transcript to existing codes. Once you have developed your codes – you need to develop a set of themes.

Themes are the overarching ideas that summarise a number of codes. Several codes can be aggregated under one code to create a theme. You may choose to visualize the themes with an image or graph which can be saved and exported into your writing-up of the data analysis. Tables summarizing the number of codes related to a theme can also be produced. Quotes attached to codes/themes can be copied into your data analysis chapter or report. There are a number of books that discuss qualitative computer analysis software in detail, such as Bryman's Social Research Methods (Clark et al., 2021) and Gibbs (2018). There are also lots of helpful YouTube clips so that you can see, for example, NVivo being used in real time. A word of caution, however – qualitative data analysis software does not do the thinking for you – you still have to identify the codes and themes yourself.

Analysis techniques derived from grounded theory

There are specific strategies and devices that the qualitative researcher can use for data analysis. Grounded theory is perhaps the best-known process for systematically analysing qualitative data. This chapter is not the appropriate place to discuss the history of grounded

TABLE 5.1 Conceptual names

Interview quote excerpt	Conceptual name
It is an accepted part of everyday school. The school organises the DM [Daily Mile] through teachers choosing when to take their class to do the DM. There is some variation – some teachers run with their class and others do not (Headteacher, Scotland)	Choice/autonomy
Since they have started the initiative the children are much more ready to learn. The attainment of the children has also improved (Headteacher, Scotland)	Attainment

theory or why some researchers find it methodologically problematic (a good starting point for this debate is the chapter by Charmaz in Denzin and Lincoln, 2011). This chapter will restrict itself to explaining some of the techniques from grounded theory which may aid your analysis.

Strauss and Corbin (1998) are two well-known authors of grounded theory research, and they give useful examples to show how they analysed their data. Examples of the data analysis process are replicated here from interviews with teachers about an exercise initiative for pupils (Shields, 2017). First Strauss and Corbin (1998) suggest highlighting the words and phrases – *conceptual names* – that are used repeatedly by participants, see Table 5.1.

Second, Strauss (1987) suggests coding for conditions, interactions among actors, strategies and tactics and consequences, see Table 5.2.

TABLE 5.2 Types of code

Interview excerpt	Type of code	Code
The school believes that through doing the DM they are helping to mitigate against sedentary lifestyles in the evenings and weekends (Headteacher, Scotland)	Conditions	Futurity
The Senior Leadership Team has been impressed with the attainment levels of the children and there is a push from the Senior Leadership Team to encourage all teachers at the school to undertake the Daily Mile with their classes. (Primary class teacher, England)	Interactions among actors	Leadership strategy
'So you know if I'm doing it with them I'll say 'right, let's run for the pink bit' and then you know we'll change and we'll do something in the yellow bit and we'll sort of make it you know, a bit easier for them and you know I don't tend to make them do the full seven laps you know I can see people flagging and things like that. I've got a few sort of boys in my class that you know like a bit of a challenge and 'I'm going to do it, I'm going to do it' and things like that' (First School teacher, England)	Strategies and tactics	Inclusivity
And the reason behind doing it is when we got out health survey back, which we do for Year 4 and Year 6 children, we found that 25% of our Year 6's came out as being obese (Deputy Head, suburban primary school, England).	Consequences	Poor health

TABLE 5.3 Memos

Interview excerpt	Memos
Ah yeah and I mean they do sit, I mean no the curriculum is the way it is you know it's quite formal and they do a lot of sitting and listening whereas in the past they have done a lot of exploring and playing and went into their own place, there is none of that now, everybody needs to be doing this, everybody needs to be achieving that…And it's working them like dogs (Reception Teacher, Coastal Primary School)	I think there is an interesting link here between a formalised curriculum and an increase in sedentary behaviours.
They, they are just a bit calm so rather than, you can see them bubbling and then they come back in they are a lot calmer and they do listen and pay attention a lot more. They seem to be able to focus on the work it's almost as if they are ready to get back on with the learning so they can work a bit better independently (Year 4 teacher, Suburban Primary School)	The DM appears to be a legitimate tool for teachers to re-engage pupils and enable them to 'let off steam'.

> **ACTIVITY**
>
> Using an interview transcript, try to code the data looking for conditions, interactions among actors, strategies and tactics and consequences as suggested by Strauss (1987).
>
> - What patterns do you notice?
> - Are there any other significant themes emerging?
> - Share your analysis with a partner – have they spotted the same themes?

In Table 5.3 there are examples of memos made on interview excerpts.

At the beginning of this chapter, data analysis was described as understanding the 'what' and 'how' of participants explaining their educational experiences. The 'how' can often be identified through considering different language devices. Three language devices which it may be useful to consider are metaphors, contrastive rhetoric and extremist talk.

Language devices for analysis

Metaphors

Although codes can take the form of a straightforward category label, the use of metaphor is a more complex way of interpreting the data (Miles and Huberman, 1994). A metaphor is a figure of speech which presents strong imagery or symbolism. The use of a metaphor can be very revealing in understanding how participants are experiencing or perceiving an event.

Contrastive rhetoric

Making contrasts is a widespread feature of interactional and conversational practice (Hargreaves and Woods, 1984). Contrasts are either explicitly or implicitly involved in all descriptions, since all our conceptions of what things *are*, must also be constructed according to what they are *not*.

TABLE 5.4 Language devices

Language device	Interview excerpt
Metaphor	We have to do end-of-term tests and the children kind of crumble (Class teacher, Suburban Primary School)
Contrastive rhetoric – 'past and present'	SLT [Senior Leadership Team] make very positive comments about the peak in data about the massive progress we've seen towards the end of this term (Class teacher, Suburban Primary School)
Contrastive rhetoric – 'us and them'	Our Key Stage 1 children they do it in an afternoon… theirs is a much smaller circuit that they do, the teacher stands, they do it a variety of ways sometimes…the teacher calls out different things so, 'walk like a crab', 'hop like a rabbit' (Deputy Head, suburban Primary School)
Extremist talk	And it's working them like dogs (Reception Teacher, Coastal Primary School)

The use of such contrastive rhetoric may be identified in many social settings, where participants create accounts based on distinctions between 'us and them', 'past and present' and 'here and there'. The use of 'past and present' is a way to compare previous and current experiences of education and may be particularly relevant for the creation of vignettes in narrative approaches to research. The use of 'us and them' can be employed as a way of differentiating between groups.

Extremist talk

Extremist talk does not involve a comparison; rather, it tends to focus on one end of a spectrum only, and it may be used by individuals who find themselves in subordinate positions or feel powerless (see Table 5.4).

ACTIVITY

- Using an interview transcript from your own data collection – can you identify any language devices being used?
- What do they tell you?

Absences in the data

So far, this chapter has concentrated on identifying what is being said, but what about information that is not mentioned explicitly? Absences in the data – topics or themes that you might have anticipated but which are not there – can tell their own story. It is important to consider whether anything is 'missing' and why that might be. Additionally, you may have anomalies in your data – that is, information from one or two participants that does not 'fit' with your overall findings. Again, you should consider why this is the case, and it is also important to consider whether these findings are important in themselves and therefore whether they should be included when reporting your findings.

TABLE 5.5 Types of variable

Type of variable	Examples	Statistical application
Nominal data	Male/female Socio-economic status Ethnicity Religion	Counting and descriptive statistics e.g. 1 out of 4 respondents was female; 35% of the sample identified themselves as Black and Minority Ethnic (BME)
Ordinal data	Ordinal data often describes perceptions and tries to gauge views. The use of the Likert Scale is a good example of the use of ordinal data, for example I think pupils in my class are good at sharing: 1 Strongly agree; 2 Agree; 3 Neutral; 4 Disagree; 5 Strongly disagree.	Literally meaning 'in order'. Counting and descriptive statistics e.g. 50% of respondents strongly agreed; 30 of the respondents disagreed that the provision of after-school activities was good.
Interval data	Interval data can be ranked on a scale because the 'gap' between each category is known, such as months or years. This means that the analysis can assess how much more or how much less, rather than just more or less.	For example, the number of grade '9' GCSE English results: 2024 – 10% 2023 – 15% 2022 – 12% In this example we could compare the schools' results year on year.
Ratio data	Income, weight, distance. Ratio data has a true zero. Comparisons can be made using multiplication and division. Ratio data is the most sophisticated type of data in terms of the types of statistical tests that can be done.	For example, you might want to compare the salary of a newly qualified teacher with that of another graduate entry profession or you may want to identify the distance travelled by pupils to school.
Discrete data	This is about naturally-forming whole units.	For example, children or teachers. Also, it does not make sense to talk about 1.4 children – we would say 1 child or 2 children etc.

Quantitative data analysis

Quantitative data is numerical, such as number of pupils or exam results. In quantitative data analysis, the focus is on variables. A variable is an attribute that describes a person, place, thing or idea. Qualitative variables take on values that are names or labels, such as school subjects or hobbies. Quantitative variables are numeric, which means they can be measured – for example, the number of children in a school (see Table 5.5).

Frequency

A questionnaire involved data collection from three Year 7 Maths classes (100 pupils in total). Question 3 asked pupils their gender – boy or girl. Question 7 asked for pupils' Maths test result when they started secondary school in September. To make sense of the data it first needs to be counted. This can be done by entering the answers from each participant into a spreadsheet or

TABLE 5.6 Exemplar frequency table

Gender	Grade A	Grade B	Grade C	Grade D	Grade E
Girl (51)	10	13	17	8	3
Boy (49)	8	14	20	6	1
Total (out of 100)	18	27	37	14	4

table. At this stage all you are doing is counting the data. The frequency table shows the number of students who achieved a particular grade in their Maths test (see Table 5.6).

If you include a frequency table, it is important to highlight to the reader the key patterns that you have identified.

Descriptive statistics

Descriptive statistics do just that – they describe. They are generally employed for univariate data which has one variable, such as the pupils' Maths test scores. For instance, looking at the frequency table (Table 5.6), we can describe this data by saying that 18 out of 100 pupils achieved a Grade A in their Maths test. We could also describe this as a percentage and say that 18% of the pupils achieved a Grade A or report it as a fraction and say that just under 1/5 of pupils achieved a Grade A.

However, you may also wish to interrogate the data further to identify other patterns. For example, of the 51 girls in the questionnaire, 10 achieved a Grade A in Maths. Therefore, you may wish to say that 19.6% of the girls achieved a Grade A in Maths. A graph can also represent this data. There are a range of different types of graphs that may be useful for visual representations, such as bar charts, pie charts, scatter graphs and line graphs. Again, it will be important to highlight to the reader the key patterns that you have identified.

Measures of central tendency

The mean, mode and median are called measures of central tendency because they identify a single score as typical or representative of all the scores in a frequency distribution (see Table 5.7).

If more than one number occurs most frequently when you are trying to work out the mode – for example, as with the dataset 4, 4, 5, 6, 6, 7 – there are two modes, in this case the numbers 4 and 6. This is because both of these numbers occur most frequently (twice). In this instance you may need to consider whether a different measure of central tendency would be more appropriate. When a dataset has an even number of measurements there is no 'middle' number to give you the median. Instead, you need to take the two middle numbers and work out the average. For example, in the dataset 4, 4, 5, 6, 6, 7 the middle numbers are 5 and 6. Working out the average of these two numbers gives you a median of 5.5.

TABLE 5.7 Measures of central tendency

Measure of central tendency	Method	Example
Mean	The mean is also known as the average. To work out the average, add all the numbers up and then divide them by the total number.	$4 + 5 + 6 + 4 + 7 = 5.2$ The mean is 5.2
Mode	The mode means the most common – that is, the most commonly occurring number in the data set.	4, 4, 5, 6, 7 The mode is **4**, since it is the most commonly occurring number.
Median	The median refers to the middle value. This means the numbers have to be placed in ascending order.	4, 4, 5, 6, 7 **5** is the median number here, since it falls in the middle.

As measures of central tendency, the mean and median each have advantages and disadvantages. The median may be a better indicator of the most typical value if a set of scores has an outlier. An outlier is an extreme value that differs greatly from the other values in the data set. However, when the sample size is large and does not include outliers, the mean usually provides a better measure of central tendency.

Standard deviation and variance

Standard deviation measures how spread out a set of numbers is. The formula for the standard variation is the square root of the variance. The variance is the average of the squared differences from the mean, see the following example:

To work out the variance of a set of reading test scores (scored out of 100):

1. Work out the average reading test score:

$$\frac{80 + 40 + 55 + 75 + 67}{5} = 63.4$$

2. Subtract the average from each measurement:

$$80 - 63.4 = 16.6$$
$$40 - 63.4 = -23.4$$
$$55 - 63.4 = -8.4$$
$$75 - 63.4 = 11.6$$
$$67 - 63.4 = 3.6$$

3. Square the results and sum them:

$$16.6^2 + (-23.4)^2 + (-8.4)^2 + 11.6^2 + 3.6^2 = 1041.2$$

4. Work out the average of the squared differences:

$$\frac{1041.2}{5} = 208.24$$

5   The variance is 208.24.

6   The standard deviation is the square root of the variance:
$$\sqrt{208.24} = 14.43$$

7   **The standard deviation is 14.**

(Decimal numbers can be rounded to the nearest whole number – round up whenever the last digit is 5 or greater).

Chi-square test

This section will outline a chi-square test since this is perhaps the most useful statistical test within educational research. The chi-square test is used to discover the relationship between two categorical variables. Your variables must be ordinal or nominal, and you need two or more groups in each variable. A quantitative data software package such as Statistical Package for the Social Sciences (SPSS) will use the correct formulae to complete the statistical test. However, it is important to know when and why you would use this test. An example of when a chi-squared test may be applied and advice on interpreting the results are given below.

A science teacher wants to know if boys or girls prefer an online game-based learning simulation or a practical experiment when learning how to create electrical circuits. Our variables are: gender – boy or girl; and preferred learning activity – online or practical. Our statistical test involves bivariate data, meaning that we have two variables. Once the teacher has collected the data it can be entered into SPSS. SPSS will identify the number of girls who prefer online learning, the number of girls who prefer practical learning, the number of boys who prefer online learning and the number of boys who prefer practical learning. The results of the chi-square test will identify if both boys and girls prefer a practical activity for learning about electrical circuits.

The chi-square test involves taking the sum of the difference between the observed (o) data and the expected (e) data, and dividing it by the expected data in all categories. The formula below shows the chi-square test calculation:

$$X^2 = \sum \frac{(o-e)^2}{e}$$

o = the frequencies observed
e = the frequencies expected
Σ = the 'sum of'

As with most statistics, the results of chi-square calculations have a significance level attached to them. If the significance level is lower than $p = 0.05$ (or one in twenty) this means that the observed effect is highly unlikely to be the result of chance. Therefore, a result of $p \leq 0.05$ is generally considered statistically significant.

Computer-assisted quantitative data analysis software

SPSS is a helpful tool for running some of the more complex statistical tests as well as calculating measures of central tendency. It also produces a wide range of graphs which can be exported into data analysis chapters and reports. Check with your university about what quantitative data analysis software may be available to you if you are a student. At the bottom of the left-hand corner of the screen on SPSS, there are two view tabs – 'data view' and 'variable view'. Click on the variable view first and complete the: 'name', 'data type', 'number of decimal places', and 'measure'. You have the choice of three types of measure: 'scale', 'ordinal' and 'nominal'. Once you have completed the variable view for each type of data you are going to input, you can click on data view. Enter your data for each column. If the numbers do not look correct – just go back to variable view to check you have set everything, for example 'decimals' appropriately.

Once all of your data has been inputted, you can go to the 'analyse' tab which is along the top of your screen. You might want to click on 'descriptive statistics' and then 'frequencies'. Drag the variables you wish to analyse into the box on the right-hand side and click 'statistics'. You can then tick the selection of statistics that you wish to produce and press continue. A set of tables with the data analysed will be produced. In addition, you may wish to click on 'graphs' which is also at the top of your screen and you can then click 'chart builder'. Remember to pick two sets of variables to create a graph. Choose your style of graph and drag your variable to label your X and Y axis. Click 'ok' to create your graph. There are a number of books that discuss quantitative computer analysis software in detail, such as Clark *et al.* (2021) and Cohen, Manion and Morrison (2018). There are also lots of helpful YouTube clips so that you can see SPSS being used in real-time.

Chapter summary

Data analysis is a significant part of a research project. The way in which data analysis is carried out will depend on whether you have qualitative or quantitative data. There are a variety of ways in which qualitative data can be analysed, but they all rely on the researcher to interpret the data. There are set ways of analysing numerical data and statistical tests can be used to show the patterns in this type of data, but it is important for the researcher to explain the meaning of these. Two popular computer-assisted data analysis software packages have been highlighted – NVivo (for qualitative data analysis) and SPSS (for quantitative data analysis).

Further reading

Bazeley, P. (2020) *Qualitative data analysis: Practical strategies*. 2nd edn. London: SAGE.
- This is a lovely book which explores the complexity of qualitative data analysis with helpful practical approaches. The book draws upon seminal authors in the field of research methods.

Bergin, T. (2018) *An introduction to data analysis: Quantitative, qualitative and mixed-methods.* London: SAGE.

- This book tackles quantitative analysis in a clear manner – enabling the most number-phobic researcher to understand both basic and more complex ways of analysing numeric data confidently.

References

Charmaz, K. (2011) 'Grounded theory methods in social justice Research', in Denzin, N. and Lincoln, Y. (eds.) *Handbook of qualitative research.* London: Sage Publications, pp. 359–380.

Clark, T., Foster, L., Sloan, L. and Bryman, A. (2021) *Bryman's social research methods.* 6th edn. Oxford: Oxford University Press.

Cohen, L., Manion, L. and Morrison, K. (2018) *Research methods in education.* 8th edn. London: Routledge.

Gibbs, G. (2018) *Analyzing qualitative data.* 2nd edn. London: SAGE.

Hargreaves, A. and Woods, P. (1984) *Classrooms and staffrooms: The sociology of teachers and teaching.* Milton Keynes: Open University Press.

Miles, M.B. and Huberman, A.M. (1994) *Qualitative data analysis: An expanded sourcebook.* 2nd edn. Thousand Oaks, CA: SAGE.

Shields, S. (2017) 'Running for success: A case study of an exercise initiative on health and "readiness to learn" in two primary schools', *ECER 2017: Reforming education and the imperative of constant change: Ambivalent roles of policy and educational research.* Copenhagen: University College UCC.

Strauss, A.L. (1987) *Qualitative analysis for social scientists.* Cambridge: Cambridge University Press.

Strauss, A. L. and Corbin, J. M. (1998) *Basics of qualitative research: Techniques and procedures for developing grounded theory.* 2nd edn. London: Sage.

CHAPTER 6

Writing up your research project

Introduction

This chapter provides practical guidance for managing the writing-up phase of a piece of extended research in education studies. This may be the first time you have taken on a large piece of writing like this, so this chapter is full of useful support and advice. It provides examples of possible chapter structures and layouts, advice for managing time and material, and hints and tips for writing effectively. If you choose your topic and your methodology carefully, your extended research project should be the best part of your degree. It is an opportunity for you to investigate an educational topic in greater depth than in other parts of the course. You will be able to use the knowledge and skills you have developed during your degree to produce an independent and original piece of work. It should be the most rewarding piece of work that you complete, but it is also the most demanding. It is therefore very important that you:

- Choose an area of study that is of real interest to you
- Ensure that you have access to sufficient and appropriate material to support your topic
- Make sure your project is realistic within your resource and time limitations
- Develop an appropriate and feasible methodological approach
- Start writing early – do not leave writing up until the last few weeks!

Getting started

Often the hardest part of writing up is getting started. Somehow your room always seems in need of a good tidy, and TV programmes seem to become much more interesting. Even the most experienced writer procrastinates – especially in the early stages of writing up.

Your research project is likely to be the longest piece of writing you will have done, and it can feel very daunting – especially at the beginning. Luckily, if you have followed the guidance from earlier in this book you will not be starting with a blank sheet of paper. You should have clear aims and objectives, research questions or a hypothesis, which you will have agreed with your supervisor quite early on. You will have lots of reference material, and you may have a draft literature review. You may have kept a 'research log' or 'diary' and undertaken substantial 'thinking on paper' (Wolcott, 1990: 21), keeping notes on your reflections about what worked well and what proved difficult throughout your research, comments on articles you have read, documenting your developing data analysis and so on. To help you make a start, consider:

- Producing a detailed chapter plan and a schedule identifying key deadline dates to complete chapters/drafts
- Taking each of your aims and objectives in turn and writing a brief description of what each means, which method you used to address it and what you discovered
- Begin writing with a chapter you already have lots of material for– this is likely to be your literature review
- Making the task seem less daunting by thinking of the final project as a series of connected short essays. It is easier to start a 2,000-word essay than a 10,000- word thesis!

Structuring your research project

A conventional structure for a research project based on empirical research consists of the following chapters:

Introduction

This chapter usually articulates and explains the project's aims and objectives, research questions and/or hypothesis. These aspects of your study are absolutely key in helping you write up – they should frame everything that follows. The introduction often includes a rationale and a justification for the study. Ask yourself why the topic is important and why you are a good person to undertake it. The chapter generally ends with an outline of the overall structure of the report and a summary of each chapter.

Context

Here you outline the political, economic, social, cultural, historical, local and personal contexts of the study. Discuss important developments in your field of educational enquiry and outline key policy developments. Think about important current factors that impact your topic – changes in technology, the wider economy, funding, participation rates, media stories and so on. In this chapter, you are providing a background to your study. If you undertook primary research in a particular school or college, provide some details about student and staff numbers, specific institutional factors and policies (remembering to adhere to conventions on anonymity).

Literature review

Use existing literature to frame your topic, to help you clarify important concepts and develop your own argument. Use a range of sources and types of literature (empirical, theoretical, conceptual, journalistic, academic, statistical, interpretive, seminal, contemporary…). Remember, you are not simply identifying important literature. You are organising and critically analysing it to help you to develop your project. Ideally, try to identify a gap in the literature that your project fills (see Chapter 3 for further guidance).

Methodology

This is a really important chapter and it has a number of functions. Firstly, you need to position your research within wider methodological debates – for instance, within the interpretivist and positivist paradigms discussed earlier (see Chapter 1). Then you need to outline and justify the choices you made – your approach to sampling, the methods you utilised, your data analysis strategies, the ethical issues you identified and the solutions you came up with. Evaluate your own research in relation to concepts like validity, reliability, representativeness, generalisability and reflexivity (see Chapter 19 for further guidance).

Results/Findings

Here you outline your main findings. Quantitative data might be presented in tables, graphs and charts. Qualitative data might be presented as quotes from respondents, extracts from fieldwork diaries, detailed life stories, or descriptions of events or encounters. The way you select and present your data demonstrates your analysis and interpretations; grouping your findings around themes is a very good strategy (see Chapter 5 for further guidance).

Discussion

This is where you critically examine your data, setting out the implications of your research. The key thing here is to refer back to the literature you discussed in your third chapter. Think about the similarities and differences between the literature and your own findings. Relate back to your aims and objectives or your research questions (see Chapter 2 and Chapter 3 for further guidance).

Conclusion

This chapter provides a summary of the overall project. It refers directly to aims and objectives/research questions as outlined in the introductory chapter. Conclusions often include a series of recommendations (for practice or for future research) that come out of your study. This chapter might also include a discussion of how your research could be improved upon, and an outline of future related research projects.

Other research project structures

Of course, this is only one way that your research project could be set out. Some prefer to embed contexts in their introduction or their literature review. Some incorporate findings and discussion into one chapter, while others prefer to have a series of 'findings' chapters, each examining different themes emerging from the data. Some have two chapters on methodology – one that deals with the theory and principles of educational research, and another that describes and justifies the practicalities of the selected research design.

If you are writing a research project based on secondary research (a library-based project, for example) you are likely to develop a very different chapter structure. You might develop four or five 2000-word essays on issues relevant to your topic, with introduction and conclusion chapters to bind them all together and create a coherent narrative. Alternatively, you might want to be original and experimental, developing your own very unique chapter structure. If you choose to do this, ask your supervisor to show you some examples of innovative structures and make sure they are happy with your proposed outline. Whichever way you choose to structure your research project, try to include all the features identified above at some stage.

Other components

Your research project should also include the following:

Title page

Along with your name or student number and the title of your project, you will be expected to include information about the assignment and your university. Check your institution's handbook for details of what should be included here.

Abstract

The abstract should appear immediately after the title page. The abstract provides a brief summary of the research project, outlining key arguments and findings. Abstracts are generally between 150 and 300 words in length. This is a really important section. As you will have discovered when doing your own literature review, the abstract is a key source of information for the reader, helping them to decide if something is relevant and interesting to them. A good abstract outlines key aims and objectives, the methodological approach, the main findings, and concludes with an indication of why the project is important. While the rest of your research project will be presented in one-and-a-half or double-line spacing, the abstract is always single-spaced. It is best to write the abstract after you have completed the whole research project.

Contents page

The contents page is a list of all chapter headings, subheadings and maybe sub-subheadings, alongside the page number that each begins on. You should also include any appendices with their page numbers. You might also include a list of tables, figures or charts. If your project contains lots of acronyms and/or subject-specific concepts, you might include a list of abbreviations and/or a glossary after the contents page.

Acknowledgements

You might take this opportunity to thank anyone who has helped you with your research project. It is usually a good idea to thank your supervisor. You might also thank any institution you visited for your fieldwork, or anybody that helped you with data collection or analysis. Finally, you might want to thank friends and family for giving you the time and space to complete such a lengthy project.

Reference list

The reference list appears at the end of the report, after the Discussion and Conclusion chapters. It includes all the sources you cited in your research project. These are presented in alphabetical order. If you have used a software package like *Endnote* or *Refworks*, it will automatically populate your reference list. A bibliography, which includes all sources read during the production of the project irrespective of whether or not they are directly cited, is used less frequently nowadays. See later in this chapter for guidance on presenting references.

Appendices

The final thing you might need to include in your research project is a list of appendices. These are supplementary documents that are of relevance to the project. As a general rule, keep them to a minimum or avoid them altogether. It is a good idea to include a copy of a questionnaire, a list of interview prompts or an observation schedule if you have used any of these. You might be asked to include your research ethics approval documentation, your informed consent form or copies of letters to head teachers or parents about your project. You might also include other official documentation – copies of school documents, official statistics tables or publicity documentation. Only include documents that you make reference to in the main body of the research report. You should not include copies of all completed questionnaires or full transcripts from interviews or focus groups, but you could provide one (or extracts from a few) as an example. Appendices do not usually count towards your word count, so there is a tendency to throw lots of things into this section if you are struggling to stay below the upper word limit.

Some useful strategies for writing-up

Over time writers develop their own strategies for ensuring they are able to submit their work on time. There are a number of tactics that you might find helpful (please also see Chapter 2):

- Draw up a *writing plan* that sets out important deadlines for completing the draft of each chapter. Aim to have a full draft completed well in advance of the final deadline. Your plan will need to be flexible, but it will provide you with a yardstick to measure your own progress.

- Identify specific *writing days*, especially in the early stages of writing up. Make sure that nothing will interrupt you on these days, so you can dedicate your time to writing. This will really help to give your writing momentum.
- Develop a *writing routine*, whether this is a daily or weekly pattern. Some people find it easy to get up early and do two hours' writing before the day begins. Others prefer doing a night shift, writing between midnight and 2.00 a.m. As a general rule, our minds are fresher earlier on in the day.
- Have regular *writing breaks*. Sitting staring at a computer screen is not the healthiest way of spending time. To avoid a stiff neck and a bleary feeling, do some exercise at regular intervals. Light exercise gets your body moving and raises your heartbeat up – but don't overdo it! Fresh air really helps, and many writers find walking to be a great activity for organising thoughts and developing new ideas.
- Set yourself *writing targets*. In a particular session, aim to write 400 words, or to complete two sub-headed sections. Make sure these targets are feasible and short-range, so that you are breaking an extended piece of writing into small manageable chunks.
- Give yourself *writing rewards*. Gift yourself a cup of tea or half-an-hour's TV viewing when you have successfully achieved a complete section or made your word target.
- Find your own ideal *writing environment*. Some writers require solitude, while others prefer to write alongside a friend or colleague (to encourage and support each other). Some need silence while others like background music.
- Identify a *writing buddy*. A 'critical friend' who can read and comment on your drafts. Preferably this would be someone who is also writing up their own research project, so that you can reciprocate – critical reading of another person's writing will really help with your own.

Ten 'top tips' for writing a successful research project

1. Aim to finish the final draft of your research project about two or three weeks before the deadline.
2. Develop research questions/aims and objectives that make the project focused and concise. For instance, do not try to explain educational inequalities; rather, concentrate on a specific issue or explanation (like young people with disabilities and their access to higher education, or social capital and the attainment of private school pupils). You might be able to refine a broad topic after you have gathered data and begun to write up.
3. Develop a detailed plan and be flexible enough to modify this as your writing develops.
4. Introduce and conclude each chapter, indicating how each section fits with those before and after.

5. Keep sentence construction simple and to the point.
6. Support your argument with references, but do not use extensive quotes or build your research project around them.
7. Present a consistent voice throughout – normally in the third person and the past tense.
8. Use chapters, subheadings and sub-subheadings to structure and signpost your arguments.
9. Do not overstate claims or overgeneralise – be tentative and moderate about the conclusions that you can draw from your findings.
10. Carefully check the criteria that your work will be assessed against, and make sure you cover each clearly.

A brief note on ethics

When you write up your research project you must take account of ethical guidelines. BERA's *Ethical guidelines for educational research* (BERA, 2024) are the standard in the UK. Most importantly you need to respect privacy, confidentiality and anonymity. If you have undertaken research in a school or another educational institution, you need to conceal its identity. Either provide it with a pseudonym, or describe it in general terms – for example, as a 'medium-sized primary school in the East Midlands'. Likewise, you must maintain the anonymity of any respondents you interview or observe. You can refer to respondents as 'Interviewee 1', 'Interviewee 2' and so on, but your research project will be a more interesting read if you use pseudonyms. It is good practice to add a footnote after the first use of a pseudonym, explaining that all names appearing in the text are fictitious to preserve the anonymity of the participants. Also, only include comments for which you have received consent! Another strategy you might choose to employ is to send the final manuscript to your respondents. Not only might their comments help you to validate your analysis and interpretations, but in ethical terms you also enable them to take some ownership of the final account (respondent validation) (see Chapter 20 for more information on these issues).

Referencing

Different departments and universities expect you to use different referencing approaches. In education, the Harvard and APA styles are the most commonly used referencing systems. Check your course or module handbook to confirm the preferred style. Most importantly, always be consistent and accurate with your references. When directly quoting a source in the main text, you should present the reference as (name, date: page number).

Plagiarism

Plagiarism is an attempt to gain an advantage by unfair means, and it is taken very seriously by universities. There are a number of potential sanctions, which will get more severe the further you are through your degree. Plagiarised work will almost certainly get a mark of zero and if you are lucky the outcome may be the dissertation being rewritten for a capped mark. Students can be thrown off the course if they are found guilty. Increasingly, Artificial Intelligence (AI) tools such as ChatGPT can be appealing in helping students to complete their university assignments. If you decide to draw upon tools such as ChatGPT, it is likely that your university will expect you to submit an 'AI declaration' as part of your assignment. An 'AI declaration' typically includes an explanation of the search terms that you have used and the responses that were generated. The general advice from academics to students (with some notes of caution) is that AI might be a helpful tool for checking key points or for guiding you on how to structure your own work. However, academics have been known to describe AI-generated responses as being equivalent to the work of a university student who did not attend any lectures! Be aware also, that academic staff may input your work into ChatGPT themselves to check for similarity. It is really important to have a good understanding of the topic of your assignment, as a search term, such as 'ethics' may generate a paragraph that is not relevant, such as one about 'social justice'. Overall, using a tool such as ChatGPT is a very poor substitute for doing your own reading and research and not acknowledging its use correctly is a form of plagiarism.

Plagiarism includes:

- Copying from a text (book, article, website) without acknowledgement
- Purchasing work from an assignment-writing website
- Copying another student's work
- Paraphrasing – putting arguments you have read into your own words without acknowledging the source
- Submitting work as your own when it has been produced with someone else or by a group.

Universities generally use a software tool like *Turnitin* to identify any correlations between your work and existing literature. Not only does this check your assignment against published work, it also checks against other students' work already submitted through the system. This is an ever-growing database, and it is certainly not worth taking any chances. To ensure you do not plagiarise, always:

- Write in your own words
- Reference accurately
- Acknowledge all sources for your material
- Make a note of any reference you use
- Clearly identify any quote you use
- Be especially careful when using material from websites. It is easy to cut and paste and then forget to rephrase and reference
- Submit a full reference list

When you have completed a full draft of your research project, you need to read it through carefully. It is worth reading aloud – this allows you to hear how your writing sounds. Because your report is an extended piece of writing, you need to be especially careful that you have written in a consistent style and in a coherent manner. When you have completed a full draft, proofread your work against the following checklist:

Presentation

- Consistency and accuracy of referencing
- Grammar, spelling and punctuation
- Follow in-house presentational guide (line spacing, font size, margins, font style)
- Consistent tense and 'voice'
- Research findings presented clearly and accurately

Coherence

- Chapters are introduced and concluded
- Aims and objectives/research questions are stated clearly and related throughout
- Conclusions refer directly to aims and objectives/research questions
- Clarity and independence of argument
- Writing is balanced, evaluative and does not overstate claims

Use of evidence

- Range of literature (current, historical, academic, theory, empirical)
- No assertions – claims that are not justified with reference to evidence
- Evidence used to develop your own argument
- Define and explain specialist language and jargon
- Research findings not simply described, but interpreted and analysed

Chapter summary

This chapter has provided support for the process of writing up your research project. It has discussed strategies to help you get started and then maintain your writing over time. It has provided 'top tips' for producing a successful piece of extended writing and outlined potential chapter structures and core components. This was followed by guidance on referencing and avoiding plagiarism. The chapter ended by offering a checklist to help you proofread your full draft.

Further reading

Bell, J. and Waters, S. (2018) *Doing your research project: A guide for first-time researchers.* 7th edn. London: Open University Press.

- Extensive practical advice and a highly accessible approach have made Bell & Waters book the 'go to' text. You will also find the practical tasks in Sharp's book really helpful as you progress with your own work.

O'Leary, Z. (2021) *The essential guide to doing your research project.* 4th edn. London: SAGE.

- This book incorporates flow charts to help you to navigate to the next part of the book that you should read. The book also includes a comprehensive glossary and useful information for writing-up your research.

References

BERA (2024) *Ethical guidelines for educational research.* 5th edn. British Educational Research Association.

Wolcott, H. (1990) *Writing up qualitative research.* London: SAGE.

PART

Research strategies

CHAPTER

7

Surveys

Introduction

Surveys enable us to collect a representation of the population of interest by the same information being collected from each participant (more information about population samples can be found in Chapter 4). Surveys may collect information on attitudes, perceptions or behaviour and they may be able to access information that is not already easily available. By the use of a survey, the researcher can make claims about a wider population based on the results from a sample. Surveys lend themselves to quantitative designs, and the large number of respondents required by the survey method means that statistical tests can be used. Therefore, survey results are generally reported in numerical form and are widely used within educational research. For example, headline findings from recent educational surveys include 'outdated facilities are harming learning. Survey findings reflect "catastrophic underinvestment" in the school estate, according to heads' union' (Norden, 2024) and 'a survey of 9,000 teachers in England found that one in four brought food into school out of concern for hungry pupils' (Fareshare, 2023). Surveys may consider educational inequality, well-being and social mobility.

Surveys can be particularly useful for looking at patterns within education and other aspects of peoples' lives. One well-known educational survey is the 'Programme for International Student Assessment' (PISA) by the Organization for Economic Cooperation and Development (OECD) (OECD, 2024). This international study is participated in by over seventy countries. It aims to evaluate education systems worldwide by undertaking three-yearly assessments of fifteen-year-olds' competencies in reading, mathematics and science. The COSMO (the COVID Social Mobility and Opportunities) study is recruiting 11,000 Year 13 pupils from England in its second wave and is weighted to be nationally representative (COSMO, 2024). This chapter will outline different types of surveys, practical issues to consider when conducting a survey and survey response rates.

DOI: 10.4324/9781003569428-9

Types of survey

There are a range of different types of surveys, and some surveys may combine more than one approach – for example, a survey may be longitudinal, but it may also use a panel of participants.

Cross-sectional

This means that responses are collected at one point in time from a sample selected to represent a larger population. A cross-sectional survey via a questionnaire research tool identified Year 5 Malaysian pupils' experiences with online games to develop their English Language vocabulary proficiency (Hasram et al., 2021). The sample was representative of pupils studying the Malaysian Language Curriculum with low intermediate English proficiency and were derived from three broad income groups. Therefore, the findings from this cross-sectional survey as to the efficacy of the online games are likely to be representative of other primary school pupils in Malaysia.

Longitudinal

Longitudinal studies are carried out over a period of time. This type of survey can be more accurate than cross-sectional surveys, and it helps us to understand changes over a period of time. This type of survey is expensive and it may be many years before results can be compared. Comparability over time can also be problematic, and so the significance of findings needs to be considered within the context they are located. For example, the proportion of individuals holding a university degree has changed significantly over the last fifty years due to shifts in the economic needs of society and educational policies, not because people are more intelligent than in the past. Over time a number of respondents are likely to drop out of any longitudinal study, thereby making it more difficult to justify comparisons over time with a diminishing number of participants. The Understanding Society study covers a wide range of topics and explores social and economic changes over time in society (University of Essex/ISER, 2023). It considers the impact of policy changes over time on the well-being of the UK population (this study replaces the British Household Panel Survey (BHPS)).

Trend

This type of survey uses a new sample population at different points in time. This can overcome the drop-out rate among respondents that may affect a longitudinal survey. However, changes in individuals cannot be identified because different populations are used each time. Comparative statistical tests are problematic if the population changes each time the survey is conducted. A rolling sample, in which a proportion of the sample in the survey is longitudinal, is a potential compromise. The Language Trends survey is delivered by the British Council (Colleen, 2022). In 2022 the trend survey asked 1600 teachers in England (primary, secondary and independent sector) about language learning and teaching. One key trend that was identified was that by 2026 Spanish will be a more popular GCSE than French. Another key finding was that the amount of time studying a language at primary school varied, with some children receiving no more than thirty minutes a week.

Cohort

A cohort survey uses the same population characteristics each time data is collected, but the samples may be different. The COSMO survey (the COVID Social Mobility and Opportunities) is a national youth cohort study and found that students in 2023 were more likely to live at home if they went to university in comparison to previous years (CLS, 2023).

Panel

A panel survey involves the collection of data at various time points with the same sample of respondents. The China Education Panel Survey uses a nationally representative data set. The China Education Panel Survey found a positive relationship between preschool attendance and cognitive skills in Grade 7 and Grade 9 and also analysed differences between rural and urban pupils (Zheng, Weng and Gong, 2021).

Retrospective

A retrospective survey asks respondents to recall past events, and it therefore has the advantage of hindsight. However, retrospective surveys can be criticized, since the accuracy of respondents in recalling past events may be called into question. In particular, attitudes may shift over time. Often reports on individuals' past actions can be prone to reconstruction according to more socially desirable recollections (Finney, 1981). A retrospective survey aimed to understand why some females became Science, Technology, Engineering and Mathematics (STEM) subject graduates (four to six years after graduation) (Luo, Stoeger and Subotnik, 2022). The retrospective survey explored the influence of parental education, teachers as mentors and peers belonging of female STEM graduates, who had attended selective science high schools. The findings suggested that becoming a female STEM graduate was strongly correlated with parental educational levels and teachers as mentors.

ACTIVITY

Read the extract below from Bubb and Jones (2020):

> The aim of the research was to find how parents, teachers and pupils (1st–10th Grade, ages 6–16) in a Norwegian municipality experienced home-school and what, if anything, they wanted to continue with after schools reopened. Our research questions were therefore:
>
> - How did pupils, parents/carers and teachers experience home-schooling?
> - What did school leaders plan to change as a result of the home-schooling experience?
>
> Key areas that related to ongoing work in the municipality were probed by asking participants to respond to statements with agreement ratings using a four-point Likert scale from 'strongly agree' to 'strongly disagree'; each had space for optional comments. The areas were digital learning; creative learning; pupil participation; progress; achievement; feedback; group work; parent-teacher relationships; and parents' ability to help children.

The approach was to involve as many individuals as possible, rather than to select any sample (Fowler, 2009). It was important to gather views of all the key stakeholders within the schools to see how their views compared and related to each other so we designed four surveys: one for parents, one for teachers and two for pupils. We considered it important to give all year groups the opportunity to participate. Younger children might be considered too immature to answer a digital survey (Lumby, 2012), but we were keen to include their views, particularly as one might imagine that they would be worst affected by the move to remote learning. To limit the demands on the younger ones, we designed a shorter survey for pupils in Grades 1 to 4, with eight questions. There were 14 questions for pupils in Grades 5 to 10, teachers and parents.

Much thought was put into survey construction (Stoop *et al.*, 2010). The questionnaires were designed to be easy and quick to complete in Norwegian, to help maximise the response rate. A key intention was to produce data which could be compared between groups so analogous statements were tailored as appropriate for each of the different groups. For instance, pupils in Grades 1 to 4 were asked how much they agreed with the statement, *I've become better at using an iPad/computer when I'm doing schoolwork;* and those in Grades 5 to 10, *I've become better at using digital tools when I'm doing schoolwork.* Parents/carers were asked how much they agreed with the statement, *My child/children have become better at using digital tools.* Teachers were asked to say how much they agreed with the statement, *I have become more adept at using digital tools during home-schooling.* In each case, a four-point Likert scale was used, ranging from 'totally agree' to 'totally disagree'. Furthermore, respondents were given the option to comment on each statement, and many took the opportunity to do so. Teachers, parents and pupils in Grades 5 to 10 were also asked one open question, which was 'What lessons can schools learn from the experience of home-school?'... To ensure that all respondents felt comfortable in completing them, all surveys were anonymous and voluntary. The only demographic data asked for from pupils and parents/carers were the name of their school and year group; teachers were asked to identify the school they worked in and which of three broad age bands (Grades 1–4, 5–7 and 8–10) they taught.

- What are the strengths of this survey design?
- Is there any part of the survey design that you would have changed? Why?

(Bubb and Jones, 2020: 211–212)

Practical issues to consider when conducting a survey

Be aware that surveys and questionnaires should not be confused. A questionnaire is a *research tool*. A survey is a *research approach* which:

- Asks standardized questions
- Uses a sample of a population
- Focuses on attitudes, perceptions and behaviour

However, to make matters slightly more complicated, a survey may use a questionnaire as a research tool. Indeed, a questionnaire is perhaps the most common tool used in surveys,

TABLE 7.1 Survey delivery approach

Survey delivery approach	Advantages	Disadvantages
Face-to-face	✓ High response rate ✓ Complex questions can be asked	× Costly × Time consuming × Interview bias × Difficult to target a large population without a lot of interviewers
Telephone	✓ Better response rate than a letter or email ✓ Quicker than face-to-face	× Not all telephone numbers or email addresses are available × Not all of the target population will respond × Difficult to target a large population without a lot of interviewers
Postal	✓ Cheap (in comparison to using interviewers) ✓ Large numbers of the survey can be posted ✓ Slower response rate than face-to-face or telephone ✓ Can access populations who are difficult to contact face-to-face or via telephone	× Low response rate × Complex questions cannot be asked × Reliant on respondents fully uncerstanding the questions × Reliant on respondent to answer questions without the interviewer present
Online survey	✓ Cheap (if survey software is already available) ✓ Professional looking survey ✓ No paper making it environmentally friendly ✓ Calculates the results for you reducing time and human error in putting the data ✓ Quick access to results	× Lower response rate than face-to-face or telephone × Populations with less access and/or confidence in technology and the internet may not be fully represented × Software compatibility issues

but it is not the only possibility – for example, surveys may also use face-to-face interviews, telephone interviews, observations or document analysis. There are also several other ways in which a survey can be conducted. Table 7.1 above highlights the different approaches and their relative advantages and disadvantages.

Response rates

Response rates will vary markedly within social research depending on the methods being used, the nature of the respondents and the types of issues being investigated. There is no hard and fast rule about what constitutes an acceptable response rate. With large-scale postal surveys it is not uncommon to get a response rate as low as 15%. Interviews arranged by personal contact between the researcher and the interviewee are at the other end of the spectrum, since very high response rates can be expected – much closer to 100%. Rather than look for a figure considered to be above or below an acceptable response rate - it is more productive to evaluate the response rate that is actually achieved in terms of whether it is in line with comparable surveys. The researcher can look to similar studies as a way of gauging whether their own response rate is acceptable. The methods, the target group, the topic of the research and the use of prior contact are all important here, each has a bearing on the level of response.

As you have already seen, the different delivery approaches of your survey are likely to influence the number of responses you receive. The delivery approach you use should reflect your target group – for example, a retrospective survey about the educational experiences of pupils in the 1950s may not be best administered via the internet but may work well using face-to-face interviews. Equally, a study of university students may not achieve a good rate of return if the survey is administered by post, but a weblink on a social media site may achieve a high response rate. The topic of your survey is also influential, because if the questions are deemed to be of a personal nature your respondents may be reluctant to complete it. Also, if the survey is not of interest or is not relevant to the respondents, they will be much less likely to respond. Finally, if you have had contact with your potential respondents before asking them to complete the survey, this may increase the response rate rather than sending the survey 'cold'. In summary, the benchmark for an acceptable response rate needs to be set by reference to the experience of similar surveys. The validity of your survey results will be measured in part by your response rate. However, the analysis of your findings also needs to be conducted carefully and should avoid overly simplistic causal links.

Non-response rate

Non-response rate is an interesting aspect to consider when analysing your survey results. In theory, the larger your number of respondents, the less likely it is that you will have missed out a significant part of a population. However, administering and analysing a survey is costly in terms of resources and time, and this has to be balanced against how many respondents you can manage. This section will consider the implications of non-response rates. The last respondents in your survey – those who returned the questionnaires at the last minute – were almost non-respondents. It is useful to identify the characteristics of your final respondents as well as those who did not respond at all.

Questions to consider with late respondents and non-respondents

- Are their characteristics any different to the earlier respondents (apart from being less organised!)?
- Do the characteristics of late respondents reflect those of non-respondents?
- Does the non-response rate and the late response rate bring an element of bias into your sample?
- Is there a significant group of a population that your survey has missed out? How does this change your results?
- Do the late responses affect the survey results?

Chapter summary

Survey checklist – *have you included…*

- An explanation of the survey instrument (e.g., is it one you have developed, or has it been used in other research projects?)
- An explanation of how validity and reliability were measured
- A blank copy of your survey tool in an appendix
- Information about your sample
- Information about non-respondents
- Data analysis

This chapter highlighted well-known examples of surveys which ask questions about educational experiences and attainment. The chapter then examined the different types of surveys that may be used and evaluated and their characteristics, such as longitudinal and cross-sectional surveys. Examples of different types of surveys were given. The differences between questionnaires as a research method and surveys as a research approach were explained. The chapter then discussed some of the practical aspects of carrying out a survey, and highlighted issues surrounding response rates. The key characteristics of a survey are:

- Asks standardized questions
- Uses a sample of a population
- Focuses on attitudes, perceptions and behaviour

Further reading

Fink, A. (2016) *How to conduct surveys: A step-by-step guide*. 6th edn. Thousand Oaks: Sage Publications.

- A friendly and accessible text with judicious use of subheadings and examples, many of which are education-related. It begins by providing an answer to the question 'What is a survey?', and moves on to give information about different types of questions and response rates. It also tackles more complex issues such as sampling, reliability, validity and analysis.

References

Bubb, S. and Jones, M.-A. (2020) Learning from the COVID-19 home-schooling experience: Listening to pupils, parents/carers and teachers. *Improving Schools*, 23(3), pp. 209–222. doi:10.1177/1365480220958797.

CLS (2023) *CLS Class of 2023 more likely to be 'stay-at-home students' - CLS (ucl.ac.uk)*. Available at: https://cls.ucl.ac.uk/class-of-2023-more-likely-to-be-stay-at-home-students/ (Accessed: 25 March 2024).

Colleen, I. (2022) *Language trends England 2022*. Available at: https://www.britishcouncil.org/research-insight/language-trends-2022 (Accessed: 25 March 2024).

COSMO (2024) *The COVID social mobility and opportunities study*. Available at: https://cosmostudy.uk/ (Accessed: 25 March 2024).

FareShare. (2023) *1 in 4 teachers bring food to school to support hungry children - fareshare*. Available at: https://fareshare.org.uk/news-media/press-releases/1-in-4-teachers-bring-food-to-school-to-support-hungry-children/ (Accessed: 25 March 2024).

Finney, H.C. (1981) 'Improving the reliability of retrospective survey measures: Results of a longitudinal field survey', *Evaluation Review*, 5, pp. 207–229.

Fowler F.J. (2009) *Applied social research methods: Survey research methods*. 4th edn. Sage Publications.

Hasram, S. *et al*. (2021) The effects of wordwall online games (Wow) on English language vocabulary learning among year 5 pupils. *Theory and Practice in Language Studies*, 11(9), pp.1059–1066.

Lumby J. (2012) 'Learner Voice in Educational research', in Briggs A.R.J., Coleman M. and Morrison M. (eds.) *Research methods in educational leadership and management*. London Sage, pp. 236–248.

Luo, L., Stoeger, H. and Subotnik, R.F. (2022) The influences of social agents in completing a STEM degree: An examination of female graduates of selective science high schools. *International Journal of STEM Education*, 9(7). doi:10.1186/s40594-021-00324-w.

Norden, J. (2024) "Outdated' facilities are harming learning', warn teachers, *Tes Magazine*, 29th February. Available at: es.com/magazine/news/general/outdated-school-facilities-harming-learning-warn-teachers (Accessed: 25 March 2024).

OECD. (2024) https://www.oecd.org/pisa/ (Accessed: 25th March 2024).

Stoop I., Billiet J., Koch A. and Fitzgerald R. (2010). *Improving survey response*. Chichester: John Wiley & Sons.

University of Essex, Institute for Social and Economic Research (ISER) (2023). *Understanding Society*. Available at: https://www.understandingsociety.ac.uk/ (Accessed: 25 March 2024).

Zheng, L., Weng, Q. and Gong, X. (2021) 'Does preschool attendance affect the urban-rural cognition gap among middle school students? Evidence from China education panel survey', *The Journal of Chinese Sociology*, 8(14). doi:10.1186/s40711-021-00150-1.

CHAPTER 8

Mixed-methods research

Introduction

It is often assumed that research is either qualitative *or* quantitative. In reality, however, much research sits somewhere on a continuum and how researchers position themselves may shift over time depending on the questions they are seeking to answer. There are many interesting research questions that require both qualitative *and* quantitative data in order to get a full picture of a given phenomenon, and mixed-methods research designs can be a pragmatic approach to answering complex research questions (McCusker and Gunaydin, 2015). Educational research studies often use either qualitative or quantitative methods. Increasingly, however, educational researchers are adopting a mixed-methods approach. This chapter explores why and how mixed methods are used in educational research. After discussing the opportunities and challenges of mixed-methods approaches, the chapter will illustrate how to design a mixed-methods study and how to analyse mixed data sets. It will end with some practical considerations.

Opportunities and challenges of mixed-methods approaches

Mixed-methods research has been popular in the social sciences for a number of years (Creswell and Creswell, 2017), and researchers who adopt a mixed-methods approach believe that both qualitative *and* quantitative perspectives are useful in addressing their research questions. There are many purposes for conducting mixed-methods research, but two of the most common ones are depth and breadth (Onwuegbuzie, Johnson & Turner, 2007). Researchers who adopt a mixed-methods approach often seek richer, more meaningful answers to research questions in order to provide a deeper understanding and fuller picture of the phenomenon they are exploring (Creswell and Creswell, 2017). It is increasingly recognised that qualitative and quantitative research methods are both important in educational research in order to capture the complexity of the field. Simply put, researchers adopting a mixed-methods approach

DOI: 10.4324/9781003569428-10

believe that the complexity of a phenomenon cannot be fully understood from a single qualitative or quantitative perspective. Quantitative methods are useful for measuring educational phenomena (e.g. educational outcomes, attainment), while qualitative methods are useful for capturing the social aspects of education (e.g. lived experiences). Researchers who adopt a mixed-methods approach are often interested in objective *and* subjective aspects of a phenomenon that require the use of both qualitative and quantitative data.

Example: Researching international student experiences

Let's take the experiences of internationally mobile students, a burgeoning research area in the field of education (see Mittelmeier, Lomer and Unkule, 2023). In their mixed-methods study, Schartner and Young (2020) set out to investigate the adaptation and adjustment of international students to life and study in the United Kingdom. They collected quantitative data through a self-report questionnaire (see Chapter 13) to measure outcomes of study abroad (e.g., academic achievement, psychological well-being, satisfaction with life). This allowed them to answer the question 'How well did international students adapt to life and study in the UK?'. The researchers were also interested in the lived experiences of individual students and collected qualitative data through semi-structured interviews (see Chapter 14). This allowed them to capture subjective experience and to answer to question 'How well did students themselves feel they were adjusting to life and study in the UK?'. In sum, mixed-methods approaches allowed these researchers to capture both outcome measures and lived experiences of international student mobility, thereby leading to a fuller and more fine-grained understanding of the phenomenon.

We have now established that mixed-methods approaches offer researchers an opportunity to answer complex research questions. There are, however, also some challenges that researchers need to be aware of regarding the philosophical, epistemological and practical aspects of mixed-methods research (see Dawadi, Shrestha and Giri, 2021):

- Data collection, analysis and write-up might be a lengthier process relative to single-method studies and therefore more expensive in terms of cost and time. For example, mixed-methods studies often involve multiple stages of data collection and separate data analysis (Wasti *et al.*, 2022). A mixed-methods design thus demands more from the researcher who needs a wider set of skills in order to conduct a rigorous study (Creswell and Plano Clark, 2011). It may also be challenging to write-up findings from two data sets into one research report and to find a journal that is open to publishing mixed-methods research (Wasti *et al.*, 2022) although many journals are increasingly sympathetic to this approach.

- Researchers might struggle to 'mix' qualitative and quantitative data. This might be due to a lack of confidence in their abilities to integrate different data sets, or could be due to a lack of strategies for data integration as existing guidance in the literature remains sparse (Casey *et al.*, 2016).

- Researchers might have difficulties in deciding which mixed-methods research design is appropriate for answering their research question. They need to decide what the purpose of their study is and which priority is given to the qualitative and quantitative elements of their study (i.e. equal priority or not). Novice researchers, or those less experienced with mixed-methods approaches may struggle to choose from a range of potential designs (see below).

- Finally, one of the biggest challenges is that qualitative and quantitative approaches are underpinned by different research philosophies (also called paradigms) and researchers might struggle to reconcile these. Quantitative research is typically underpinned by the assumption that there is one single real world out there that can be measured (positivism). Qualitative research, however, is usually based on the assumption that we all experience the world differently (interpretivism) (Wasti et al., 2022). Remaining with our international student research example above, quantitative research would address question such as "What proportion of higher education students in the UK are from overseas?" Qualitative research, on the other hand, would ask questions such as "How do overseas students experience study abroad?" Researchers who adopt a mixed-methods approach thus take an 'ecumenical' (or pragmatic) stance by bringing together questions from two different philosophies. Some refer to mixed-methods approaches as a third research paradigm (Johnson, Onwuegbuzie and Turner, 2007).

Despite these challenges, mixed-methods approaches are increasingly popular and it is relatively easy to find educational research studies that have adopted a mixed-methods approach.

ACTIVITY

Explore what types of educational research have combined qualitative and quantitative methods into a single study.

- Select an educational database (e.g. ERIC) or use Google Scholar and carry out a search using your own areas of interest (e.g. experiences of international students) and the term 'mixed-methods'.
- Scroll through the search results and identify educational research that has adopted a mixed-methods approach.

As you become familiar with mixed-methods research, consider which kinds of questions you may wish to explore in your own area of interest from a mixed-methods perspective.

Designing a mixed-methods study

There are different types of mixed-methods designs and researchers need to consider carefully which is most appropriate for the purposes of their study. Creswell and Clark (2018) put forward the following three core designs:

Design 1: Convergent mixed-methods design

Researchers adopting a convergent design collect and analyse quantitative and qualitative data separately (and often at the same time) with the 'intent of obtaining a more complete understanding of a problem' (Creswell and Clark, 2018: 65). The findings from both data sets are then brought together to see whether they tell the same story (converge) or different stories (diverge). Simply put, the aim is to get the two data sets to 'talk to each other' in order to get as full a picture of a phenomenon as possible. As such, this design can help researchers to get a more nuanced understanding of the phenomenon under study and can enhance the validity and reliability of their findings. The main advantage of using a convergent design is that it allows researchers to capture both numerical insights and trends as well as subjective lived experiences and context. It is also a relatively efficient design as two data sets can be collected at the same time. Finally, it lends itself to team-based research with team members bringing a range of skills. This design is not, however, without its challenges. Firstly, integrating text-based and numeric data can be complex and researchers need to consider their analysis techniques carefully. Secondly, this design can be resource intensive as data collection and analysis can be time consuming and may require specialist expertise. Finally, researchers need to think carefully about how to present findings from a convergent design effectively, catering to a readership with varying levels of methodological expertise.

Example: Exploring loneliness among international students

Adopting a convergent parallel design, Wawera and McCamley (2020) explored loneliness among international students studying in Australia. This approach meant that quantitative and qualitative data were collected separately and at the same time. The quantitative strand of the study consisted of a self-report questionnaire (Jong Gierveld Loneliness Scale) to measure the degree of loneliness among a group of international students. This allowed the researchers to answer the question 'What are the levels of loneliness among international students at the university?'. The qualitative strand consisted of semi-structured interviews to explore experiences of loneliness from the students' perspectives. This allowed the researchers to answer the question 'How do students themselves talk about and experience loneliness?'.

Design 2: Explanatory sequential design

This design consists of two phases. Researchers adopting this design typically collect and analyse quantitative data first. The first phase is usually followed by a second phase of qualitative data collection and analysis. At a basic level, the aim of this design is to 'use a qualitative strand to explain initial quantitative results' (Creswell and Clark, 2018: 77). The main advantage of this design is that it allows researchers to achieve both depth and breadth in a singly study. An initial quantitative phase can offer numerical trends while the following qualitative phase can uncover underlying reasons or contextual factors. Explanatory sequential designs are most appropriate when the research is more quantitatively oriented and the researchers have time to conduct data collection sequentially (Creswell and Clark, 2018: 78). A challenge of this design is the relatively lengthy timeframe needed to complete two subsequent data collection phases which may extend the overall duration of a study relative to single-method designs. Researchers also need to be mindful of potential for bias as they may unconsciously seek to confirm quantitative findings in the qualitative data, potentially overlooking contradictory findings.

Example: Exploring the link between teacher–student relationship and student engagement

In a mixed-methods study set in Sweden, Thornberg et al. (2022) used an explanatory sequential design to investigate the links between teacher–student relationship quality and student engagement in two high schools. The initial quantitative phase consisted of an online questionnaire which was completed by 234 students. This was followed up with a qualitative phase of focus group interviews with 120 participants in total. The aim of the first phase (quantitative) was to test whether there was an association between teacher–student relationship quality and student engagement over time. The aim of the second phase (qualitative) was to give the students a voice by exploring what they considered to be a 'good teacher'. The explanatory sequential design allowed the researchers to obtain a 'general understanding of the research problem' (Thornberg et al., 2022: 844) first through the quantitative data, whereas the qualitative data allowed them to explain the quantitative findings in greater depth and from the students' perspectives.

Design 3: Exploratory sequential design

This design typically consists of three phases. In the first phase, researchers collect qualitative data, for example through interviews or focus groups (see Chapter 14). This exploratory data is then used to inform the design of a quantitative data collection instrument such as a self-report questionnaire (see Chapter 13). This design is especially appropriate when there is a need to develop a new research instrument. As with other sequential designs, a challenge for researchers is the time it takes to complete multiple phases of data collection.

Example: Exploring international students' experiences during the COVID-19 pandemic

Zhang, Kuek and Wu (2023) examined the academic and non-academic experiences of international students studying in China during the COVID-19 pandemic. In the first phase the researchers collected qualitative data through focus group interviews with nine (3 × 3) international students studying at three Chinese universities. The themes identified in the interview data then informed the development of a quantitative questionnaire (phase 2) which was then administered to 410 international students (phase 3). This approach allowed the researchers to answer questions such as 'How did the students experience online learning during the pandemic?' (qualitative) and 'What was the level of satisfaction with online learning?' (quantitative).

Analysing mixed-methods data

Data analysis in mixed-methods research is often more complex than in single-method studies as researchers need to employ different analytical techniques to the quantitative and qualitative data sets respectively. Quantitative data typically require statistical analysis which can be either descriptive (for example to compute percentages of responses or average scores) or inferential (for example to establish relationships between variables or differences between groups). Descriptive statistics help the researcher to describe their sample, while inferential statistics are analyses that allow generalisation to a larger population (Whatley, 2022). Qualitative data, on the other hand, require analytical approaches that can deal with text-based data, for example thematic analysis (Clarke and Braun, 2017). Unless they work as part of a multi-skilled team, researchers conducting mixed-methods studies need to be well versed in both statistical analysis and text-based analysis. They need to be able to make sense of two data sets independently and need to be able to integrate or 'mix' them. Ultimately, in mixed-methods research, inferences are drawn from the whole study rather than an individual component and it is thus useful for researchers to ask themselves 'Where is the mixing?' (Halcomb, 2019). It is also important that researchers are explicit in their write-up of findings about how data mixing was done. Published mixed-methods studies often lack a detailed description of how the integration of quantitative and qualitative data was achieved (Zhang and Creswell, 2013). The examples below illustrate how educational researchers can go about analysing mixed-methods data.

Example 1: Stress and family relationships among student parents

In a study of university students who are also parents, Dotterer *et al.* (2021) used a convergent mixed-methods design to study the association between student parents' stress and distress in their relationships with their children and explored how student parents managed their multiple roles. Eighty student parents completed an online questionnaire and a sub-sample of 14 respondents also took part in semi-structured interviews. The researchers analysed the quantitative questionnaire data using both descriptive and inferential statistics. Correlation and regression analyses were computed to answer the question 'Is student parent stress related to distress in parent-child relationships?'. Open coding was used to explore themes emerging in the qualitative interview data related to the question 'What stressors do student parents report and how do they balance their family, school and work roles?'. The quantitative and qualitative data sets were analysed independently, and the findings were presented separately. Data integration ('mixing') occurred in the discussion of the findings.

Example 2: Academic burnout in nursing students

Using an explanatory sequential mixed-method design, Ghods *et al.* (2023) investigated burnout in nursing students in Iran. In an initial quantitative phase, a questionnaire was completed by 91 nursing students. In the subsequent qualitative phase 13 nursing students took part in individual interviews. The quantitative data were analysed by computing descriptive statistics using the Statistical Package for the Social Sciences (SPSS). Additionally, a t-test and analysis of variance (ANOVA) were computed to examine any group differences. Content analysis was used to analyse the qualitative interview data until. The data were presented separately, and data integration ('mixing') occurred in the discussion of the findings.

Example 3: Food consumption in English households

Using an exploratory sequential mixed-methods design, Filimonau, Beer and Ermolaev (2022) explore the effect of the Covid-19 pandemic on food consumption in English households. In an initial qualitative phase, interviews were conducted with 16 heads of household. The qualitative data were analysed using thematic coding. In a second phase, the themes emerging from the interview data were then used to design items for a quantitative questionnaire. Descriptive analysis and regression analysis were used to analyse the questionnaire data. The two data sets were analysed, presented and discussed separately.

Data analysis in mixed-methods studies can be resource-intensive and time-consuming, especially if there are multiple sequential data collection phases. It is thus important that researchers allocate sufficient time and resources for data analysis. Given how complex data analysis and interpretation can be, reporting findings from mixed-methods studies can be challenging. It is thus important that researchers develop coherent narratives in their write-up that help the reader understand how the two data sets relate to each other and to the research question(s).

Dealing with practical and logistical aspects

Researchers employing a mixed-methods design need to be aware of several practical and logistical issues in the lifecycle of their project. Some key challenges are discussed below.

Research design

As discussed above, researchers need to decide which type of mixed-methods design is most appropriate for their study. This decision may be driven in part by the methodological emphasis of the research study. In other words, the researchers may decide to emphasise the quantitative *or* qualitative strand of their research, or they may feel that quantitative and qualitative data are of *equal importance*. If the latter is the case, then a convergent design may be most appropriate. It allows researchers to assign equal weighting to their quantitative and qualitative data with the aim of achieving a holistic understanding of the phenomenon under study. In a more quantitatively oriented project, the researcher may opt for an explanatory sequential design. This allows them to use qualitative insights to explain or add context to quantitative findings. Finally, if the development of a new research instrument is the aim, then an exploratory sequential design may be most practical. It allows researchers to collect qualitative data and use these to inform the development of a new data collection tool (e.g., a quantitative self-report questionnaire).

Ultimately, decisions around research design are driven by the research question(s) but also by constraints around resources, time and researcher skills.

Sampling

Decisions around sampling can be more complex in a mixed-methods study relative to single-methos studies. The sampling strategy is in part determined by the research design (see above), but researchers need to also be aware of more general principles regarding sampling in quantitative and qualitative research respectively. In qualitative research, sample sizes are typically smaller than in quantitative research as the aim of qualitative studies is depth of understanding rather than breadth. As such, a sample size as low as one can be justifiable (Boddy, 2016). In quantitative research, on the other hand, researchers need to determine a sample that is an appropriate representation of the wider population under study. Sampling in a quantitative study is partly determined by the statistical tests the researchers wish to carry out as some tests require a certain threshold in order to have statistical power (Kraemer and Blasey, 2016). In a mixed-methods study sample sizes can be different for qualitative and quantitative strands, but researchers need to be aware that size differentials may impact the synthesis ('mixing') of their findings (Dawadi, Shrestha and Giri, 2021).

Example 1: The effect of study abroad on intercultural competence

In a mixed-methods longitudinal study, Schartner (2016) tracked a multinational group of international postgraduate students studying in the United Kingdom in order to explore possible changes in their intercultural competence over time. A sample of 143 students completed a self-report online questionnaire twice, approximately nine months apart. Additionally, 18 students, all of whom had also completed the questionnaire, took part in three waves of semi-structured interviews.

Example 2: Social contact patterns of international students

Using an explanatory sequential design, Pho and Schartner (2021) examined the role of social contact in the academic adaptation of a sample of international students at British universities. Data were collected over a five-month period (May to September) using quantitative self-report surveys ($N = 110$) and qualitative semi-structured interviews ($N = 17$). The interviewees were a sub-sample of the survey respondents.

Resource, time and skill constraints

Collecting, analysing and integrating qualitative and quantitative data can be time-consuming and resource intensive. This may mean that researchers employing a mixed-methods design work under tight budget and time constraints (McCusker and Gunaydin, 2015). Researchers may also need to consider the limitations of their own skills and understanding of quantitative and qualitative research (Riazi and Candlin, 2014). Researchers conducting mixed-methods studies need to be skilled in both qualitative and quantitative research methods and thus be 'methodologically bilingual' (Teddlie and Tashakkori, 2012: 777).

Write-up and dissemination

In the latter stages of a research project, researchers may encounter challenges in writing up findings emerging from mixed-methods studies. They need to be proficient in communicating both numerical and narrative data in a meaningful and effective way. This means that they need to be familiar with techniques for reporting and illustrating statistical findings in a concise and accessible manner, while at the same time being able to report more nuanced text-based data that reflects the 'voice' of their participants. Following on from writing up their findings, researchers might also find that they encounter problems during the dissemination process as many publishers have particular methodological preferences. Although this is increasingly less common, some journals, continue to explicitly exclude mixed-methods research (Cameron, 2011).

Chapter summary

In conclusion, researchers employing a mixed-methods design need to be multi-skilled and versatile. There are frameworks and toolkits available to researchers wishing to embark on mixed-methods research. There are also academic journals specifically dedicated to mixed-methods research (see examples in Further reading).

Further reading

- The *Journal of Mixed Methods Research* published quarterly by Sage is an international publication that welcomes empirical, methodological and theoretical articles as well as research notes and commentaries about mixed-methods research from across the social, behavioural, health, and human sciences.

- The *Journal of Mixed Methods Studies* is an international, peer-reviewed open-access journal that is published bi-annually. It welcomes submissions from across the social, behavioural, health, and human sciences employing a variety of mixed-methods research designs.

- The *International Journal of Multiple Research Approaches* is a triannual, international publication that published both multi-method and mixed-methods research from across the social, behavioural, business, education, health, and human sciences.

Cresswell, J.W. (2021) *A concise introduction to mixed methods research*. 2nd edn. London: SAGE.
- A renowned author of research methods books provides a succinct introduction to all the key information required to undertake a mixed-methods research study.

Cresswell, J.W. and Cresswell, J.D. (2023) *Research design - international student edition: Qualitative, Quantitative, and mixed methods approaches.* 6th edn. London: SAGE.
- A classic text which is highly informative and now in its sixth edition.

References

Boddy, C.R. (2016) 'Sample size for qualitative research', *Qualitative Market Research: An International Journal*, 19(4), pp. 426–432.

Cameron, R. (2011) 'Mixed methods research: The five ps framework', *Electronic Journal of Business Research Methods*, 9(2), pp. 96–108.

Casey, D., O'Hara, M.C., Meehan, B., Byrne, M., Dinneen, S.F. and Murphy, K., (2016) A mixed methods study exploring the factors and behaviors that affect glycemic control following a structured education program: The Irish DAFNE Study, *Journal of Mixed Methods Research*, 10(2), pp.182–203.

Clarke, V. and Braun, V. (2017) 'Thematic analysis', *The Journal of Positive Psychology*, 12(3), pp. 297–298.

Cresswell, J.W. and Plano Clark, V.L., (2011) *Designing and conducting mixed methods research*, Thousand Oaks, CA: SAGE.

Creswell, J.W. and Clark, V.L.P. (2018) *Designing and conducting mixed methods research.* 3rd edn. Thousand Oaks, CA: Sage Publications.

Creswell, J.W., Clark, V.L.P., Gutmann, M.L. and Hanson, W.E. (2003) 'Advanced mixed', *Handbook of mixed methods in social & behavioral research*. Thousand Oaks, CA: SAGE, p. 209.

Creswell, J.W. and Creswell, J.D. (2017) *Research design: Qualitative, quantitative, and mixed methods approaches.* Thousand Oaks, CA: SAGE.

Dawadi, S., Shrestha, S. and Giri, R.A. (2021) 'Mixed-methods research: A discussion on its types, challenges, and criticisms', *Journal of Practical Studies in Education*, 2(2), 25–36.

Dotterer, A.M. et al. (2021) 'Stress and family relationships among college student parents: A mixed methods study', *Journal of Social and Personal Relationships*, 38(3), pp. 888–911.

Filimonau, V., Beer, S. and Ermolaev, V.A. (2022) 'The COVID-19 pandemic and food consumption at home and away: An exploratory study of English households', *Socio-Economic Planning Sciences*, 82, p. 101125.

Ghods, A.A., et al. (2023) 'Academic burnout in nursing students: An explanatory sequential design', *Nursing Open*, 10(2), pp. 535–543.

Halcomb, E.J. (2019) 'Mixed methods research: The issues beyond combining methods', *Journal of Advanced Nursing*, 75(3), pp. 499–501.

Kraemer, H.C. and Blasey, C. (2016) *How many subjects?: Statistical power analysis in research.* Sage Publications.

McCusker, K. and Gunaydin, S. (2015) 'Research using qualitative, quantitative or mixed methods and choice based on the research', *Perfusion*, 30 (7), pp. 537–542.

Mittelmeier, J., Lomer, S. and Unkule, K. (eds.). (2023) *Research with international students: Critical conceptual and methodological considerations.* London: Routledge.

Onwuegbuzie, A.J., Johnson, B.R. and Turner, L.A., (2007) 'Toward a definition of mixed methods research', *Journal of mixed methods research*, 1(2), pp.112–133.

Pho, H. and Schartner, A. (2021) 'Social contact patterns of international students and their impact on academic adaptation', *Journal of Multilingual and Multicultural Development*, 42(6), pp. 489–502.

Riazi, A.M. and Candlin, C.N. (2014) 'Mixed-methods research in language teaching and learning: Opportunities, issues and challenges', *Language Teaching*, 47(2), pp. 135–173.

Schartner, A. (2016) 'The effect of study abroad on intercultural competence: A longitudinal case study of international postgraduate students at A british university', *Journal of Multilingual and Multicultural Development*, 37(4), pp. 402–418.

Schartner, A. and Young, T. (2020) *Intercultural transitions in higher education: international student adjustment and adaptation*, Edinburgh: Edinburgh University Press.

Teddlie, C. and Tashakkori, A. (2012) 'Common "core" characteristics of mixed methods research: A review of critical issues and call for greater convergence', *American Behavioral Scientist*, 56(6), pp. 774–788.

Thornberg, R. *et al.* (2022) 'Teacher–student relationship quality and student engagement: A sequential explanatory mixed-methods study', *Research Papers in Education*, 37(6), pp. 840–859.

Wasti, S.P., Simkhada, P., van Teijlingen, E.R., Sathian, B. and Banerjee, I., (2022) 'The growing importance of mixed-methods research in health', *Nepal journal of epidemiology*, 12(1), pp. 1175–1178.

Wawera, A.S. and McCamley, A. (2020) 'Loneliness among international students in the UK', *Journal of Further and Higher Education*, 44(9), pp. 1262–1274.

Whatley, M. (2022) *Introduction to quantitative analysis for international educators*. Springer.

Zhang, W. and Creswell, J. (2013) 'The use of "mixing" procedure of mixed methods in health services research', *Medical Care*, 51(8), pp. e1–e57.

Zhang, S., Kuek, F. and Wu, Y. (2023) 'International students' satisfaction with online learning and faculty engagement during the COVID-19 pandemic in northwestern Chinese universities', *International Journal of China Studies*, 14(1), pp. 79–107.

CHAPTER

Case studies

Introduction

Case studies are a very popular research strategy, often used by researchers in education and other social sciences and by researchers in various legal and health-related professions. They are also commonly used by university students undertaking research projects for dissertations and theses. This chapter looks at the key purposes of case study research, examines the different types of case studies (single and multiple) and outlines their key characteristics. It considers when case studies should be used, how they can be designed and conducted and what types of data collection methods can be used. It also covers the strengths and limitations of case study research.

What is the purpose of case study research?

The purpose of a case study is to explore a specific example of a phenomenon or situation that can help illuminate whatever research question is under investigation. The complexity of defining case study research is highlighted by Cohen, Manion and Morrison (2018) and it is important to have a strong understanding of what you recognize as case study research and why it is the relevant approach for the study you are planning to undertake. However, it is likely to be an 'in-depth' and 'bounded' study – that is providing a holistic understanding with clear parameters of what constitutes 'the case', such as a teacher, a classroom or a school. Yin (2018: 15) argues that case study research would be undertaken 'to understand a real-world case and assume that such an understanding is likely to involve important contextual conditions pertinent to your case'.

Types of case study

Similarly to the challenges of defining case study, the different types of case study are also characterised slightly differently by different researchers. Again, the most important consideration for your own research is being clear about the type of case study that you are undertaking. Personally, I find Stake's (1995) characterization of case study research a helpful starting point:

- Intrinsic: An intrinsic case study aims to understand more specifically about the particular case being researched. Therefore, this type of case study might be interested in the novelty or uniqueness of this case.
- Instrumental: This case study might have been picked because it can exemplify the issue being researched or might enable a theory to be applied.
- Multiple case studies: This enables a more detailed understanding of the research questions and can provide more depth, as well as cautioning against the critiques of case study not being generalizable.

CASE STUDIES IN PRACTICE

1 Pupils' understandings of interreligious learning and teaching (Foley, Thompson and Caltabiano, 2024)

This case study explored pupils' understandings of interreligious learning and teaching. The research was a qualitative single-case design with the Australian, multicultural, Catholic primary school being a bounded case. The case was chosen for its potential to illuminate the phenomena under investigation. The key research question was: 'How do students describe their role in interreligious learning and teaching?' (Foley, Thompson and Caltabiano, 2024: 63). The case study used two group interviews with pupils reflecting the diversity of the students.

'The diversity of the school context was acknowledged by the students. They appeared proud of the fact there was such a variety of cultures and religions within the school. The plurality was spoken of as an asset, something that made their school a better place. Students highlighted:

> We have people that come from the Christian religion, and we have people that come from many different religions all over the world.
>
> (Interview Group 2)
>
> We learn a lot from our students. . . they share a lot of what they do with their culture and background information.
>
> (Interview Group 1)

The learning from the religious and cultural diversity was acknowledged and appreciated.

(Foley, Thompson and Caltabiano, 2024: 64–65)

This case study has provided suitable demographic context from this school, so that it may be possible to transfer the findings to similar schools.

2 A Scottish school case study of environmental and sustainability education (ESE) and character education (CE) (Jordan, 2023)

> The case study was at a Scottish, independent (fee paying) school for pupils aged between 3 – 18 years old. This case study was an instrumental case study – that is it was chosen specifically because it was a school which brought together an emphasis on environmental and sustainable education (ESE) and character education (CE). The data were gathered through teacher interviews, observations at the school, document analysis and field notes.
>
> > 'This case study takes a broadly contextualist orientation to the data (Huxley *et al.*, 2016; Terry *et al.*, 2017), and interviewees' responses were viewed within the specific context of the school and educational setting, as well as the local and Scottish background…The researcher particularly acknowledges that, as a non-Steiner–Waldorf educator, they will interpret data as an outsider'.
> >
> > Jordan (2023: 297)
>
> An ethos of environmental and sustainability awareness that was embedded throughout the school was identified through the use of case study research.

ACTIVITY

Consider the two examples of case study research mentioned above.

- Did this approach to the topics under consideration make sense?
- Why do you think the researchers opted for a case study approach?
- Would you have done things differently if you were the researcher?

How to design and implement case studies

There is no one set way to design a case study. The design that is used in a particular study should reflect the purpose for which it is intended, since the case study is an approach to research as opposed to a set of specific strategies. Therefore, the design of case studies is open to creative interpretation, which means that researchers can be imaginative in how they construct their studies. There are a number of issues to take into consideration when designing a case study:

- Define the 'case' clearly: Although it is difficult to entirely remove ambiguity from any study, try and be as specific as possible.
- Ensure that the case is researchable: Think about the extent to which the 'case' will also value the research being conducted and that you can use a range of research methods to understand the case you are researching.
- Choose your sample and location(s) wisely: Consider whether or not the sample and the site(s) of study will provide enough evidence in appropriate forms for your study. If you focus on the wrong case(s), the success of the research project would be open to serious question. Cases are not all the same; some are strategically more effective than others. For example, if you are studying the impact of curriculum change on teacher morale, choosing

a school or schools that is currently undergoing curriculum change would make much more sense than targeting sites that can only offer retrospective accounts of their experiences.

- Ensure access to the site(s): If the study involves physical access to spaces such as schools, universities, etc., ensure that appropriate access has been granted. This is especially important in case study design, since you are relying on a smaller number of cases to do the work for you. Being granted access early on will make the job of the researcher much easier. Permission to research at this stage is also important because of the issues surrounding anonymity and the ethics of your research – the smaller the research sample, the more important these issues become.
- Ensuring anonymity: If the results are to be anonymous, take special care in case study research – avoid concentrating on aspects or characteristics that may potentially allow readers to identify specific institutions, organisations or individuals.

ACTIVITY

Think of a research topic that you are interested in exploring further.

- Would a case study approach be an appropriate one to take? Consider all the points mentioned above – is the 'case' you have in mind clearly defined, or does it have the potential to be so?
- Is it a researchable topic?
- Will it provide sufficient evidence to deliver appropriate findings and support a convincing argument?
- Will you to able to access the 'case' whilst also ensuring the anonymity of your participants?
- Use these points as a checklist against your preferred research topic, and consider whether or not the case study approach is right for you.

Analysing data from case studies

Depending on the kinds of data collection methods utilised in a case study, analysing the data can prove a challenge. While this is true for all forms of research, it can be especially problematic for researchers who have used multiple methods or who have researched a number of sites. Throughout the analysis stage it is vital that the 'case' remains central at all times, because it provides the rationale for the entire project. However, as Yin (2018: 5) notes:

> the case study's unique strength is its ability to deal with a full variety of evidence – documents, artifacts, interviews, and direct observations, as well as participant observation.

Case study research is often (but not always) qualitative – so consideration of qualitative data analysis (see Chapter 5), and a clear focus on the phenomena being researched and the research questions that you hope your case can illuminate, are an important starting point for making sense of your data.

Advantages and disadvantages of case study research

With case studies, there should be no doubt that what you gain in depth, you lose in breadth; this is the unavoidable compromise that needs to be understood from the beginning of the research process. This is neither an advantage nor a disadvantage, since one aspect cancels out the benefits and drawbacks of the other. However, there are other positives and negatives that need attention.

Advantages

- Flexibility: Case studies are popular for a number of reasons, one being that they can be conducted at various points in the research process. Researchers are known to favour them as a way to identify and develop themes for more extensive research in the future – pilot studies often take the form of case studies. They are also effective conduits for a broad range of research methods; in this sense they are non-prejudicial against any particular type of research – focus groups are just as welcome in case study research as questionnaires or participant observation.
- Understanding complexity: The in-depth nature of case studies allows for different understandings of social reality by participants and can offer alternative perspectives and viewpoints (Cohen, Manion and Morrison, 2018).

Case study research is able to embrace the complexity of educational settings which arguably offers holistic research findings as variables are not artificially disaggregated.

Disadvantages

- The challenge of generality: At the same time, given their specificity, care needs to be taken when attempting to generalise from the findings. While there's no inherent flaw in case study design that precludes its broader application, it is preferable that researchers choose their case study sites carefully, while also basing their analysis within existing research findings that have been generated via other research designs. No design is infallible, but so often have arguments against case studies been raised that some of the criticism (unwarranted and unfair in many cases) has stuck: 'They are not easily open to cross-checking, hence they may be selective, biased, personal and subjective' (Cohen, Manion and Morrison, 2018: 379 adapted from Nisbet and Watt, 1984).
- Suspicion of amateurism: Case studies, a long-time favourite method of education researchers, tend to carry with them the unfortunate whiff of a suspicion that they offer the time and finance-strapped education researcher a convenient and pragmatic source of data, providing findings and recommendations that, given the nature of case studies, can neither be confirmed nor denied in terms of their utility or veracity. However, alongside this suspicion is another more insidious one – a notion that 'stories' are not what social

science research should be about. Miles (2015) argues that rather than seeing case study research as 'less valid', we should appreciate its strengths in helping us to understand educational practices.

However, there are a range of objections that can and should be made against such a bias. So much research is based either on peoples' lives or on the impact of other issues (poverty, institutional policy) on their lives, so the stories of what actually occurs in their lives or in professional environments tend to be an invaluable and rich source of evidence. The fact is that stories (individual, collective, institutional) have a vital role to play in the world of educational research. To play the specific vs general card against case study design suggests a tendency towards forms of research fundamentalism, as opposed to any kind of rational and objective take on the strengths and limitations of case studies.

- Preciousness: Having said that, researchers should not fall into the surprisingly common trap of assuming that case study data speaks for itself. Rarely if ever is this the case, and it is an assumption that is as patronising to research subjects as it is false. The job of the researcher is both to describe social phenomena and also to explain them – i.e. to interpret. Without interpretation the research findings lack meaningful presentation; they present themselves as fact when of course the reality of 'facts' is one of the reasons why the research is being carried out in the first place.

- Conflation of political and research objectives: Another trap that education case study researchers sometimes fall into is presenting research findings as if they were self-evidently true, as if the stories were beyond criticism. This is often accompanied by a vague attachment to the notion that research is a political process, one that is performed as a form of liberation – for example against policies that seek to ignore the stories of those who 'suffer' at the hands of overbearing political or economic imperatives. Case study design should not be viewed as a mechanism for providing a 'local' bulwark against the 'global', but rather as a mechanism for checking the veracity of universalist claims (at least, this should be one of its objectives). The valorisation of particularism can only get you so far in educational research. In this regard, it is important that the researcher maintains an appropriate distance from the case being studied. Otherwise, as Mark (2004: 214) points out, there is the '*possibility that the observer will lose their perspective and could become blind to the peculiarities that they are supposed to be investigating*'. Research validity can be affected as a result.

Chapter summary

This chapter explored the key characteristics of case study design, while also providing some examples of research that have used case study as their framework. Some of the advantages and disadvantages of case studies were outlined, including a focus on the 'generalisability' of case studies and also the potential of this form of research to capture the lived experience of those who are being researched. The important message to take from this chapter is that the case study is as valid an approach to research as any other, but the merits of such studies can often be taken for granted. The case study is an excellent approach to educational research, but it is also wise to be aware of its shortcomings.

Further reading

Gerring, J. (2017) *Case study research: Principles and practices*. 2nd edn. Cambridge: Cambridge University Press.

- This book includes information on quantitative case studies. The book provides useful context as to the origins of case study research. The book includes a range of examples, including educational case studies.

Hancock, D.R., Algozzine, B. and Lim, J.H. (2021) *Doing case study research: A practical guide for beginning teachers*. 4th edn. New York: Teachers College Press.

- This book provides a useful overview of seminal texts on case study research. This book provides comprehensive information about some of the research methods most likely to be employed in case study research.

References

Cohen, L., Manion, L. and Morrison, K. (2018) *Research methods in education*. 8th edn. Abingdon: Routledge.

Foley, T., Thompson, M.D. and Caltabiano, N. (2024) 'A case study of primary students' perspectives of engagement in interreligious learning and teaching: A community of learners', *British Journal of Religious Education*, 46(1), pp. 59–70. doi:10.1080/01416200.2023.2259112.

Huxley, C., Clarke, V. and Halliwell, E. (2016) Report 2: Are lesbian and bisexual women 'protected' from sociocultural pressure to be thin? A reflective account of a thematic analysis study. In E. Lyons & A. Coyle (Eds.), *Analysing qualitative data in psychology* (2nd ed., pp. 306–321), London: Sage.

Jordan, K.E. (2023) 'The intersection of environmental and sustainability education, and character education: An instrumental case study', *British Educational Research Journal*, 49, pp. 288–313. doi:libproxy.ncl.ac.uk/10.1002/berj.3843.

Mark, R. (2004) 'The case study approach to research in adult literacy, numeracy and ESOL', in Osborne, M., Gallacher, J. and Crossan, B. (eds.) *Researching widening access to lifelong learning: Issues and approaches to international research*. Abingdon: RoutledgeFalmer, pp. 207–230.

Miles, R. (2015) 'Complexity, representation and practice: Case study as method and methodology', *Issues in Educational Research*, 25(3), pp. 309–318. http://www.iier.org.au/iier25/miles.pdf

Nisbet, J. and Watt, J. (1984) Case Study. In J. Bell, T. Bush, A. Fox, J. Goodey and S. Goulding (Eds.), *Conducting Small-Scale Investigations in Educational Management*, London: Harper & Row, pp. 79–92.

Stake, R.E. (1995) *The art of case study research*. London: SAGE

Terry, G., Hayfield, N., Clarke, V. and Braun, V. (2017) Thematic analysis. In C. Willig & W. Stainton Rogers (Eds.), *The SAGE handbook of qualitative research in psychology* (2nd ed., pp. 17–37), London: Sage.

Yin, R.K. (2018) *Case study research and applications: Design and methods*. 6th edn. London: SAGE.

CHAPTER

Ethnography

Introduction

Ethnography is a fashionable approach to modern educational research. It involves in-depth study of a particular group or setting over an extended period of time. Ethnography requires the researcher to immerse herself within the site of study and attempt to experience it from the perspective of an inhabitant. This chapter identifies important and recent examples of ethnographic research in education. While acknowledging that the term is used in a variety of ways, the chapter outlines some of the common characteristics of the approach. Strengths and limitations are examined and three distinct branches are considered – practitioner ethnography, critical ethnography and autoethnography.

Ethnographic research attempts to develop an understanding of the shared cultural meanings of a particular group or setting. This might be the culture of an institution (a school or college, for example) or a distinct subculture within the institution – like a gang, a classroom or a friendship group. A group's 'culture' includes their shared behaviours, values, interpretations, artefacts, symbols, norms, assumptions, expectations and meanings. While some aspects of culture are easily identifiable, others lie below the surface – and it is these that the ethnographer attempts to uncover and understand. The ethnographer:

> will usually spend quality time 'out in the field' with people, getting to know their behaviours and practices intimately.
>
> (McDonough, 2021: 30)

To gain an understanding of this shared culture, the ethnographer immerses herself in the day-to-day experiences of those who inhabit or participate within it. She attempts to conceive the *world-view* of these actors, to see the world through their eyes.

DOI: 10.4324/9781003569428-12

Some of the most significant studies in education – generally within the discipline of the sociology of education – have been based on ethnographic research within a particular institution. Among the most influential UK studies are the following:

- David Hargreaves identified a link between streaming, labelling and school subcultures in '*Social Relations in Secondary School*' (1967).
- Paul Willis explored the school experiences of 'the lads' as preparation for working-class employment in '*Learning to Labour*' (1977).
- Stephen Ball identified the impact of teachers' stereotyping, banding and pupil behaviour at '*Beachside Comprehensive*' (1981).
- Peter Aggleton examined middle-class underachievement at college in '*Rebels without a cause*' (1987).
- Mairtin Mac an Ghaill uncovered the hegemonic 'macho' school cultures in '*The Making of Men*' (1994).
- Heidi Mirza explored black girls' positive self-esteem and approaches to study despite teachers unwitting failure to meet their needs in '*Young, Female and Black*' (1992).
- Beverley Skeggs examined the lives of working-class women undertaking 'caring courses' in FE as they negotiated social and cultural power relations in '*Formations of Class and Gender: Becoming Respectable*' (1997).

Ethnographic research in education continues to be popular, for example:

- Shamus Khan carried out a study into an elite school in the USA and identified the entitlement fostered in the environment and the maximization of life chances in '*Privilege: The Making of an Adolescent Elite at St. Paul's School*' (2011).
- Kat Simpson focused on teachers' perceptions of deindustrialization on pupils at a primary school in a former coalmining community in England in '*Social haunting, education and the working class. A critical Marxist ethnography in a former coalmining community*' (2021).
- Zi Wang considered social organization and hierarchy in secondary school clubs in Japan in '*The discursive construction of hierarchy in Japanese society. An ethnographic study of secondary school clubs*' (2020).

ACTIVITY

- Have a look at some of these important ethnographic studies in education.
- Using an educational database, try to identify three or four contemporary ethnographic studies.
- Make a list of the kinds of educational research topics most suited to an ethnographic approach.

Characteristics of ethnography

There is much disagreement about what counts as ethnographic research. While ethnographic studies vary considerably, they share a number of features in the main:

- Exploring the shared culture of a group: Ethnography developed out of early twentieth-century anthropology. Anthropologists like Malinowski believed the best strategy for understanding newly discovered tribes was to go and live among them, and to experience their cultural interpretations first-hand. This enables an understanding of their 'way of life' – the shared interpretations and understandings that are considered 'normal' and meaningful within the group. The role of the ethnographer, then, is to get close enough to the group to uncover this 'way of life' or culture, and it is this focus on groups and their shared culture that differentiates ethnography from the other approaches outlined in Part 2 of this book.
- Significance of meaning: The ethnographer is especially interested in the shared meanings that social actors attach to their behaviour, language, events, contexts and lives. Different groups might attach different cultural meanings to the same object or event. For instance, the ASBO (anti-social behaviour order) was designed to attach a cultural stigma to the holder within mainstream society, but many subcultural groups appropriated its meaning, redefining it as a 'badge of honour'. Therefore, the ethnographer will repeatedly ask social actors why they act in particular ways, what their environment means to them, how they understand events and so on.
- Insider approach: To uncover shared culture, the ethnographer attempts to live as a member of the group – to experience the world from the perspective of its participants. This is an 'insider' approach. Rather than standing back as an expert, impartial, social scientist, the ethnographer tries to immerse themselves within the cultures they study, viewing participants as the true experts concerning their own lives.
- 'Thick descriptions': Ethnographers develop detailed descriptions of activities, events and interpretations. Distinguishing between ethnographic and everyday descriptions, Hammersley and Atkinson argue:

  The methods used by ethnographers are not far removed from the means that we all use in everyday life to get information and to make sense of our surroundings…what is distinctive is that ethnography involves a more deliberate and systematic approach than is common for most of us most of the time.

  (Hammersley and Atkinson, 2019: 4)

  Geertz used the term 'thick description' (1973) to identify the specific features of ethnographic description. He argued that understanding culture involves studying specific events in their contexts and uncovering the meanings of these events to the social actors involved.
- Making the familiar strange: While the ethnographer takes on the role of an 'insider' within the research site:

  ethnography exploits the capacity that any social actor possesses for learning new cultures, and the reflexive understanding to which this process can give rise. Even where he or she is researching a familiar group or setting the participant observer is required to treat this as 'anthropologically strange', in an effort to make explicit the presuppositions that culture members take for granted.

(Hammersley and Atkinson, 2019: 9)

It is the capacity to maintain a distance that enables the ethnographer to uncover and make explicit the commonsense knowledge of the group.

- Naturalistic settings: Ethnographers are interested in experiencing the world as it actually is. To do so, they employ methods that enable them to view real people in authentic situations and settings. Most commonly, they use participant observation and in-depth interviews.
- Longitudinal: To uncover 'lived experience' ethnographic studies usually take place over an extended period of time, sometimes over a number of years. It takes a long time to uncover levels of reality beyond the surface, so ethnographic research is usually prolonged and repetitive.
- Range of data collection techniques: While participant observation and in-depth interviews are the most common data collection techniques employed by the ethnographer, other methods are frequently utilised. For instance, ethnographers might use surveys to examine issues they have identified during observations. They are highly likely to employ multiple methods to add context and depth to their study, such as diaries, films, photographs, analysis of institutional documentation and so on.
- Evolving study: The ethnographer does not enter the site of study with pre-existing research structures. As the study develops, aspects of culture will be identified and appropriate data collection techniques will be employed to study these aspects in further depth.
- Theory deriving from data: Likewise, theories to emerge from ethnography derive from the data that is collected. The ethnographer does not enter the research site with a hypothesis to 'test'. Rather, she develops theories from her experiences within the site and from the conversations she has with participants. Like other qualitative approaches, ethnographers generally employ what Glaser and Strauss term 'grounded theory' (1967), whereby early observations give rise to theory that is explored further by additional data collection. Frequently, ethnographers will take their descriptive accounts back to social actors to check that they are recognisable as accurate reflections of their culture.
- Reflexivity: Because of the kinds of methods commonly employed, ethnographers are very likely to consider issues of reflexivity. Their research is inevitably shaped by existing assumptions, relations, prejudices, values and experiences, as well as by the data collection processes. 'Personality' will impact on choice of topic, who takes part in the research, which events are considered important, and how events are analysed, interpreted and reported. Many ethnographers today would accept that the account they produce is one of numerous possibilities. Therefore, ethnographers are generally reflexive – taking

themselves, and their role in the field of study, as a serious object of research. This involves being thoughtful and open about their own position and the impact of their methodological choices and processes on the final account they produce (see Chapter 19 for a more detailed discussion of reflexivity).

> **ACTIVITY**
>
> Ethnographers frequently adopt a role of 'acceptable incompetence' in the site of study – cultivating and conveying an identity of friendly inept tude.
>
> - Given the characteristics identified above, why might a role like this be of benefit to the educational ethnographer?
> - What other qualities might an effective educational ethnographer require?

Evaluating ethnography in educational research

Because the ethnographer immerses herself in the cultures she studies, she is able to elicit rich, detailed insights. She can understand complex and fluid meanings and interpretations within settings such as the classroom, a friendship group or the playground. Developing relationships with inhabitants of these settings (such as pupils and teachers) gives a human face to the research. By utilising a range of methods over an extended period of time, she is able to uncover meanings and understandings under the surface of everyday life. The combination of commonly- used methods like participant observation and informal interviews means that patterns and discrepancies between what people do and say become apparent. For ethnographers, educational theories that emerge from experiences within the field have greater authenticity, validity and value.

Nevertheless, there are a number of difficulties with the approach. Ethnography is dismissed by those who favour a more positivist or scientific approach to educational research. Selected methods are generally flexible, open-ended and unstructured, making them open to the charge that they are unsystematic and lack reliability. Close engagement with small groups makes it difficult to claim that findings are representative. It is also more difficult to generalise claims to wider society – that is, findings from a detailed ethnography in one school might be very different to findings from another school.

Moreover, the ethnographer's approach is entirely at odds with scientific ideals of the detached and impartial researcher. She attempts to immerse herself within the culture of study, often reflexively introspecting on her own changing attitudes, behaviours and feelings. Many would challenge the veracity of the ensuing interpretation, questioning the legitimacy and validity of an account so dependent on the subjective experiences, choices and interpretations of a particular ethnographer. Others would challenge how ethical she is when she joins and then leaves the group she studies, suggesting that she is effectively using people as a means toward her own ends.

These difficulties make ethnography a non-starter for some educationalists. Nevertheless, it remains a very popular choice for research. Questions the education ethnographer might ask herself to ensure she has done a good job might include the following:

- Does the account derive from direct contact with the group being studied?
- Have aims and objectives developed responsively and flexibly?
- Does the account generate or contribute to educational theory?
- Is the account open and critical about the author's identification and selection of 'relevant' data?
- Is the account reflexive – open and thoughtful about the ways that the researcher's personality and the research process have shaped findings and interpretations?

> **ACTIVITY**
>
> There are lots of recent examples of ethnographic research with children and young people. Read Besse-Patin (2023) and Black and Down (2023) and consider the roles of children in educational ethnography.
>
> ■ Now have a look at the journal 'Ethnography and Education' in more detail. Look at the most-read articles and draw a diagram identifying strengths and weaknesses of the approach.

Branches of ethnography

Earlier in the chapter we mentioned that there is no clear agreement in terms of how ethnography is defined. There are a number of branches within ethnography, each with their own contested meanings, definitions and uses. Three branches that have proved of interest to educational researchers are:

- Practitioner ethnography
- Critical ethnography
- Autoethnography

Practitioner ethnography

Practitioner ethnography entails the researcher studying a cultural setting that they already participate in. Drawing from Stenhouse's influential call for 'teachers-as-researchers' (1975), it commonly involves the teacher conducting ethnographic research in the institution that she works in, working with the group she teaches. Alongside action research, practitioner ethnography is widely used by people who are studying as well as practicing – for example, working part-time in a school while completing their studies.

There are many advantages of this approach to ethnography. Problems associated with gaining and maintaining access are avoided – existing relationships facilitate integration and immersion within the site of study. Familiarity with the research site helps the ethnographer to collect and analyse data. As Griffiths has argued in relation to teacher-researcher studies, events that occur during fieldwork can be contextualised by pre-existing knowledge, and 'subtle and diffuse' links can be identified as well as more obvious ones (Griffiths, 1985: 212). Analysis can gain 'sureness' due to this 'subsidiary awareness' and 'tacit knowledge' (Pollard, 1985: 221) – the researcher and researched are 'people-who-know-each-other-and-have-experienced-the-same-experiences' (Pollard, 1985: 226). This is especially true for research with children; as Pollard has argued, the teacher-pupil relationship is one of the only 'natural' relationships between adults and youngsters (Pollard, 1985: 226). While there are clearly benefits to this practitioner approach, there are also concerns. Insider accounts can be considered to be partial, limited and constrained by the viewpoint of one actor within a site.

Critical ethnography

As we have seen during this chapter, ethnography is concerned with developing descriptions of existing cultures and meanings. Over the last twenty years critical ethnography has emerged, which concerns itself with theorising about cultures as they *could be*. Drawing on critical theory and the work of Paulo Freire (1973) and critical pedagogy, critical ethnography begins with a moral or political commitment to tackle social injustice or unfairness. The critical ethnographer takes on the role of advocate, using ethnography as a tool for articulating the interests of a marginalised or disempowered group.

Critical ethnography entails:

- An explicit purpose to contest hegemonic oppression
- Perceiving cultures as positioned unequally within power relations
- Disrupting taken-for-granted assumptions
- Interrogating underlying discourses of power and control
- Challenging the status quo
- Developing emancipatory knowledge and skills
- Attempting to change the world for the group studied
- The researcher as an *activist*

Critical ethnographers like Carspecken (1996) and Thomas (1993) argue that the approach offers the possibility to impact positively on the education system, making the lives of students and teachers more free, fair and equal. It moves from the description and understanding of culture to the challenge and transformation of it. Critics view the overt political nature of the approach as problematic, claiming that data collection is really a means to articulate and justify the pre-existing (left-wing) biases of the researcher.

Autoethnography

Autoethnography places the subjective experiences of the researcher at the forefront of the process. It is a cross between ethnography (exploration of culture) and autobiography (exploration of the self), starting from the perspective that the self is socially constructed within culture. A narrative is developed that critically reflects on the researcher's self as situated in relation to others and to social, political and cultural settings. Personal stories, feelings, experiences, anecdotes, observations and reflections become the means by which cultures are interrogated.

Autoethnography has been widely criticised for lacking any scientific credibility. Some claim it is not real educational research, being rather a self-indulgent activity. Others argue that the approach is very useful as a means of exploring the meanings and experiences of educational processes. Starr argues that autoethnography, like critical ethnography, offers the potential for educational transformation, suggesting that it is:

> a valuable tool in examining the complex, diverse and sometimes messy world within education where we stress cooperation, teamwork and distributed leadership but are mired in hierarchy and power tensions.
>
> (Starr, 2010: 7)

ACTIVITY

The following extract is taken from Higgins (2024):
The article describes workplace bullying of colleagues working with international students at a higher education institution:

> Theme one: I don't even recognize myself anymore. Who is this that is accepting living in fear. I feel like I am living on eggshells–trying to be quiet, be "good". I'm silenced. This is reminiscent of living in an abusive relationship—always afraid to do something that will "wake the beast." So, I sit here with questions that need answers so I can actually get some work done and yet I am afraid to go ask her (Jackie, director). I am not this timid person and I am suffering with this weight of living dualistic lives. I reflect on being in this field that I love, that I am passionate about, that can do so much good and be meaningful in so many important ways, and yet I am miserable. I still find working with international students and programs meaningful and I feel honored and recognize my privilege in getting to know international students, refugees, and immigrants through this journey. How is it that something so integral to my life for so many years has now become so toxic to my soul? Daniella and Constance (co-workers) came to me today to talk about something that Jackie(director) did while I was out yesterday. Evidently, Constance needed to ask a question about what Jackie's preferences were to reschedule a part of one of our study abroad programs. She finally went to ask Jackie about it and Jackie exploded.
>
> (Higgins, 2024: 34)

- What do you think of the first extract as a piece of academic writing?
- In what ways does this autoethnographic account challenge your understanding of 'educational research'?
- How representative do you think this extract is of workplace cultures in higher education?

Chapter summary

This chapter outlines the main characteristics of ethnographic research, providing examples of influential studies in the sociology of education that have utilised the approach. Ethnographers describe and explain the social and cultural lives of groups or institutions, uncovering the perceptions and interpretations of social actors within those settings. Three branches of ethnography that are commonly used in educational research are outlined – practitioner ethnography, critical ethnography and autoethnography. While there are many reasons to adopt an ethnographic approach to educational research, it may be difficult to uncover 'taken-for-granted' meaning, and over-familiarity can hamper validity. Most significantly, ethnographic researchers must be open, honest and reflexive with regard to their own values and assumptions and how these impact on the stories they tell.

Further reading

Fetterman, D. (2020) *Ethnography step by step*. 4th edn. London: SAGE.
- An overview of ethnography is provided, as is information about theoretical underpinning, research methods and data analysis.

Fitzpatrick, K. and May, S. (2022) *Critical ethnography and education: Theory, methodology and ethics*. Abingdon: Routledge
- This book makes a strong case for adopting a critical ethnographic approach and discusses issues such as positionality as well as ethical issues. The book offers an important discussion of theoretical developments, such as those related postcolonialism and posthumanism.

Woods, P. (1986/2005) *Inside schools: Ethnography in educational research*. Abingdon: Routledge.
- Woods' book provides an excellent starting point for students interested in undertaking an ethnographic study. It outlines and explores many of the strategies employed by teachers who utilise the approach.

References

Aggleton, P. (1987) *Rebels without a cause*. London: Falmer Press.
Ball, S. (1981) *Beachside comprehensive: A case study of a secondary school*. Cambridge: Cambridge University Press.
Besse-Patin, B. (2023) 'How play becomes educational: case study in an out-of-school club in France', *Ethnography and Education*, 18(4), pp. 376–392. doi:10.1080/17457823.2023.2252951.
Black, A. and Down, B. (2023) 'Social class and streaming in contexts of educational disadvantage: What young people have to say', *Ethnography and Education*, 18(4), pp. 411–426, doi:10.1080/17457823.2023.2262069.
Carspecken, P. (1996). *Critical ethnography in educational research: A theoretical and practical guide*. London: Routledge.
Freire, P. (1972) *Pedagogy and the oppressed*. London: Continuum.

Geertz, C. (1973) *The interpretation of cultures: Selected essays*. New York: Basic Books.

Glaser, B. and Strauss, A. (1967) *Discovery of grounded theory: Strategies for qualitative research*. London: AldineTransaction.

Griffiths, G. (1985) 'Doubts, dilemmas and diary-keeping: Some reflections on teacher-based research', in Burgess, R. (ed.) *Issues in educational research: Qualitative methods*. London: Falmer Press, pp. 197–215.

Hammersley, M. and Atkinson, P. (2019) *Ethnography: Principles in practice*. 4th edn. Abingdon: Routledge.

Hargreaves, D. (1967) *Social relations in the secondary school*. Abingdon: Routledge.

Higgins, P. (2024) '"I don't even recognize myself anymore": An autoethnography of workplace bullying in higher education', *Power and Education*, 16(1), pp. 29–41. doi:10.1177/17577438231163041.

Khan, S.R. (2011) *Privilege: The making of an adolescent elite at st. Paul's school*. New Jersey: Princeton University Press.

Mac an Ghaill, M. (1994) *The making of men: Masculinities, sexualities and schooling*. Maidenhead: Open University Press.

McDonough, B. (2021) *Flying aeroplanes and other sociological tales an introduction to sociology and research methods*, Abingdon: Routledge.

Mirza, H. (1992) *Young, female and black*. Abingdon: Routledge.

Pollard, A. (1985) 'Opportunities and difficulties of a teacher-ethnographer: A personal account', in Burgess, R. (ed.) *Field methods in the study of education*. London: Falmer Press, pp. 217–233.

Simpson, K. (2021) *Social haunting, education and the working class. A critical marxist ethnography in a former coalmining community*. Abingdon: Routledge

Skeggs, B. (1997) *Formations of class and gender: Becoming respectable*. London: Sage.

Starr, L.J. (2010) 'The use of autoethnography in educational research: Locating who we are in what we do', *Canadian Journal for New Scholars in Education*, 3(1), pp. 1–9

Stenhouse, L. (1975) *An introduction to curriculum research and development*. London: Heinemann Educational.

Thomas, J. (1993) *Doing critical ethnography (Qualitative research methods)*. London: Sage.

Walford, G. (2020) 'Ethnography is not qualitative', *Ethnography and Education*, 15(1), pp. 122–135.

Wang, Z. (2020) *The discursive construction of hierarchy in Japanese society. An ethnographic study of secondary school clubs*. Boston/Berlin: Walter de Gruyter.

Willis, P. (1978) *Learning to labour: How working class kids get working class jobs*. Farnham: Ashgate.

CHAPTER

Action research

Introduction

Action research refers to practitioners carrying out research on their own practice in order to enhance it. This typically involves classroom teachers testing and trialling changes to their pedagogic practice and evaluating the effectiveness of these changes. Arguably practitioners are the people who have the best understanding of *what* and *how* practice needs to be developed, and therefore they are ideally placed to do this. Because it is the teacher who generally decides what they wish to research and how they are going to go about it, action research can be seen as an empowering process for those involved, since they are taking control of making the changes they perceive to be necessary.

This approach is quite different from a seasoned researcher arriving in a school to carry out a piece of research 'on' the teacher and their pedagogic practice. Lawrence Stenhouse (1975) was one of the key advocates for teachers to be actively involved in research. He claimed that it is not sufficient merely to study teachers' work; teachers also need to study their own work. There is a concern that not enough teachers are involved in research to improve teaching and learning (Hancock, 1997). This concern in itself is not new; Stenhouse himself conceded that 'it will require a generation of work … if the majority of teachers – rather than only the enthusiastic few' are to be involved in research (1975: 142). This chapter is split into three sections: First, we will examine the cyclical nature of action research, followed by a discussion of different types of action research. Finally, we will note a number of potential constraints to using this research strategy.

Cyclical nature of action research

The concept of action research can be explained by the notion of doing experiments in the field, rather than the laboratory. Its creation is attributed to the work of the social psychologist Kurt Lewin (1946), who discussed a model of action research in his article 'Action research and minority

DOI: 10.4324/9781003569428-13

problems' which addressed intergroup relations in some American communities in the 1940s. Following Lewin's ideas, action research involves a 'spiral of steps each of which is composed of a circle of planning, action and fact-finding about the result of the action' (Lewin, 1946: 38). According to Cousin (2009), the stages within the action research cycle are reconnaissance, planning, preliminary research, formulating research questions, implementing, observing, recording and reflecting.

1   Reconnaissance

Reconnaissance can be described as 'fact-finding'. This process has four functions. Firstly, action needs to be evaluated to see if it has met expectations. Secondly, based on this evaluation the strengths and weaknesses of an action can be considered. This leads to the third step, using this information to plan the next steps, and finally the overall plan can be amended accordingly.

2   Planning

Planning is a key idea in all research practice, and it is not unique to action research. Nevertheless, it worth pointing out that it is necessary to move from a general idea of what the research is hoping to achieve to a series of stages which will enable this to be achieved. The actions that must be taken in order to achieve the aims of the research need to be identified. This may also mean that the original idea has to be modified to make it achievable or viable.

3   Preliminary research

Many pieces of research carry out a pilot study. This is often a small-scale piece of research to test the methods being used and to evaluate the impact or findings of the research. An example of this might be a school which decides to embed drama into aspects of the curriculum. Rather than every teacher in the school trying to do this straight away, it makes more sense for one or two teachers in the school to trial the new approach by making changes to their planning and perhaps identifying key subjects where drama can be integrated. Once they have trialled the use of embedding drama in certain subjects within the curriculum, they will then evaluate the practice – has it improved the children's learning, engagement or confidence? Based on these findings the pilot study teachers are likely to make further changes to the ways in which they have embedded drama in the curriculum, and then they will be able to support other teachers in a school-wide initiative if this is indicated by the preliminary findings.

4   Formulating research questions

Based on the pilot research findings, the project may be implemented on a wider scale. It will be underpinned by research questions emerging from the preliminary findings, for example:

1   What is the impact of using drama on boys' motivation to write stories in literacy lessons?
2   To what extent has the use of 'hot-seating' encouraged children to become confident in asking and answering questions?
3   How effectively can drama techniques be integrated into cross-curricular planning?

5   Implementing

Based on the planning and with reference to the research questions, the changes to pedagogic practice are made – in this instance, the development of the use of drama in the classroom.

6   *Observing*

In the action research cycle the impact of the implemented changes needs to be observed (different observational strategies are noted in Chapter 15). It is possible for the teacher/researcher to note these observations themselves simply by reflecting on the changes taking place – for instance, when marking literacy books they may note an improvement in the quality of the stories written by boys. Alternatively, they might wish to work with a colleague who may come in and make observations about how the classroom practice has changed. Alternatively, teachers may engage in discussions with each other about their experiences, or they may ask children for their views.

7   *Recording and reflecting*

The changes that have taken place need to be recorded to aid further changes. This may mean writing field notes or recording interviews. The data can then be systematically analysed so that the changes that have been made can be further enhanced. This indicates the cyclical nature of action research, and it is not unusual to repeat each step in the process two or three times. The cyclical nature of this type of research offers opportunities for comparative data to be measured over time, giving a strong sense of reliability and validity within the research findings (Reason and Bradbury, 2006).

Practical example of the cyclical nature of action research

The cyclical nature of other pieces of action research can offer a practical illustration of the different phases. Twelve educational practitioners (five teachers and seven teaching assistant - community volunteer parents) met weekly over a two year period to discuss their ambition, plan the project, implement and evaluate (Wood and McAteer, 2023). The participatory action research project focused on how teachers and parents could work together more effectively to support the learning of children. The project was undertaken at a South African primary school in a low-income area. The project team gathered data from parents about what help they needed in supporting their children at school. The team designed modules for parents which were amended through feedback. Ten parents were recruited to trial the modular programme, this was then evaluated and final adjustments were made (Wood and McAteer, 2023).

ACTIVITY

- Can you think of an educational research topic that would be suitable for an action research design?
- What factors would you need to consider?
- What vision do you have for changes to educational practice upon completion of the project?
- Are there are any potential challenges to consider in adopting an action research design?

Different types of action research

Although all action research approaches follow these broad cyclical stages, there are different types of action research.

Emancipatory

Emancipatory action research aims to empower all the research participants. This is very much a 'grassroots' approach to the research, giving those involved the power and control to change their educational experiences for the better. Emancipatory action research encourages joint responsibility for the research from all parties, such as the practitioner, students and the facilitator (Carr and Kemmis, 1986). The researchers from project discussed above (Wood and McAteer, 2023) noted the emancipatory impact of their participatory action research (PAR) design:

> My parents did not have the chance to be part of my education. I used to think my part was just sending him to the school – it was 'him and the teacher', now I see I have to work hand in hand with him and the teacher' (FG2:4).
>
> (Wood and McAteer, 2023: 70)

Reflective

Reflective action research is very much about the practitioner being in control and making changes to their own practice. The practitioner can then reflect on the impact of these changes for themselves and their students. Reflection is a key part of the cyclical nature of action research, but it can also support the goals of action research. In this PAR (Bjørke, Førland Standal and Moen, 2023), three teachers were recruited with an interest in developing more student-centred approaches to the teaching of physical education (PE). The first author was an external researcher facilitator with a background of teaching physical education. Bjørke, Førland Standal and Moen (2023) argue that the addition of an external researcher facilitator can encourage greater reflection in participants through offering alternative perspectives.

Technical

Emancipatory and reflective action research is ideally instigated by the practitioner themselves. However, teachers are less likely to have the opportunity to publish their findings in research journals, so it is likely that much of the action research one can read about has some element of participation from a university academic in its design. Technical action research is often instigated by a facilitator rather than the practitioner. Technical action research tries to improve the efficiency and effectiveness of practice. Furthermore, technical action research is often measured by the facilitator's criteria, tending not to involve the practitioner in this process. Whittle *et al.* (2020) report on an action research project that explored educational practitioners working with university students who were impacted by a fear of failure at university. The educational practitioners involved in the project highlighted the challenges that they had encountered in engaging student participants from some subjects. This article provides a good example of how more technical approaches to action research whilst having excellent intentions, are not always able to develop practice as anticipated. Swann and Ecclestone (1999) and Munns and Woodward (2006) used a collaborative approach in their projects, recruiting several teachers from different schools to be action researchers on their project. The authors themselves acted as facilitators and co-ordinators within the project. It was hoped that all the teachers involved in the project would attend meetings, develop and test ideas within their own practice and contribute to guidelines and materials for other teachers. Sometimes researchers are not in a position to carry out research on their own practice and may ask practitioners to trial implementations to practice.

Potential constraints

If you are interested in carrying out action research with teachers or as a teacher yourself, it is worth reflecting on how to overcome potential barriers. There are several reasons why teachers may find it difficult to be involved in research. The everyday business of teaching is not necessarily underpinned by the acknowledgement of how important educational theory is to practice. Teachers may not become actively involved in research – unless, for example, they are working for a higher degree, or they have been asked by a local university to be participants in a piece of active research. Indeed, the very intensity of a teaching day and the never-ending multitude of tasks that need to be done means that there is barely any time to eat a sandwich at lunchtime, let alone get involved in carrying out a piece of research. In addition, being involved in research requires an innate sense of confidence that your research is a worthwhile activity. For many teachers, the potential erosion of their professional identities through government interventions has meant that they do not always feel that they can say anything worth hearing, or have any control in making changes to pedagogic practice.

One of the key problems is that research requires some level of objectivity to enable the researcher to reflect on what is happening, but when you are caught up with caring for the children in your class it becomes very difficult as an 'insider' to step away from this. There are good examples of teachers being involved in action research projects particularly when they have been guided and supported by universities who have lent 'researcher expertise'. McNiff (1988: xiii) comments: 'Action research presents an opportunity for teachers to become uniquely involved in their own practice'. Although practitioners have the opportunities to carry out reflective action research on their own practice, perhaps the most popular model within education research is a more technical approach. This often involves practitioners and researchers working together. Such a collaboration can undoubtedly be rewarding and fruitful for all involved. However, there are some key caveats that perhaps should be considered before working alongside practitioners to develop a piece of action research, and equally for practitioners it is important to consider the implications of this type of research. Implementing a methodology can be a complex process, and in the case of action research there are three issues – communication problems, differences in expectations and changing priorities – that may prevent successful implementation.

- Communication: When using a technical approach to action research it is important to recognise the significance of communication between the practitioner(s) and the researcher(s) if the project is to proceed successfully.
- Differences in expectations: For the researcher and practitioner to work effectively together on a piece of action research, clear expectations and guidelines are needed. At the outset of the project you need to give consideration to the importance of trust, respect and openness between the researcher and practitioner. It is important not to underestimate the issues of power, control and reputation that can make participants feel vulnerable and exposed at times. Messiou and Ainscow (2020) report on an action research project developing dialogue amongst teachers and pupils to make lessons more inclusive, supported by university teams. They note that at times power relationships between teachers and pupils and pupil sensitivity to upsetting their teachers was a challenge. However, differences in perceptions can emerge in any type of research; this problem is not specific to action research.
- Changing priorities: When working with practitioners, changes in the priorities of team members can make it difficult to continue with a research project. Therefore, it is important to consider how to communicate effectively and to ensure that expectations are aligned.

Chapter summary

A key tenet of action research is that it is not done *on* people, but *with* people (Cousin, 2009: 151). Action research is a cyclical process with each stage being visited and revisited two or three times. There are different types of action research: Emancipatory, reflective and technical. A popular action research approach combines reflective and technical aspects. As with all types of educational research, good communication and trust among all those involved in the project are important to ensure success.

Further reading

Glenn, M. et al. (2023) *Action research for the classroom: A guide to values based research in practice*. Abingdon: Routledge.

- This book is aimed at teachers, but is helpful for anyone conducting classroom based action research. The book provides useful suggestions, such as working with a critical friend, considering your values and writing up your findings.

McNiff, J. (2016) *You and your action research project*. 4th edn. Abingdon: Routledge.

- This accessible guide will explain exactly what action research is, as well as working with others and analysing data.

References

Bjørke, L., Førland Standal, O.F. and Mordal Moen, K. (2023) 'What we have done now is more student-centred': An investigation of physical education teachers' reflections over a one-year participatory action research project', *Educational Action Research*, 31(5), pp. 946–963. doi:10.1080/09650792.2022.2062407.

Carr, W. and Kemmis, S. (1986) *Becoming critical: Education, knowledge and action research*. London: RoutledgeFalmer.

Cousin, G. (2009) *Researching learning in higher education: An introduction to contemporary methods and approaches*. Abingdon: Routledge.

Hancock, R. (1997) 'Why are class teachers reluctant to become researchers', *Journal of In-Service Education*, 23 (1), pp. 85–99.

Lewin, K. (1946) 'Action research and minority problems', *Journal of Social Issues*, 2(4), pp. 34–46.

McNiff, J. (1988) *Action research: Principles and practice*. London: Routledge.

Messiou, K. and Ainscow, M. (2020) 'Inclusive inquiry: Student–teacher dialogue as a means of promoting inclusion in schools', *British Educational Research Journal*. 46, pp. 670–687. doi:10.1002/berj.3602.

Munns, G. and Woodward, H. (2006) 'Student engagement and student self-assessment: The REAL framework', *Assessment in Education*, 13(2), pp. 193–213.

Reason, P. and Bradbury, H. (eds.) (2006) *Handbook of action research: Participative inquiry and practice*. London: Sage.

Stenhouse, L. (1975) *An introduction to curriculum research and development*. London: Heinemann Educational.

Swann, J. and Ecclestone, K. (1999) 'Improving lecturers' assessment practice in higher education: A problem-based approach', *Educational Action Research*, 7(1), pp. 63–87.

Whittle, R. *et al.* (2020) 'The 'present-tense' experience of failure in the university: Reflections from an action research project', *Emotion, Space and Society*, 37. doi:10.1016/j.emospa.2020.100719.

Wood, L. and McAteer, M. (2023) 'The affordances of PAR for a school-community partnership to enhance learner support in socio-economically challenged communities', *Action Research*, 21(1), pp. 62–80. doi:10.1177/14767503211023133.

CHAPTER

12

Narrative inquiry

Introduction

Narrative inquiry is a methodological approach that draws on the fact that humans are all 'storied' – we all tell stories about our lives. Narrative inquiry does not interpret participants' stories as a straightforward re-telling of the 'truth', but recognises that stories are shaped by the audience, our perception of 'what happened' and our ability to accurately recall the past. Therefore, narrative inquiry tends to focus on meanings and recognises that our stories are shaped by the social, economic and historical context that we are situated in. The chapter begins with a discussion of 'telling stories' in everyday life. Second, narrative inquiry, life history and life story as biographical approaches to research are explained. Third, narratives in the experiences of learners are considered; fourth narrative analysis techniques are highlighted; and finally, ethical issues are reflected upon.

Telling stories

We all tell stories about our lives. Narrative research focuses on the fact that we are all 'storied'. The interview quote from Matt below is a story about his experience of not getting the A Level grades he needed for university:

> So the [familial] education level is fairly low and I suppose that meant when I was in Clearing that I was sort of trying to sift through the options going it alone, although they were all very supportive, but they didn't know how to support because they hadn't been there, nobody had been there in the family and I sort of stumbled across this [*degree programme] which I took fairly badly at the time. I gained a ton of weight, I stopped sleeping, I didn't go out much. I took it badly, I thought I had basically blown it because I really wanted to teach, but then that is why I started from September with my Mam and

DOI: 10.4324/9781003569428-14

Dad's working attitude. I saw Uni not as a socialising experience, but as a job, sort of as a road to redemption if you will. (Matt, interview)

Stories might be 'small' – explaining an event or an experience, such as the quote above. Alternatively, they may be 'big' stories – recounting significant experiences throughout the lifecourse (Murray, 2009). Stories can emerge from participants' responses to interview questions or the research approach can focus specifically on the telling of stories. Narratives may relate to things that have occurred recently or experiences from the past. There may be some disagreement over defining a 'narrative' in research – however it is generally considered to be an event or experience that is recounted, which will have a logical order like a story plot. O'Toole (2018: 177) suggests that a 'central idea of narrative inquiry is that stories are collected as a means of understanding how people construct their experiences as lived and told'. Narratives are likely to explain events and experiences with a consideration of the past, present and future and are told sequentially (Wells, 2011).

Narrative inquiry

Education and related disciplines often focus on understanding experiences and we tend to recount our experiences as stories. Clandinin and Connelly (2000) used narrative inquiry to describe the personal stories of teachers. Narrative inquiry according to (Clandinin, 2022) is about stories 'lived and told'. Clandinin (2022) argues that we use stories in our everyday lives to recount anecdotes and to provide both solicited and unsolicited advice to others. Consequently, if we make sense of our lives through stories, it makes sense to research lives in this way too. Narratives tend to focus on temporality – past, present and suggested future. A narrative has a beginning, middle and end. It may include direct quotations of speech. It may also use metaphor. Narratives are retrospective and present the story through a current evaluation of the experience or event. The account of the story may be partial and is likely to emphasise elements that the narrator wants to highlight to the audience/listener. However, Murray (2009: 47) argues 'narrative inquiry is conducive to documenting the changing conditions of lives and the impact these new conditions can have over time on all aspects of an individual's life'.

Life history

The boundaries between narrative and life history can be blurred. The distinction between narrative inquiry and life history is not always clear. However, Coles and Knowles (2001: 20) highlight 'whereas narrative research focuses on making meaning of individuals' experience, life history research draws on individuals' experiences to make broader contextual meaning'. Life history uses other sources, such as diaries, letters and photographs alongside interviews. The method emphasizes the experiences of individuals – changing events and phases throughout the lifecourse. The events are assumed to have happened, but the narrator may be able to tell more than one version of the event. Oral history is slightly different as participants are asked to recall specific events and reflect upon them in relation to specific research topic, rather than covering the entire biography of the interviewee (Clark *et al.*, 2021).

Life stories

Life stories are not generally checked for veracity against other documents such as photographs or diaries. However, like a life history, the life story asks the interviewee for an account of their life, spanning childhood, family, education, work, retirement. Life stories can capture the experiences of marginalised voices in relation to cultures, social factors and historical events (Brannen, 2020). There is of course, concerns about lapses in memory or distortion in the recounting of events (Clark *et al.*, 2021). Spoken or written accounts of a person's life and events throughout their lifecourse will capture their experiences of these events. Life story telling might be prompted by a particular point or event in the lifecourse and educational transitions may be an example of this.

Learner experiences

Narrative inquiry is a useful approach to understanding educational transitions, such as 'school to university' or 'learners' experiences', such as exam stress or bullying. Narrative inquiry has also been used very effectively in feminist studies to understand the experiences of women in the education system. Narrative inquiry can provide a narrative analysis emerging from a particular set of learners reflecting the commonalties and differences in stories about educational experiences. Often within biographies these stories are likely to be 'big stories' or 'grand narratives' (Brannen, 2020: 112). Equally we may wish to focus on a specific aspect of an individual's life, for example the transition to starting university and the stories captured here might be 'small narratives' (Brannen, 2020), for example, their parents insisting on an early morning start to attend a university open day or the jokes made about the six different brands of teabag in the kitchen when meeting their flat-mates for the first time. Brannen (2020) contends that these smaller narratives are the way in which individual's construct their identities over time. Biographical research methods, such as narrative inquiry can be powerful for understanding developmental trajectories among learners, such as transitions from school to college. Critical 'turning points' can also inspire stories, such as particular events like bullying or exam pressures.

CASE STUDY STORY: APPLYING TO UNIVERSITY AND MISSING MY EXAM – INTERVIEW EXCERPT

S: I was the first person in my family to go to university… New Labour had very helpfully changed the rules around fees and maintenance and I was due to go in 98 but went in 99, but I will tell you that story in a minute. But, basically they had changed the rules, there was a tuition fee of a £1000 that New Labour brought in, but my family weren't eligible to pay it - so the Local Authority paid it. They'd got rid of any kind of grant and it was all loans. I looked at the loan and it probably would have covered my Halls, but not even the bus fare to the university because the Halls were out of town and I wasn't sure how I'd manage financially. My parents weren't like 'oh that's a good idea' kind of thing. So, I ended up commuting and I went to Cook University and the reason

I went to Cook University was because originally, I realised that I was probably going to have to live at home that was only way financially I was going to be able to realistically manage it. I'd put Midland University down as my first choice because 'Midland' is a good uni and I was going to do History. Yeah I was going to do History at Midland University and then it came to do my A Levels – I did History, English Language and Sociology. And obviously very exam based and I think they drifted away to being more modular and more coursework based and they have now gone back to being very exam based. So basically mine were all exams apart from maybe 10% coursework and maybe this is just a background thing – your parents are not really following what you are doing. I'd mis-read my exam timetable.

L: Oh dear

S: AM/ PM I thought my History exam was in the afternoon. And it wasn't – it was in the morning and it was already too late to get there. So basically I ended up with 'ABE'. An E on one paper is actually pretty good. So I also needed a 'ABB' to get into Midland University and they were like well if you get 'AAD' we'll take you, but there was no way I was going to get that - a 'D' with one exam – there was just no way I was going to get in, but at that point my second choice was East University because I'd gone like Midland University, East University. I'd gone you know what - I don't want to go to a Post-92 - I don't think that's going to be the right thing you know longer term. So, I had a year out, reapplied [1st Choice Midland University; 2nd choice Cook University]. Did my A Level again as a private candidate because obviously college are quite keen to get rid of you really because obviously you are not really great on their stats. They were like why don't you get a job and just turn up and do the exams with everybody else. So managed to successfully turn up, but equally hadn't done any work for a year thinking I was going to be fine, I was doing well anyway. So got the same grade but this time it was worse because it was on two exam papers so anyway I was like I don't know what I am going to do. This is awful. Then I saw, I got a copy of the [news]paper because you know UCAS didn't really exist online, and the internet wasn't quite what it is now and I saw that Cook University were taking people and I was like maybe I can phone up and do a different course or something. And I phoned them up on Clearing day and they were like 'oh it's fine you've got a place with us'. We've offered you a place. So obviously they were a bit desperate, I guess. So, I had a place to do History, but the first year you did History and Politics. Well, there was a choice of subjects you could do but I picked History, Politics, Sociology. I didn't do that well in History, I did okay, but not great, also the History lecturers weren't very nice. So, in the end I transferred and did my degree in Sociology, so it all worked out in the end it was all okay in the end. But I also have that overhang of a horrible A Level and even though I've got a doctorate it will never really go away I suppose I've still got an E in History.

ACTIVITY

- Think about an education related story about yourself e.g. applying to university
- How might you tell this story?
- How might it change depending on the audience?
- Are there bits of this story that you might choose to edit, adapt, extend, repress depending on the audience?
- Do you think your story might share 'like events' with others?

TABLE 12.1 'Problem-solution' coding approach

Code	Example
Characters	Personality, behaviours of individuals
Settings	Place, year, environment/context
Problem	Phenomena being described/explained in relation to the question being answered.
Actions	Movement through the story, feelings, intentions, actions/reactions of the characters. Failure/success
Resolution	Explains turning points.

Narrative analysis

Narrative analysis involves making sense of experiences based on stories. Narrative analysis focuses on content, structure and the context of the story holistically (Wells, 2011). Ideally, these stories are treated analytically as a 'whole' rather than being fragmented into thematic categories. Some research approaches may be less concerned with the actual events and experiences that are relayed and are more interested in the narrative form of the data. The qualitative analysis could be both the descriptions of the story and the themes emerging from it. Ollerenshaw and Cresswell (2002: 335) suggest a 'problem-solution' coding approach (see Table 12.1).

An alternative approach is the three-dimensional space narrative structure (from Clandinin and Connelly, 2000 cited in Ollerenshaw and Cresswell, 2002: 340) (see Table 12.2).

Ethics

In addition to adopting good ethical practices that are required in all educational research, such as informed consent, confidentiality and anonymity (discussed in more detail in Chapter 20). Clearly, researchers do not wish to cause participants any psychological distress and it is important to recognise the potential for stories to surface difficult emotions for participants.

TABLE 12.2 Three-dimensional space narrative coding approach

Theme	Example
Interaction: Personal & Social	Personal – look inward to internal feelings, hopes etc. Social – other people in the environment – intentions, purposes, assumptions, point of view.
Continuity: Past, present, future	Past – remembered experiences, stories from earlier points in time Present – current experiences and feelings, stories relating to current events/situation Future – look forward to possible future experiences
Situation/place	Context, time, place – how this was bounded up with characters, intentions, purposes, viewpoints.

Therefore, it is recommended that participants are fully aware of the nature of the research and of their control over which narratives they tell or of the emphasis that they choose to place when retelling stories. Furthermore, it is important to send analysis of the stories to participants to avoid misinterpretation and misrepresentation.

Chapter summary

This chapter has explored the storied nature of our lives and provided some differentiation between biographical research approaches and examples relating to the suitability of narrative research to educational experiences are outlined. In addition, the chapter has highlighted two approaches to analysing narrative data. The chapter has also emphasized the potential ethical issues related to participants telling stories about their lives.

Further reading

Eichsteller, M.J. and Davis, H.H. (2022) *Biographical research methods*. London: SAGE.

- This comprehensive book explores theoretical approaches to biographical narratives, explains data analysis, research design and conducting autobiographical research.

Kim, J.-H. (2015) *Understanding narrative inquiry: The crafting and analysis of stories as research*. London: SAGE.

- This detailed book helpfully defines 'narrative' as well as discussing a wide range of possible philosophical and theoretical underpinnings to narrative research, the book also explains how to design narrative research and how to analyse data.

References

Brannen, J. (2020) 'Life story and narrative approaches in the study of family lives', in Parsons, J. and Chappell, A. (eds.) *The palgrave handbook of Auto/Biography*. Cham: Palgrave Macmillan. pp. 97–117. doi:10.1007/978-3-030-31974-8_5.

Clandinin, J. (2022) *Engaging in narrative inquiry*. 2nd edn. Abingdon: Routledge.

Clandinin, J. and Connelly, M. (2000) *Narrative inquiry: Experience and story in qualitative research*. San Francisco: Jossey-Bass

Clark, T., Foster, L., Sloan, L. and Bryman, A. (2021) *Bryman's social research methods*. 6th edn. Oxford: Oxford University Press.

Cole, A.L. and Knowles, G.J. (2001) *Life in context: The art of life history research*. Oxford: Altamira Press.

Murray, G. (2009) 'Narrative inquiry', In Heigham, J. and Croker, R. (eds.) *Qualitative research in applied linguistics: A practical introduction*. Basingstoke: Palgrave Macmillan, pp. 45–65.

Ollerenshaw, J.A. and Creswell, J.W. (2002) 'Narrative research: A comparison of two restorying data analysis approaches', *Qualitative Inquiry*, 8(3), pp. 329–347. doi:10.1177/10778004008003008.

O'Toole, J. (2018) 'Institutional storytelling and personal narratives: Reflecting on the 'value' of narrative inquiry', *Irish Educational Studies*, 37(2), pp. 175–189.

Wells, K. (2011) *Narrative inquiry*. Oxford: Oxford University Press.

PART

Methods of data collection

CHAPTER

Questionnaires

Introduction

It is easy to assume that questionnaire design is straightforward and quick because we all have some experience of completing questionnaires, whether they are 'personality trait' quizzes in magazines, market research surveys on the high street or a medical questionnaire at the doctor's office. In reality, however, there are many issues that need to be considered when designing a questionnaire to ensure a successful response rate and the collection of meaningful data. This chapter explores some of the advantages and pitfalls of questionnaire-based research. It is divided into four sections: What are questionnaires?, advantages and pitfalls of questionnaires, designing questionnaires and practical issues.

What are questionnaires?

Questionnaires are one of the most popular data collection tools in the social sciences but are also among the most misused (Young, 2015). The term 'questionnaire' is also known by other labels including 'inventory', 'test', 'battery', 'checklist', 'scale' or 'index' (Dörnyei, 2007) and, most commonly, 'survey'. Although at times used interchangeably, surveys and questionnaires are not one and the same. A survey (see Chapter 7) is the '…systematic collection of information from individuals using standardized procedures' (Stockemer, 2019: 23) while questionnaires are instruments 'that present respondents with a series of questions or statements to which they are to react either by writing out their answers or selecting among existing answers' (Brown, 2001: 6). Essentially, 'survey' refers to the broader process of collecting data while 'questionnaire' refers to the data collection tool. Questionnaires are most commonly associated with quantitative (numerical) data, but they can also include open-ended questions that collect qualitative (text-based) data. If the questionnaire produces numerical data, statistical methods

DOI: 10.4324/9781003569428-16

are typically used for analysis. If the questionnaire data is text-based, then a more qualitative approach such as Thematic Analysis may be appropriate.

Questionnaires are used by a wide range of individuals, groups and organisations including academic researchers, students, political parties, governments, civil society organisations, marketing research agencies…the list goes on. Various types of information can be collected using questionnaires, including for example:

- Demographic information (e.g., age, biological sex, years of education)
- Behaviours (past, present or future e.g., how often students use social media on a typical day)
- Attitudes (e.g., towards certain groups such as immigrants)
- Opinions (e.g., about the desirability of immigration)
- Factual knowledge about something (e.g., what proportion of primary school children in England receive free school meals)
- Psychometric properties (e.g., how extroverted or introverted a person is)
- Intentions or aspirations (e.g., about whether they will, or would like to, go to university) (for more examples, see Young, 2015).

Questionnaires can be practical as they allow educational researchers to make inferences about a larger population by examining a sample of that population (see below for examples). It would never be possible for researchers to capture everyone in a target population (this would be the aim of a census and is large scale). Therefore, a sample is a feasible way of learning something about the wider target population. It is important that the sample is as representative of the wider population as possible in order for the researcher to be able to make valid claims.

Examples: Population versus sample

- Population of interest: Primary school pupils in England using English as an additional language (EAL)
- Sample: EAL pupils in two primary schools in the Northeast of England
- Population of interest: International students who studied in the United Kingdom during the coronavirus pandemic
- Sample: International students who studied at one British university during the coronavirus pandemic

Once they have decided on an appropriate sample, researchers using questionnaires can opt for different types of research designs. Two common designs are cross-sectional and longitudinal designs. In cross-sectional designs (also known as 'snapshot' designs), researchers collect data at a single point in time. In longitudinal designs, researchers repeat the same questionnaire multiple times to explore changes or patterns over time. Examples of large-scale longitudinal questionnaires include:

- The World Values Survey (WVS), a cross-national questionnaire that has been carried out since the 1980s and explores people's values and beliefs over time.
- The European Social Survey (ESS), a biennial cross-national questionnaire that measures attitudes, beliefs and behavioural patterns in over 30 European countries.
- The National Child Development Study which has been following the lives of a group of people all born in a single week in March 1958 in Britain.

For novice researchers or students conducting dissertation projects cross-sectional designs are usually more feasible and efficient. They demand less time from the researcher and are less resource intensive.

Once researchers have determined an appropriate sample and design, they need to administer their questionnaire to the target population. Most questionnaires are administered in a self-report format (i.e., the respondents complete the questionnaire themselves) either online (researcher is not present) or in-person (researcher is present). However, less commonly, questionnaires can also take the form of a structured interview (see Chapter 14) where respondents complete the questionnaire verbally with the researcher asking the questions. In order to determine which questionnaire format is most appropriate, researchers need to consider several aspects (Ruel, Wagner and Gillespie, 2018):

- Their research question(s), for example, certain questions may require more interactivity (a focus group interview setting)
- Their target population, for example, an online questionnaire might not be appropriate for certain groups such as the elderly or hard-to-reach groups like refugees and asylum seekers
- Their available resources, for example, cost and efficiency of online versus in-person (pen and paper) questionnaires

Advantages and pitfalls of questionnaires

A well-designed questionnaire can be an efficient way of collecting data, but it relies on:

- A carefully considered design
- Representative sampling
- Appropriate and effective administration (Ruel, Wagner and Gillespie, 2018)

Novice or less-experienced researchers (e.g., students doing dissertation projects) may find questionnaires especially appealing for the following reasons (see also Young, 2015):

- They are relatively easy to construct
- There may be existing freely available questionnaires that can be used or adapted
- They can be administered online at no direct cost to the researcher
- They can be used to collect large data sets in a relatively short timeframe
- The data can be processed relatively quickly using statistical analysis software (e.g., Statistical Package for the Social Sciences)
- They allow for data to be collected anonymously which may be especially useful for sensitive data (e.g., drug use, alcohol consumption, sexual activity) and when used with vulnerable or hard-to-reach groups (e.g., refugees, asylum seekers)

Due to the many (perceived) advantages of using questionnaires it is relatively easy to find studies in all educational fields that have incorporated them into the design of projects.

ACTIVITY

- Investigate what types of educational research have used questionnaires in your own area of interest.
- Choose an education database such as ERIC or use Google Scholar and search using educational-related terms, for example, 'questionnaire' and 'creativity'.
- Scroll through the journal article abstracts to identify educational research in your area that has used questionnaires.
- As you become familiar with other research in your area which has used questionnaire tools, if you decide to incorporate one into your own research you will need to start considering the questions to include in your own instrument.

Questionnaire-based research is, however, not without its challenges. One common criticism is that questionnaires lead to relatively superficial, 'thin' data.

Designing questionnaires

What questions should I ask?

A sensible starting point for deciding what questions to include in your questionnaire is to read relevant literature in your topic area. You may find it useful to focus on journal articles that have used questionnaires with the same research emphasis. Also, check whether there are any existing questionnaires that you could use or adapt for the purposes of your study. Go back to your research questions or project aims and consider what issues you are trying to find out about, and then consider how you can formulate questions related to these issues.

> **ACTIVITY**
>
> - Explore existing questionnaires in the field of education studies. Choose an education database such as ERIC or use Google Scholar and search for questionnaires using your topic of interest, for example, if you are interested in the intercultural competence of teachers, search for 'intercultural competence measure' and 'teachers'.
> - Scroll through journal articles to identify whether the authors have published their questionnaire tool (these can often be found in the appendix or in the methods section of a paper).
> - Once you have found a questionnaire tool you can look at it in detail to decide whether it fits your purposes or can be adapted for use.

If you are designing your own questionnaire, you need to decide which questions to ask and also how to ask them. There are several different types of questions. To illustrate these, we will consider the practical example of a research project interested in the professional identity of newly qualified teachers. Two of the project aims were:

- To explore the meanings that participants attach to 'professional' identity and how these shifted from the time students achieve QTS to the end of their NQT year.
- To identify the impact of the ITE context and the work environment on developing professional identity in relation to pedagogic practice within the classroom.

Your questions should be formulated based on the aims of your research and the different types of questions you could use to do this will be discussed.

Question type

From looking at the project aims above it is clear that a variety of questions could be asked. Using the project aims, examples of the different types of questions and their relative advantages and disadvantages will be discussed below.

- ***Closed question*** Have you been offered your first teaching post? Yes/No

The advantage of closed questions is that it is easy to analyse responses – for example, 67% Yes and 33% No. The disadvantage of closed questions is that the choices on the questionnaire may not allow participants to choose their 'real' answer because the researcher has made assumptions about the participants' answers through the choices provided. There are scenarios that closed questions may not cover. A trainee teacher may have decided to not apply for teaching jobs after completing their course, or they may have an interview tomorrow which could change their response! In addition, closed questions can only provide a limited amount of information – for example, we do not know from this question whether NQTs who answered 'no' have had any interviews, or if those who answered 'yes' have been offered fixed-term or permanent contracts.

- Open-ended question: Why did you want to become a teacher?

The advantage of open-ended questions is that they can provide 'qualitative' data and let participants respond in their own words. The themes that emerge from open-ended responses can be followed up in interviews. The pitfalls of open-ended questions can include a lack of space provided for written responses, problems with reading handwritten responses and poor spelling and grammar, which can all make responses tricky to decipher. In addition, participants may not answer the question you have asked, writing about something else instead. Meanwhile, some respondents will leave this type of questions blank. If you decide to use open-ended questions, read up on qualitative data analysis because this section of your questionnaire will require a specific analytical approach.

- Multiple-choice questions: Please tick the year groups in which you undertook your three school experience placements:

    Foundation ☐
    Year 1 ☐
    Year 2 ☐
    Year 3 ☐
    Year 4 ☐
    Year 5 ☐
    Year 6 ☐

Multiple-choice questions are easy to analyse. Their drawback is that if the responses you provide are not relevant and do not cover all the options, your data will be skewed or incomplete. A good example of this is the fact that mixed year-group classes are not included in the options above. Therefore, potentially a different number of responses than the anticipated three might be picked. Responses of 'Year 5' and 'Year 6' would not tell us if the student was in a mixed Year 5/Year 6 class, or if these were two separate placements and their other selection was a mixed year class. Additionally, the specification of three choices would be problematic for a student who failed a placement and had to retake it, giving them four school placements. For these types of questionnaires, it is useful to include an 'Other' option with a space for participants to provide information, which will allow participants to state their answers if it has not been included in the possible choices.

- Likert scale questions: I feel well supported by my mentor as a NQT

    5. Strongly agree
    4. Agree
    3. Neither agree nor disagree

2. Disagree
1. Strongly disagree

Likert scale questions are useful for finding out about perceptions, emotions and feelings. Traditionally five categories are used, but it is not unusual to see seven or even nine options to choose from. Arguably an even number of choices, such as 1–4, means respondents cannot choose the middle number (usually the neutral option). One problem with a Likert scale response is that sometimes respondents may circle two numbers, which is problematic in the analysis stage. In addition, Likert scales often encounter an 'end-aversion' bias among adults, where people tend not to mark the two extreme ends of the scale. Pantell and Lewis (1987) also identified a position bias among children's responses in questionnaires where they tended to choose the first answer among the response options.

- Category questions: What type of teacher training did you undertake?

BA Primary Teaching with QTS
BEd
PGCE
SCITT

Category questions are useful for collecting demographic information. However, ensure that participants understand the categories available – for example, the initials above are only likely to be understood by those who move in educational circles. Also, be clear in your own mind about how demographic data collection is relevant to your research. Try not to make overly deterministic causal links between demographic data and other questionnaire responses, such as that those with a PGCE have better relationships with their NQT mentor than those with BEd training.

Practical issues

Think carefully about how you want to analyse the data before sending out your questionnaire. The types of questions you ask will influence the type of data analysis you can do. Therefore, you need to know how you are going to process the results before you receive the completed questionnaires back. A closed 'Yes/No' question will allow you to give a percentage – 35% of respondents said 'yes'. On the other hand, open-ended questions do not lend themselves to number-crunching and require a different type of analysis, but they may give you more in-depth responses. A Likert scale question allows for more sophisticated statistical analysis.

Layout and sequence

It is important to get the overall 'look' of your questionnaire right:

- Give the respondent clear instructions on how to complete the questionnaire, such as 'tick the box', 'circle all choices that apply' or 'if no, go to question 10'.

- Keep the layout simple and use a font that is easy to read. Also, think about the size of the font. It can be tempting to use a small font to get all your questions on one side of A4, which will make your questionnaire look relatively short. However, if respondents struggle to read the questions this will put them off.

- If your questionnaire is for children you need to make sure that they are able to read the questions, or that an adult will be on hand to read the questions aloud.

- Think about the number of questions you include. Respondents may suffer from 'questionnaire fatigue' if there are too many questions. Therefore, you need to be realistic about the time and effort required to fill in a questionnaire. 'When designing a questionnaire, then, the researcher has to walk a tightrope between ensuring coverage of all the vital issues and ensuring the questionnaire is brief enough to encourage people to bother answering it' (Denscombe, 2003: 96).

- Make sure that the printing or photocopying is of good quality if you use a paper-based questionnaire. Alternatively, an online questionnaire may avoid the prohibitive costs of printing and look more 'professional'.

- The jury is out on the sequence of questions. Some researchers recommend putting the easy questions, such as gender and age categories, at the start to encourage the respondents to fill in the questionnaire. Others recommend putting the easier questions at the end when the respondent has already invested in the questionnaire and is therefore more likely to complete it. Whichever way you decide to organise your questionnaire, put questions of a similar theme together and try not to include too many open-ended questions.

- A disadvantage of questionnaires is the lack of depth and detail that they can provide, but you can compensate for this by including open-ended question responses and complementing the questionnaire data with other research methods.

- It is worth leaving space at the end of the questionnaire to include your contact details for the option of a follow-up interview, or in case respondents have any further comments they wish to make.

ACTIVITY

As a starting point for considering the significance of questionnaire design for an effective piece of research:

- Think about a time when you have completed a questionnaire.
- What was good or bad about the questionnaire you had to complete?
- Compile a list and discuss it with a partner.
- Now, use this list to analyse the strengths and weaknesses of the questionnaire you have designed for your own research project. Is there anything you need to amend before giving it to research participants?

It is important to be aware of the practical issues of administering a questionnaire. An online questionnaire that was used with families of school-age children during the Covid-19 lockdown in Spain (Bonal and González, 2020) will be used as an example of dealing effectively with consent, pilot testing and bias. In their study, Bonal and González (2020) investigated the impact of school closures on the learning gap between children from different social backgrounds in Catalonia. Data (35,419 responses) were collected from families with children between 3 and 18 years of age.

- Consent: Bonal and González (2020) included an ethics form in their questionnaire which included information about the aims of the study, anonymity and confidentiality. It also informed the respondents that they were giving consent by answering the questionnaire. Data were collected from consenting adults and not their children. For more information on informed consent see Chapter 20 and for the ethics of conducting research with vulnerable groups see Chapter 21.
- Pilot testing: Bonal and González (2020) piloted their questionnaire by asking 10 families with children of different ages and on different school pathways to complete the questionnaire. Due to the exceptional circumstances of the coronavirus pandemic, the authors opted for this informal piloting strategy. Pilot testing is vital to check that respondents understand the questions, that the questions are appropriate, and that the questionnaire is a reasonable length to encourage a good return rate. For example, you might discover that respondents' experiences may not be sufficiently described by the pre-set multiple-choice responses, or the questionnaire may have little relevance or personal interest to respondents. You need to ensure that the questionnaire is completed by the target audience. Respondents may make up answers or leave out certain questions completely, and this will skew your data. Through piloting your questionnaire, you should be able to iron out any difficulties concerning the likelihood of respondents misunderstanding or misinterpreting questions.
- Bias: For any questionnaire there is the possibility of bias. For example, if a questionnaire is being used to elicit the views of pupils about their own teacher, then there is the potential for bias – for example, if pupils wish to answer positively to please their teacher. It is important that respondents feel able to express their opinions safely and honestly. The use of an independent researcher should reduce any possible bias. Bonal and González (2020) administered their questionnaire on various social media channels (Twitter [X], Facebook and WhatsApp) as well as through contacts they had in more deprived areas where families were less likely to engage with online communication platforms. This helped to mitigate against any sampling bias linked to the use of social networks.
- Response rate: Response rate is often the biggest issue with using questionnaires, making good questionnaire design crucial to increase participation. We've already highlighted the fact that asking too many questions can be very off-putting for respondents, which will reduce your response rate. To work out how many questionnaires to send out, you need

to decide how many questionnaires you need for analysis. Questionnaires, especially those administered by post, have a notoriously low return rate and this means you will need to send out a lot more questionnaires than you actually need for analysis. Broadly speaking, you can expect a response rate of about twenty to thirty percent. This means that if you are hoping to have fifty questionnaires to analyse, you may need to send out at least two hundred questionnaires. Questionnaires can be delivered to the respondents by various means including post, email or online. Postal questionnaires often have a low response rate, but they also have advantages such as wide coverage and eliminating any bias that may be introduced by interaction with a researcher.

The most common mode of delivery for questionnaires is now online and it is becoming increasingly sophisticated and cost-effective to design, collect and analyse questionnaire data using online platforms (Young, 2015). Online software helps you design the questionnaire in a professional way and will let you send out a link to respondents. In addition, the software will collate the findings and allow you to perform basic statistical tests. Online software often has a subscription fee, but many institutions do subscribe. However, if this is not a possibility at your institution, online software often lets you have a free 'trial', sending a limited number of questionnaires without the need to pay for the service.

There are several strategies you can use to increase the number of responses – for example:

- Offer a suitable prize, such as a book token, or say you will send out the results to interested respondents (but you must make it clear in your write-up that an incentive was offered).
- Target your audience by name, such as Ms. Jones, rather than 'the head teacher'.
- You may be able to get a 'captive' audience, for example by handing out your questionnaires at the beginning of a seminar and collecting them at the end of the session.
- Send email reminders.
- If it is a postal questionnaire, include a stamped and self-addressed envelope.
- Explain the purpose of the questionnaire and why the responses are important.
- Structured interview questionnaires – where you read out the questions to respondents and complete their responses, these can be effective but they are time consuming.

Dealing with problem responses

Most people will answer all the questions in the way that you have requested. However, some respondents may miss out a question. When coding your questionnaire responses, it is better to record something on your grid rather than nothing, but you may want to differentiate the responses, for example between missing (M) and don't know (DK). This is important because when you are calculating your statistics at a later date it is important to know how many responses you are dealing with. For example, you may have 160 questionnaires returned, but perhaps only 143 people answered question 7. This means that if 87 respondents said 'yes' to question 7, you need to base your calculations on 87 out of 143, not 87 out of 160.

Checklist

- Have you piloted your questionnaire?
- Does the questionnaire give instructions for completion?
- Is the questionnaire a sensible length that will not require too much time to complete?
- Will the respondents understand the questions?
- Are the choices for response appropriate and comprehensive?
- Have you decided how you will analyse the data?

Chapter summary

Questionnaires are a useful tool for gathering responses from a large number of participants. The design of a questionnaire instrument can allow statistical analysis to be applied. It is crucial to pilot your questionnaire to ensure that respondents will be able to understand the questions and will not suffer from 'questionnaire fatigue'. There are lots of different types of questions, such as multiple-choice items, Likert scale questions and open-ended responses. However, do not worry about trying to include every possible type of question– this can be confusing for participants.

It is a good research method for ensuring anonymity and confidentiality, but you can include your contact details (typically an email address) and ask participants who wish to be further involved in the research to get in touch. There are also several disadvantages of using questionnaires, such as low response rates and the limited amount of information that can be obtained using this approach. Therefore, using questionnaires to complement other research methods in a research project can compensate for these drawbacks (see Chapter 8 on mixed-methods). For instance, your questionnaire may offer a broad overview of the research area, while other methods such as interviews or observations provide in-depth detail.

Further reading

Vannette, D.L. and Krosnick, J.A. (2017) *The Palgrave handbook of survey research*. Cham, Switzerland: Palgrave MacMillan.

- This book offers a comprehensive overview and discussion of survey-based research, including best practices for questionnaires design put forward by leading scholars in the field.

Williams, M., Wiggins, R.D. and McCoach, B. (2021) *The SAGE quantitative research kit*. Lo Angeles: SAGE.

- This collection of books offers clear and accessible information on theories, methods and techniques for quantitative research.

Young, T.J. (2015) Questionnaires and surveys, in Hua, Z. (ed.), *Research methods in intercultural communication: A practical guide*. West Sussex: John Wiley & Sons, pp. 163–180.

- This chapter helps less experienced researchers in identifying the potential pitfalls of questionnaire-based research and offers tried-and-trusted techniques that can help avoid them. It also details approaches to data analysis and illustrates how questionnaires can feature in a mixed-methods research design.

References

Bonal, X. and González, S. (2020) The impact of lockdown on the learning gap: Family and school divisions in times of crisis. *International Review of Education*, 66(5), pp. 635–655.

Brown, J.D. (2001) *Using surveys in language programs*. Cambridge: Cambridge University Press.

Denscombe, M. (2003) *The good research guide for small-scale research projects*. Buckingham: Open University Press.

Dörnyei, Z. (2007) *Research methods in applied linguistics*. Oxford: Oxford University Press.

Pantell, R.H. and Lewis, C.C. (1987) 'Measuring the impact of medical care on children', *Journal of Chronic Diseases*, 40(1), pp. 99–108.

Ruel, E., Wagner, W.E. and Gillespie, B.J. (2018) *Introduction to survey research in: The practice of survey research: Theory and applications*. Lose Angeles: Sage, pp. 2–10.

Stockemer, D. (2019) 'A short introduction to survey research', in Stockemer, D., Stockemer, G. and Glaeser, J. (eds.) *Quantitative methods for the social sciences*. Cham, Switzerland: Springer, pp. 23–35.

Tourangeau, R. (2018) 'Maintaining respondent trust and protecting their data', in Vannette, D.L. and Krosnick, J.A. (eds.) *The Palgrave handbook of survey research*. Cham: Palgrave Macmillan, pp. 135–141.

Williams, M., Wiggins, R. and Vogt, P. (2022). *Beginning Quantitative Research* (1st ed.). London: SAGE Publications.

Young, T.J. (2015) 'Questionnaires and surveys', in Hua, Z. (ed.) *Research methods in intercultural communication: A practical guide*. West Sussex: John Wiley & Sons, pp. 163–180.

CHAPTER

Interviews and focus groups

Introduction

Interviews are a popular research tool within education (for instance, Murphy, 2022; Pace, 2024; Scholes et al., 2024; Yeoh and Cheong, 2023 are all recent examples). An interview can broadly be defined as being conducted on a one-to-one basis, with a range of questions to be asked and answered. Some of these questions may be fairly straightforward and some will take a great deal of thought and consideration. Interviews generally fall into three main categories: Semi-structured, unstructured and structured. The type of interview that you conduct is dependent on your underlying methodology and the focus of your research (please refer back to the introduction for a discussion of these issues). After examining the different types of interviews, this chapter discusses power dynamics in the interview process and illustrates how interviewing principles can mediate this, before exploring the practical aspects of interviewing. The chapter finally explores focus group interviews.

Semi-structured interviews

These are perhaps the most commonly used type of interview within education research and in social science research more widely. The questions are pre-set but do allow some flexibility into your schedule. If a participant starts talking about something which you had not previously considered, this is not generally thought to be problematic. In addition, this type of interview normally encourages participants to add their own thoughts – after all, this approach believes that it is important to identify what is most significant for the participants. The quote below is an example of an extract from a semi-structured interview conducted with a teacher:

> Going out on a limb, I'd probably say 90% of private tutoring is based on parental aspiration to get their child into grammar school. The tutoring tends to happen from the

DOI: 10.4324/9781003569428-17

middle of Year 5 to the beginning of Year 6. It finishes after the Kent test, the 11+. The grammar test isn't like the SAT [Scholastic Aptitude Test]. It's not part of the curriculum. For the children to be able to have experience of it and pass it, the parents often hire a private tutor for that…I can't recall a child ever saying, 'I attend tutoring because I want to do this' or 'Because I want to learn more' (Teacher 1).

(Hajar, 2020: 468)

The teacher candidly discusses the use of personal tutoring to prepare children for the 11+ exam in East Kent, where there is the option to attend a Grammar School. The interview participants need to feel comfortable with the interviewer in order to discuss their views honestly and this requires rapport between the interviewer and interviewee. A good interview technique relies on 'rapport'.

Rapport is the development of a sense of trust and empathy. This means that you will need to get the interview participant to 'like you' enough to give honest and detailed answers. In this type of approach, it is okay to go 'off topic' or answer questions not directly pertaining to the interview questions, and this may partly facilitate the rapport-building process. Although it is not specific to education research, a seminal discussion on rapport in interviews can be found in Ann Oakley's work (2005).

Unstructured interviews

It may appear tempting to use an unstructured interview – after all, very little preparation is required beyond thinking about the broad themes you want to discuss and hoping the participant has something to say on them. If you have very chatty participants, this type of approach may work. On the other hand, if your participants are less forthcoming you will still need a prepared range of probes to elicit the information. During semi-structured interviews it is not unusual to ask additional questions to subsequent participants if you feel that particular themes are emerging, but you may feel that this is inappropriate if you are using an unstructured approach. Unstructured interviews are more likely to produce disparate accounts and themes, which may create difficulties in the analysis stage, although you may want to explore a grounded theory approach (see Strauss and Corbin (1998) for more information).

Structured interviews

On the other hand, structured interviews require the same questions to be asked of each interview participant. The answers given tend to be very short and to the point – the questions do not allow for any flexibility. The focus is on the uniformity of question delivery, and in many ways a structured interview can be likened to reading out a questionnaire to a participant. This approach is underpinned by beliefs in objectivity and researcher neutrality. Interviewers who conduct this style of interview are less concerned about rapport. If a participant asked the interviewer a question, they are less likely to engage in a conversation and may respond with answers such as, '*Sorry, I'm just here to ask you questions*'. Additionally, the interviewer is likely to be only concerned with answers to their pre-planned questions and will not give opportunities for the participant to add additional information or thoughts. This type of interview may be used in survey research (see Chapter 7).

Interview participants and power dynamics

You may interview a range of participants within educational settings: Teachers, senior management, governors, children, support staff and parents. It is important to reflect on your own identity and how this will influence the interview process. Czerniawski (2023) discusses the experiences of thirty teachers in relation to their positionality and the power dynamics that they have had to navigate as they undertake research in their schools for professional doctorates. The range of possible participants is likely to shape the interviews, particularly in relation to the power dynamics involved in interview research. The power dynamics within the interview process can have a real impact on what questions you feel that you can ask, as well as the types of responses you are likely to get from participants.

ACTIVITY

These are a useful set of questions to consider before you start the interviews:

- Are you older or younger than the participants?
- Do you have more or less experience in the educational field?
- Do you have any 'common ground' with the participants, for example, are you a parent or a student teacher?
- Is your gender, socio-economic background and ethnicity the same or different from participants?
- Do you see yourself as an 'outsider' or an 'insider'? Are you part of the educational community that you are researching? Are you looking in on the educational community from the position of someone who is not closely aligned with this group?
- Do the participants see you as an 'outsider' or as an 'insider'? How do you think this will affect the interview process?

Interviewing principles

The ways in which you deal with these power dynamics will be shaped by your own beliefs about research and how these translate into your interviewing principles. Oakley (1981) highlighted that interviewing is a masculine paradigm which does not include characteristics such as emotion and sensitivity. She was not inclined to continue interviewing women as 'objects' and thereby not understanding them as individuals. Although this unwillingness arose from Oakley's moral and ethical convictions, it is also significant methodologically. Interviewing has been widely used by feminist researchers and has often been regarded as the most appropriate method for 'producing the kind of knowledge that feminists wish to make available as being more in keeping with the politics of doing research as a feminist' (Maynard and Purvis, 1994: 11). Ann Oakley moved away from traditions in interviewing which were seen as ways of avoiding bias – for example, not answering questions from interviewees, or sharing experiences which would facilitate rapport-building (Oakley, 2005). As Oakley states (1981: 49), there is 'no intimacy without reciprocity', meaning that unless the interviewer shares their own identity and experiences with the interviewee, it is unfair to expect participants to share such information about themselves. Oakley's research was about women becoming mothers, but her belief in a non-hierarchical, non-exploitative interviewing process lends itself to educational research.

The use of interviews in a non-hierarchical way does enable the development of a more democratised research process and facilitates the formation of more reciprocal relationships between the researcher and the participants. The term 'conversational partner' (Rubin and Rubin, 2005: 14) allows for the interviewee to shape the topic and the direction of the research themes, suggesting ways in which the interviewer and interviewee may work together to develop shared understandings. The concept of a 'conversational partner' captures the idea of a non-exploitative, non-hierarchical relationship. The term 'conversational partner' also emphasises the uniqueness of each person with whom you talk, his or her distinct knowledge, and the different ways in which he or she interacts with you (Rubin and Rubin, 2005). Sometimes principles of non-hierarchical and reciprocal relations can be difficult to apply, especially when this does not reflect participants' wider experiences within society. A case in point would be interviews with children.

The idea that children should be given a voice is a relatively new one. Historically children have been subsumed within the 'family' in sociological research. However, a new sociology of childhood has emerged in the last 30 years, particularly through the work of Allison James, Chris Jenks and Alan Prout (James, Jenks and Prout, 2001). Based on this acknowledgement that children have their own voice, it is now much more common to see research that has explored children's perspectives. In addition, the advent of the United Nations Convention on the Rights of the Child (UNCRC) (1989) has meant that children have begun to be seen as individuals in their own right. However, adults clearly have more power in society than children, and this is particularly apparent within a school setting.

This power dynamic will have a significant impact when interviewing children (Eder and Fingerson, 2002). Experienced researchers are more likely to carry out interviews with children, so do not be surprised if your research supervisor is hesitant about you conducting interviews with children and advises against this. Nevertheless, if you do get ethical clearance to interview children there are a variety of strategies that can enable children to feel more comfortable:

- Interacting with children informally in a natural setting, such as the classroom, before carrying out an interview.

- Using language which children are familiar with and avoiding technical terms.
- Pictures, toys and other practical resources are helpful in making young children feel comfortable and encouraging discussion.
- Draw on what children already know. For example, they may not be able to tell you their parents' occupations, but perhaps they can say where they work or what types of tasks their job entails.
- Be patient. It can sometimes take children a while to articulate what they want to say, especially with an unfamiliar adult.

ACTIVITY

A master student undertakes interviews with teaching assistants in their own homes, asking about their training and qualifications. The student is a young, white female. The teaching assistants are also white, but perhaps 20 to 30 years older than the interviewer. The student does not mention that she is also a teacher.

- Who do you think had the most power during the interviews?
- Why do you think the student did not tell the teaching assistants she was a teacher?

The view that researchers occupy a more powerful position than participants has long been a concern within research (Olesen, 1994). However, this debate has evolved as researchers have looked more closely at the relationship between interviewers and participants. The image of the powerless respondent has been superseded by notions that power is only partial, and transitory and often shifts between the researcher and the participants throughout the research process. Fine and Weiss (2000: 115) suggest that 'they [the participants] recognised that we could take their stories, their concerns and their worries to audiences, policy makers and the public in ways that they themselves could not because they would not be listened to'. This highlights that it is possible that participants recognise and exploit power inequalities within the research process.

Practical aspects of interviewing

This section of the chapter will be divided into five subheadings:

- Interview questions
- Technique
- Location
- Recording
- Transcribing

Interview questions

It is often a good idea to start with questions which do not put the interview participant under too much pressure – for example, some relatively straightforward introductory questions such as 'why are they studying this course?', 'where did they do their teacher training?' or 'what is their favourite subject at school?'

You want your interview participants to answer your questions as fully and as honestly as possible. However, the way that you ask questions can influence their responses. For example, if you asked: 'Why do you think boys present more challenging behaviour in the classroom?', this would tell us something about the attitude of the interviewer and the types of response they are looking for. This may put pressure on the interview participant to agree with the interviewer and say things that they do not necessarily believe. Therefore, when you are designing your interview schedule check that you are not unfairly influencing the responses of your participants.

Interview technique

Sometimes one of the hardest aspects of conducting an interview is not saying too much. It can be difficult because you often feel that you should not make the interview a one-sided affair and that you want the interview participant to know that you are interested in what he or she is saying. However, when you are transcribing your interview data you do not want to find that you actually said more than the participant! It is important to listen carefully, and perhaps listening is a skill that we often take for granted when in reality we are not always very good at it. There are lots of ways you can show the interview participant that you are listening and therefore that you are interested in what they are saying. This may simply be with the verbal cues that you give to them: Eye contact, a nod of the head or an encouraging smile. Sometimes you may ask them to clarify or expand a point. This is really important because the point may fit with the tentative themes that are emerging from your interviews. Alternatively, you may simply not understand what they mean, and if this is the case during the interview itself, it is unlikely to be any clearer when you analyse the data. Therefore, do not be afraid to ask for clarification if needed. If you are interested in reading more about different interview techniques you may find the books by Lincoln and Guba (1985) and Rubin and Rubin (2005) helpful.

It is also useful to give the interviewee a bit of time at the end. Ask the participant if there is anything they would like to add – maybe something that they feel is important, but which they have not had a chance to raise during the interview. Often at this stage, it is tempting to think that the participant is unlikely to have anything to add. Initially, they may say 'not really, I can't think of anything'. However, given a brief pause to reflect, it is surprising how many participants have some additional information to impart. Don't worry if they haven't, though – if you use the 'member checking' procedure, participants often have something to add at a later date. It is also useful to give the interview participant your contact details in case they do remember something later on.

Location

The ideal room for interviewing should be quiet and private. Hopefully, this will provide a relaxed and informal setting in which to conduct the interviews. This is particularly important because you will wish to preserve your participants' anonymity and confidentiality. It is better to try and arrange a time for the interview when the participant has enough time to talk to you fully. It is good practice to reiterate why you are carrying out the research and what your research is about. It is also helpful to double-check that it is okay to record the interview. Also, from a practical standpoint it is very difficult to transcribe data when there is a lot of background noise – so shut the window. However, if you are interviewing children, it may not be appropriate to be in an enclosed space alone with them, and you may wish to leave the door open and ensure that you are clearly visible. This contradicts our earlier advice about location, but it is certainly something you will need to consider in your research.

Recording interviews

Digital voice recorders (dictaphones) can be bought for approximately £30. However, if you have a smartphone, it is worth looking to see if it has a voice recording facility. Have a play around with your digital recorder before you start the interview. Record yourself speaking – it is a little eerie listening to yourself saying 'hello, hello', but at least you can be confident that:

A   You know how to use the recorder.
B   It is recording.
C   The volume is correct.

There is nothing worse than finding out that the hour you have spent talking to someone has not recorded (it has been known to happen!), or that you can barely hear what is being said. In addition, check batteries and mains sockets. The advantage of having a plug-in recorder is that you know the batteries won't run out. The disadvantage is that you may not be in a location where a mains socket is readily available or accessible. The key message here is to *be organised*. Preparation is everything to guarantee a successful interview recording. Not all participants will feel comfortable being recorded, and it is important to double-check this before you begin the interview. If participants do not wish to be recorded, you may be able to take notes during the interview (so remember to bring a notepad and pen). Once you have typed up these notes you can then ask the participant to confirm, amend or add to them. If you conduct interviews online via Zoom – it is possible to audio record the interview and Zoom will send you a transcript. It is unlikely that this transcript will be 'perfect' and it may cope with some languages better than others. However, given the time and cost of conducting interviews (particularly for an individual research project) with some note-taking and careful amendments in conjunction with the interview participant, this is a pragmatic approach for those without research funds to support the transcription of interviews (see below).

Transcribing

Once you have recorded an interview it can then be transcribed. Transcription is the process of listening to a voice recording and typing the words verbatim (word for word). This can be a tricky skill to learn – it helps if you are a quick typist (or alternatively if you can slow the voice recording down to make it easier to type). Sometimes in bigger research projects a professional transcriber may be employed. However, in small-scale projects, it is more likely that the person carrying out the research will transcribe their own data. The advantage of this is that you can often start to analyse the data as you go, as you think about what you are typing. It also ensures that you really 'know' your data.

It is also helpful to check the final transcript with the participant. Email the file to your participants and ask them to add or change any aspects that they are unhappy with. Alternatively, if you have conducted the interview with children, it is worth sitting down and checking it through with them. The advantage of this is that you can be sure that the participant feels that the information is valid; they may want to add more detail, and perhaps most importantly, they are happy for you to use their words.

Focus groups

Focus groups are a popular way to interview children, as they help to minimise power dynamics between adults and children. In addition, it can feel much less threatening when you are not the only person being asked questions. An advantage of focus groups is that they can help others in the group by sparking thoughts and ideas. Power dynamics in a focus group are often a concern in terms of having a very vocal or opinionated participant, that other members of the group do not feel that they can challenge. Therefore, conducting a focus group requires an effective level of facilitation from the interviewer in order to check that everyone has had the opportunity to speak and that all voices are fairly represented. Another challenge of focus groups is the complexity of transcribing a multitude of voices. Typically, transcription companies charge more for the transcription of focus groups because of their complexity. The ideal number of participants in a focus group is debated. However, an interview with two participants might be best described as a 'paired interview'. Therefore, somewhere between three and six participants are probably ideal, as many as eight participants may make it difficult to fully listen to all participants. It can be difficult to get all participants in a room together at the same time. Ideally, it is also probably best to offer participants the choice of a focus group or an interview. It is important to avoid the use of focus groups for very sensitive topics. However, there may be a degree of camaraderie and reflection amongst participants in a focus group say on school uniforms or choosing a university.

Focus groups with pupils may be a helpful way to understand issues that are important to them, and it can also enable greater anonymity – both increasing pupil confidence to speak, but also in the presentation of the data analysis. Keisu and Ahlström (2020) conducted ten focus groups with 43 children from four different Swedish schools about gender equality and diversity. They report on some of the comments made by pupils in the focus groups:

As one pupil describes it:

Well. It feels like they never cared about our opinions. Or, of course there are individual teachers who really care. But in general they see our engagement as we just want to complain. 'Why are you complaining?' Like we're not supposed to complain. 'We live in Sweden, we're doing all right, we've got food on the table, and so on and so forth. But we want more.

(Keisu and Ahlström, 2020: 10)

Chapter summary

Overall interviewing can be a rich way to gain insights into aspects of educational experiences and perspectives. To ensure that the interview process is successful you need to consider how to develop a rapport with your participants. The power dynamics within the interview process will play a large role in shaping the success of your interview and you need to minimise these power differentials as far as possible. Make sure that you are really organised in terms of equipment and suitable locations. Most importantly, you need to be appreciative of the fact that participants are giving up their time and perhaps sharing very personal stories.

Further reading

Flick, U. (2021) *Doing interview research: The essential how to guide*. London: SAGE.
- This comprehensive and accessible book discusses the process of conducting interviews including focus groups. The book gives helpful information about the analysis process for interview research.

King, N., Horrocks, C. and Brooks, J. (2018) *Interviews in qualitative research*. London: SAGE.
- This book explores epistemology and ontology in qualitative interviews, as well as outlining the key aspects of qualitative interviews. The book incorporates helpful recommended reading.

References

Czerniawski, G. (2023) 'Power, positionality and practitioner research: Schoolteachers' experiences of professional doctorates in education', *British Educational Research Journal*, 49, 1372–1386. doi:10.1002/berj.3902.

Eder, D. and Fingerson, L. (2002) 'Interviewing children and adolescents', in Gubrium, J. F. and Holstein, J. A. (eds.) *Handbook of interview research: Context and method*. Thousand Oaks, CA: SAGE, pp. 181–201.

Fine, M. and Weiss, L. (2000) 'Compositional studies in two parts: Critical theorizing and analysis on social (In) justice,' In Denzin, N. K. and Lincoln, Y. S. (eds.) *The SAGE handbook of qualitative research*. 2nd edn. London: SAGE.

Hajar, A. (2020) 'The association between private tutoring and access to grammar schools: Voices of year 6 pupils and teachers in South-East England', *British Educational Research Journal*, 46, pp. 459–479. doi:10.1002/berj.3587.

James, A., Jenks, C. and Prout, A. (2001) *Theorizing childhood*. Cambridge: Polity Press.

Keisu, B.-I. and Ahlström, B. (2020) 'The silent voices: Pupil participation for gender equality and diversity', *Educational Research*, 62(1), 1–17. doi:10.1080/00131881.2019.1711436.

Lincoln, Y.S. and Guba, E.G. (1985) *Naturalistic inquiry*. Beverly Hills, CA: Sage.

Maynard, M. and Purvis, J. (eds.) (1994) *Researching women's lives from a feminist perspective*. London: Taylor and Francis.

Murphy, R. (2022) 'How children make sense of their permanent exclusion: A thematic analysis from semi-structured interviews', *Emotional and Behavioural Difficulties*, 27(1), pp. 43–57, doi:10.1080/13632752.2021.2012962.

Oakley, A. (2005) *The Ann Oakley reader*. Bristol: The Policy Press.

Oakley, A. (1981) *Becoming a mother*. Oxford: Martin Robertson.

Olesen, V. (1994) 'Early millennial feminist qualitative research: Challenges and contours', in Denzin, N. and Lincoln, Y. (eds.) *Handbook of qualitative research*. London: SAGE.

Pace, J.L. (2024) 'Tensions in teaching balanced controversial history: Competing voices within a student teacher in Northern Ireland', *British Educational Research Journal*, pp. 1–18. doi:10.1002/berj.4008.

Rubin, R.J. and Rubin, I.S. (2005) *Qualitative interviewing: The art of hearing data*. 2nd edn. London: SAGE.

Scholes, L. et al. (2024) 'Many truths, many knowledges, many forms of reason: Understanding middle-school student approaches to sources of information on the internet', *British Educational Research Journal*, 50, pp. 53–72. doi: 10.1002/berj.3909.

Strauss, A.L. and Corbin, J.M. (1998) *Basics of qualitative research: Techniques and procedures for developing grounded theory*. 2nd edn. London: SAGE.

UNCRC (1989) 'UN convention on rights of a child (UNCRC) - UNICEF UK', Available at: https://www.unicef.org.uk/what-we-do/un-convention-child-rights/ (Accessed: 13 June 2024).

Yeoh, H.N. and Cheong, H.F. (2023) 'What do the children and teachers say?: Voices on gender stereotyping in children's literature for Malaysian ESL classrooms', *Review of Education*, 11, p. e3427. doi: 10.1002/rev3.3427.

CHAPTER

Observations

Introduction

This chapter outlines and compares some of the distinctive forms that observation might take – for instance, participant and non-participant, overt and covert, structured and unstructured. It identifies some of the chief reasons for observation's popularity as a method in educational research, and highlights some of the technical considerations that frame how observations are carried out. It goes on to consider different approaches to recording data from observations. Finally, the chapter discusses the main difficulties for the researcher who chooses observation – namely, issues of access, viability, visibility and the 'observer effect'.

What is observation?

Observation involves looking and collecting data by systematically recording interactions between people, patterns of behaviour, speech, rituals, routines and/or environments. Therefore, unlike other primary methods of data collection, observation does not depend on the respondents providing information to the researcher. Rather, the researcher gathers data from naturally-occurring situations, viewing social reality as it actually takes place. Many of the most influential pieces of educational research have utilised a variety of observational approaches to uncover characteristics of learning, culture and identity. For example, Paul Willis' exploration of 'the lads' in *Learning to Labour* (1978), Stephen Ball's *Beachside Comprehensive* (1981), Heidi Mirza's *Young, Female and Black* (1992) and Mairtin Mac an Ghaill's *The Making of Men* (1994) all used observational methods.

DOI: 10.4324/9781003569428-18

Why use observation?

Observations are an attractive method of data collection in educational research for many reasons. Among the four most important advantages are:

- Ecological validity: Observations provide the researcher with a direct view of behaviour in natural settings. The researcher can develop observations with little experimental control, so that what takes place would do so with or without the researcher's presence. This leads to high levels of ecological validity – the researcher can (quite) confidently claim a correspondence between what they observe and what really happens. For instance, a classroom observation is likely to provide a more accurate picture of the strengths and weaknesses of a lesson than an interview with a teacher or a survey of the pupils.

- Combines with other methods: In the previous example, the classroom observation will almost certainly increase the validity of the survey or interview – the presence of the researcher can minimise exaggeration in subsequent responses. If observations take place prior to other methods, they can help inform the topics and structure of questioning. Used after other methods, observations can be used as a check on the validity of previous responses. Exploring the similarities and divergences between 'what you said' and 'what you did' are especially fertile grounds for the educational researcher.

- Uncovering the 'taken-for-granted' and 'unexpected': More than any other method, observations enable the researcher to enter the research site without prior classification or categorisation. This makes observations more likely to uncover the unexpected, which is especially beneficial in grounded theory. Likewise, much of our behaviour is habitual and involuntary, and therefore it is difficult to articulate or explain during an interview. Importantly, observations help the researcher to identify what is 'taken-for-granted', what 'goes-without-saying', or what an 'insider' knows.

- Gathering data that other methods cannot reach: Observations can enable the researcher to access settings, groups and events that other methods are unable to. For instance, very small children are unable to complete a survey and might be difficult to interview, but it is possible to observe them playing and interacting in playschool or nursery.

Technical considerations

Observational research takes a wide variety of forms, each producing very different data and each with its own set of strengths and limitations. Among the decisions which the researcher utilising observation must make are:

- How to gain access to the research site.
- 'What', 'who' and 'when' to observe.
- Finding the right place to observe.
- What and how to record.

- How to manage and handle data.
- How to leave the research site.

These technical decisions are largely shaped by the researcher's approach to observation, including the researcher's role, position and closeness to the research site, as well as levels of involvement, disclosure and structure.

Different roles in observation

Gold (1958) outlined an influential continuum that distinguished between observer roles:

- Complete participant
- Participant as observer
- Observer as participant
- Complete observer

At one end of the spectrum is the *complete participant* – a total insider who conceals her identity from the other members of the group. One famous example of this approach was James Patrick's *A Glasgow Gang Observed* (1973), where the researcher became a full member to directly experience the language, rituals and behaviour of a gang. At the other end, the *complete observer* is entirely detached and unknown to the group. An example of this might be the researcher who places a video camera in a classroom to record interactions. In between, the *participant as observer* might normally have a connection to the group that exists outside the research. Theirs is a partial membership, like that of a volunteer classroom assistant who writes a fieldwork diary of her observations at the end of each week. Likewise, the *observer as participant* is also a partial member of the group, although this membership is not natural or normal. Typically, this is the kind of role an Ofsted inspector might have within the classroom. Gold's continuum starts to demonstrate that there are a number of alternative approaches you need to consider if you are to employ an observation method.

Participant or non-participant observation?

Perhaps the most important decision is the extent to which the researcher takes part in the activities of the group or research site. Ethnographers, as we saw in Chapter 10, believe in the value of full immersion within the group being studied, and the importance of experiencing the world as the group members do, so they tend to favour participant observation. This form of observation is commonplace in educational research; when researchers observe an educational setting, they already inhabit as a teacher, classroom assistant, school manager or student.

Of course, there is a danger that by participating, the researcher might influence behaviour within the research site. Because of this risk, other educational research employs a non-participant approach, where the researcher observes behaviour but does not take part in it. In adopting this approach, the researcher might find it easier to record observations, but conversely, she might find it more difficult to observe what she wants to.

Covert or overt?

A second important decision is whether or not the group should be aware that they are being observed. If the group members are aware, the research is overt; if they are unaware, it is covert. Both approaches give rise to important difficulties. An overt observation is likely to impact on the group's behaviour – pupils and teachers are likely to alter their behaviour in response to the presence of an observer. A covert approach provokes ethical concerns such as deception and a lack of informed consent. It is very unlikely that an ethics committee would grant ethical approval for a covert observation today because it breaches serious ethical principles.

Naturalistic or artificial?

In general, observations in educational research aim to look at interactions as they normally take place, i.e. as they naturally occur. Unlike other methods, observations allow the researcher to see activities and behaviour as they really happen, so researchers are likely to try to minimise the contamination of what they observe. Nevertheless, if a researcher is interested in a specific aspect of educational activity, she might attempt to contrive an artificial scenario to observe how different people respond. For example, a teacher-researcher might choose a particular educational resource to understand how different pupils respond to it. This approach blurs the boundary between observation and field experiment.

Structured or unstructured?

As we saw in the Chapter 14, interviews might take either a structured, unstructured or semi-structured form. Likewise, observations might take various forms, from entirely unstructured on the one hand to fully structured on the other. Unstructured observations mean that the researcher starts with a blank sheet of paper and records what she observes, often in the form of a fieldwork diary. Structured observations generally use an observation schedule or a tally chart (see below) to identify pre-specified patterns of behaviour. Of course, there is a whole continuum in between, and many researchers who employ observations will combine a fieldwork diary with an observation schedule.

Gathering quantitative and qualitative data

While the famous educational research examples mentioned above used observations to produce qualitative data, the method is equally able to produce quantitative data. Close scrutiny of a group's behaviour can elicit rich, detailed 'thick' description. However, it is equally possible to use observations to identify trends, patterns and comparisons – for example, the number of times a teacher communicates with girls versus boys, or the number of 'positive' interactions compared with 'negative' ones. Walford (2020) reminds us that some of the best observational studies in education have drawn upon both qualitative and quantitative observational techniques.

Reflective or neutral

While the majority of current educational researchers would deny the possibility of researcher neutrality or objectivity, many observations will try to minimise the researcher effect – for instance, by specifying observational criteria or by using a number of different observers. Others will adopt a reflexive approach, considering the impact of their own values and positions on the patterns of behaviour they look for and the ways they interpret them. The latter approach will generally make use of reflective fieldwork diaries, where researchers record their observations and their thoughts on those observations.

Closeness or distance

Similarly, some observers will choose to maintain a detachment or distance from their observations, perhaps by making use of one-way mirrors, video cameras or other 'surveillance' technologies in order to minimise their impact on the research site. Others, believing in the significance of studying the minutiae of social interactions, will favour a mode of observation that gets them as close as possible.

Recording observational data

There are various ways a researcher might choose to record her observations, depending on her topic of research, her access to the research site, and the kind of data she intends to gather. If the researcher does not know what she plans to observe prior to commencing observations, she might use:

- Video recording: It creates a permanent record of the observation and can mean the 'observer' does not have to be present ('indirect observation') which might minimise the extent that the researcher contaminates the research site. However, the presence of a researcher with a camera can prove rather inhibiting, and a camera attached to a wall or tripod can only observe what takes place in front of it.
- Audio recording: Again, this produces a permanent record and means the data collection is not limited to what the researcher can write during an observation or remember after it. A tape recorder might be less inhibiting than a video camera, but tape-recorded observations are unable to capture anything silent or visual, notably non-verbal communication.
- (Reflective) fieldwork diary: Perhaps the most common means of recording participant observation and ethnographic research, fieldwork notes or diaries are written accounts of observations. These are likely to be detailed and include the viewpoints and feelings of

the researcher, making them more subjective than either of the above. Non-participants might write their diaries during observations; participants might leave the research site at regular intervals to update their diary, or they might write at the end of each day or week.

If the researcher intends to develop a more structured and systematic approach to observation, she is likely to develop an observation schedule. This involves operationalising or 'coding' behaviour or events, specifically listing what to focus on and how to define it. An influential example of coding in education research was developed by Flanders (1970). His list of 'interaction analysis categories' was an observational tool to code or classify verbal communication among pupils and teachers in the classroom, with two main categories of 'teacher talk' and 'pupil talk' and ten subdivisions.

- Event or interval sampling: It involves recording the number of times particular events take place or making notes about observations at specific time intervals – for instance, every fifteen minutes. Event sampling might record 'critical incidents' such as examples of disruptive behaviour or pupils receiving negative feedback.
- Checklists or tally charts: Event or interval sampling usually involves developing checklists or tally charts to produce quantitative data. Table 15.1 below illustrates how a tally chart can help the observer identify patterns – in this case, to examine the use of questions in the classroom.
- Rating scales: They enable the researcher to make judgements about activities or events. For example, they might rate classroom behaviour on a scale from 5 to 1 with 5 being 'exceptional' and 1 'unacceptable'. Alternatively, as Table 15.2 below illustrates, a ratings scale might allow the researcher to evaluate classroom activities across a continuum:

TABLE 15.1 Using a tally chart for recording observations

Event	Tally
Teacher asks a pupil specific a question	///
Teacher asks whole class a question	///// /////
Pupil asks teacher a question	////
Pupil asks another pupil a question	///

TABLE 15.2 Using a rating scale for recording observations

	5 4 3 2 1	
Pupil-centred		Teacher-centred
Active learning		Didactic
Group work		Independent task
Engaging		Dull

ACTIVITY

You are going to conduct a non-participant observation of classroom behaviour, contrasting three approaches:

- Event sample
- Rating scale
- Fieldwork diary

1. Draw out your event sample and rating scale observation schedule (Tables 15.1 and 15.2 might give you a good starting point)
2. Identify a TV programme set inside a classroom, for example, 'Waterloo Road' or 'Gilmore Girls' or a classroom-based clip from YouTube.
3. Try out your three approaches on the same clip for approximately 5–10 minutes.
4. Compare the data you have collected. How is it similar and different?
5. Which observational method did you prefer? Why?

Some difficulties for the observational researcher

Despite their obvious appeal to the educational researcher, observations carry with them a number of difficulties:

- Lack of reliability: Data gathered via observations is less reliable than many other methods. If a different researcher observed the same group on a different occasion, they would almost certainly collect different data. To maximise reliability, research might use more than one observer and/or repeated observations on a number of occasions.
- Observational bias: Similarly, what a researcher 'sees', as well as how they interpret what they see, will inevitably be partial and subjective. The researcher brings with them their own values and expectations, and these frames what, when, where and how they observe. To mitigate against this bias, some researchers develop systematic tools such as observation schedules to add scientific rigour to the method. They might focus on recording 'low-inference' behaviour (like occurrences of teachers asking open-ended questions or praising learners) rather than 'high-inference' behaviour (like instances of teacher kindness or learner creativity). Other researchers might take a different approach. Researchers may choose to develop a personal and reflective account of their own position and highlight the ways that this has impacted upon the research.
- Gaining entry, maintaining access and exiting: One of the more difficult tasks for the observer is accessing the research site. This is especially difficult when attempting observation of a 'closed' group or space such as a school gang or a staffroom. Once they are

'in', the researcher needs to maintain their position, not causing any disruption or other adverse effects. In covert observation, this entails not arousing suspicion. Finally, they need to find a way to leave. Strong attachments might develop, and these can result in emotional discomfort for both the researcher and the observed participants as the fieldwork comes to an end. To avoid such difficulties, people who already occupy a position within the research site frequently undertake observations in education.

- Observer effect: Anyone who has sat in a class during an Ofsted inspection will know that people behave differently when they are being observed. This change in behaviour is often termed the 'Hawthorne effect' after a famous study that found workers in an electricity plant became more productive because they were being observed. To minimise observer effects, researchers might communicate with people ahead of observations to assuage their fears, conduct observation over an extended period of time so that it becomes a normal part of daily life, or conceal observation by adopting a covert approach.

- Balancing familiarity and strangeness: In order to gain rich insights, the observer attempts to develop familiarity with the research site. The closer they can get, the greater the visibility of behaviour and events – although, of course, researchers can only view what happens in front of them. Especially in participant observation, the researcher risks 'going native', losing sight of the research as they become immersed within the group they study. Although observers require familiarity, they also need to maintain their distinct researcher identity, 'stepping inside and outside' of the research setting to uncover meanings and interpretations.

- Ethical considerations: Observational research typically requires ethics committee approval. Covert observations are especially difficult to justify because they violate guidelines on informed consent and invasion of privacy. Observations, whether they are participant or non-participants, risk altering the natural setting. Without due care, they can impact negatively on the people who are observed. Before commencing observations, researchers must consider how they will react if they witness bullying, illegal, abusive or violent behaviour (see Chapter 20 for a full discussion of ethics in educational research).

ACTIVITY

Read the following two extracts of observational research:

> My participation in each class varied depending on the age of the children and the wishes of the class teacher. In younger classes and the separate EAL provision, this meant actively supporting pupils most of the time, while in older secondary classes I had less to offer and thus tended towards the 'observer' end of the participant-observer spectrum. I took abbreviated notes whenever possible throughout the school day, then typed and expanded the notes when I got home each evening.
>
> (Prentice, 2022: 1130)

Following preliminary pilot studies, an observational study was carried out on the amount of time infant school children spend waiting for teacher attention during seatwork. This involved teachers and children in 20 infant classes. Each class was observed on four occasions and the number of children signalling and waiting for help was noted at the end of each successive minute. In addition, the length of time individual children spent waiting was sampled. The results showed that on average 2.66 children were waiting for assistance at any time and that this number increased as the lesson progressed. The average time spent waiting was 84 seconds. There were no appreciable differences between the numbers of boys and girls waiting. It appears, however, that children in classes whose teachers operate a queue system wait for shorter periods than in classes where hands-up signalling is employed.

(West and Wheldall, 1989: 205)

- What kind of observation techniques are employed?
- What challenges might have been encountered with these two approaches to observation?
- What advantages does observational research offer in these two pieces of research?

Chapter summary

Observations are the best way for a researcher to view educational activities as they actually take place, and they work especially well when combined with other methods of data collection, like interviews, documentary analysis and surveying. As we have seen during the chapter, there are a wide variety of approaches that the researcher might utilise to collect and record observations; the choice between these methods is dictated largely by practical constraints regarding the research setting, and the topic and types of data the researcher seeks. Each brings its own advantages and disadvantages. In general, observations have high levels of ecological validity and enable an 'insider' viewpoint on activities and behaviour. However, there is also a range of important limitations and difficulties, most notably in relation to bias and the danger that the observer might contaminate the research site. More than any method with the exception of experiments, the observer must be conscious of the ethical concerns that shape and constrain their practice.

Further reading

Clark, T. et al. (2021) *Bryman's social research methods*. 6th edn. Oxford: Oxford University Press.
Cohen, L., Manion, L. and Morrison, K. (2018) *Research methods in education*. 8th edn. Abingdon: Routledge.
- Both of these comprehensive research methods texts provide excellent chapters on observational research.

Woods, P. (2005) *Inside schools: Ethnography in schools*. Ebook: Taylor & Francis.
- Peter Wood's classic text is available electronically with a chapter devoted to observation within classrooms, in addition to a useful overview of ethnographic research in the classroom.

References

Ball, S. (1981) *Beachside comprehensive: A case study of a secondary school*. Cambridge: Cambridge University Press.

Flanders, N. (1970) *Analyzing teaching behavior*, New York: Addison-Wesley.

Gold, R. (1958) 'Roles in sociological field observations', *Social Forces*, 36(3), pp. 217–223.

Mac an Ghaill, M. (1994) *The making of men: Masculinities, sexualities and schooling*. Maidenhead: Open University Press.

Mirza, H. (1992) *Young, female and black*. Abingdon: Routledge.

Patrick, J. (1973) *A Glasgow gang observed*. London: Eyre Methuen.

Prentice, C.M. (2022) 'Educators' positive practices with refugee pupils at two schools in England', *British Educational Research Journal*, 48, pp. 1125–1144. doi:10.1002/berj.3818.

Walford, G. (2020) 'Ethnography is not qualitative', *Ethnography and Education*, 15(1), pp. 122–135.

West, C. and Wheldall, K. (1989) 'Waiting for teacher: The frequency and duration of times children spend waiting for teacher attention in infant school classrooms', *British Educational Research Journal*, 15, pp. 205–216. doi:10.1080/0141192890150208.

Willis, P. (1978) *Learning to labour: How working class kids get working class jobs*. Farnham: Ashgate.

CHAPTER

Documents

Introduction

A wide variety of existing documentary materials can be obtained and analysed by education researchers, and documentary analysis can be used either as part of a research project (alongside other methods of data collection) or as the primary research tool. Analysing documents as a research tool is different from analysing documents for a literature review, which is discussed in Chapter 3. This chapter looks at a range of written documents (such as records, government publications, diaries) and considers how and why they might be used and analysed by educational researchers. The advantages and disadvantages of using and evaluating documents are also discussed.

What is documentary research?

There are a number of definitions of documentary research (Tight, 2019); however, for the purpose of this chapter, we borrow the definition of Dolowitz, Buckler and Sweeney (2008: 39 cited in Tight, 2019: 8): 'A document is simply any written, printed, photographed, painted or recorded material that can be used to provide information or evidence'. Documentary-based research (sometimes called desk-based research) is just as valid as any other research method, so long as it fits the purpose of the study in question. It is an attractive method for those influenced by postmodern or poststructuralist approaches in understanding educational policy and practice, for example using the work of Michael Foucault and Jacques Derrida as ways to examine or 'deconstruct' government policy documentation. At the same time, qualitative documentary research tends to be underutilised in education (Morgan, 2022). The relative invisibility of documentary research should not be taken at face value; just because other methods are currently more popular does not negate the potential that this form of research has for the modern researcher. The use of documentary research has a rich and productive history in the social sciences; as Ahmed (2010: 8) points out, it was a method greatly favoured by one of the most famous social scientists, Karl Marx:

Marx made extensive use of documentary sources and other official reports, such as Her Majesty's Inspectors of Factories reports made between 1841 and 1867, reports by the Medical Officer of the Privy Council, Royal Commission and Inland Revenue reports, as well as reports on the employment of children in factories, the Banking Acts, the Corn Laws, the Hansard and Census Reports for England and Wales. He also referred to various Acts and Statutes, such as the Factory Regulation Acts of between 1833 and 1878. Marx also used newspapers and periodicals such as '*The Times, Economist* and *New York Daily Tribune*'.

The internet has made documentary research all the easier, and there are plenty of resources for your searches if you wish. What was once a laborious activity has now been made more manageable by the development of highly efficient search engines that can access documents instantly. The rise of open access research, although it is still up against a firewall of 'closed' or privileged access rights, has helped to nudge documentary research ever closer to the heart of research methodologies. It should never be thought that desk-based research is in some way a poor cousin of 'field' work: Oftentimes, documentary research requires 'field' work anyway, in the shape of visits to museums, libraries, galleries or archive collections.

So, when you combine this technological revolution with its close cousin, the digital revolution, it becomes evident that the possibilities for valuable and exciting forms of documentary research are practically endless. The advent of the digital age with its capacity to shift and store documents and information means that the power of access gets combined with the power of analysis and storage. This is even evident in how we use and research via journal articles; where considerable amounts of time were once spent photocopying individual articles and painstakingly writing notes from them, now one can access these materials online in PDF form while note-taking digitally from the same sources.

Of course, none of this means that documentary research has turned into a failsafe approach to evidence gathering – the same historical caveats still apply. Digital and online access come with their own set of anxieties. While access, evidence gathering and storage have all become much more efficient, it is also wise to be aware of the potential downsides of this access – one of the key ones being plagiarism, especially of the unwitting variety. As researchers increasingly copy and paste excerpts from journals and online digital books, the chances are magnified that people will confuse someone else's work with their own. It is also much easier to lose track of the source for the documentary evidence you have accumulated – this is important for your evidence base, because you need to provide a source for all forms of evidence. More efficient access to documents also means that it is much easier to be in breach of copyright. Publishers take such breaches seriously, so be careful how you use copyrighted work, especially if you are looking to distribute it for research dissemination purposes.

> **ACTIVITY**
>
> - Do a Google search on the internet for documents related to your chosen topic area.
> - Keep a list of the kinds of documents that you can find online, such as books and newspaper articles.
> - What other kinds of documents exist related to your topic, for example, government publications and school policies?
> - Is there sufficient documentation to make documentary research viable in your area?

What kinds of documents are there?

Documents come in all shapes and sizes; a fact reflected in the research that has used documents as a primary data collection method. It is rare that you will find a study that has not used some form of documentary analysis as part of its research design, given that sources come in formats such as:

- Newspaper articles: The way that educational issues are reported in the newspapers can say a great deal about the attitudes and values associated with education at any one time among the public.
- Biographies: These can be an excellent source of historical information, and not just in the traditional published format – they can also come in the form of individual life histories, career biographies, etc.
- Diaries: These may be kept for the specific purpose of the study, such as teacher diaries (Altalhab, Alsuhaibani and Gillies, 2021), or these may be diaries that have been kept independently of the study and are related to biographical research approaches.
- Field notes: These notes are taken at the site of the research project, whether it is a school or a playground, libraries or community groups.
- Reflective journals: Mercieca (2013) used the reflective journals of student teachers to help explore the ways in which novice teachers understood what reflective practice was all about.
- Minutes of meetings/memos/emails: As most organisations are required to keep records of their activities and their decision-making processes, minutes can prove a powerful and also a reliable source of research data. They are particularly useful if the research relates to issues such as organisational change, institutional culture and/or educational management and leadership. Caution should be taken with minutes, however, because they are always intended as both an accurate and a formal record of the issues discussed and actions taken. Much tends to be left out of the formal record for the sake of both efficiency and

diplomacy. This is often not the case with emails, but caution should be adopted here too, given that the use of email (which is nearly always a personal form of communication) highlights ethical as well as privacy issues. Memos, still used in some organisations (and some more private than others), have been used to have a good effect in various types of investigative forms of research, especially in relation to government policy.

- Books/articles: Many researchers use previously published academic papers, including books, as an evidence base for their research questions, and it is not unusual for whole research projects (at both UG and PG levels) to be entirely based on desk-bound academic research. This is particularly true in research on the philosophy of education.

- Policy documents: The use of policy documents as a device for gathering evidence is a popular approach for researchers who are interested in how educational arguments are presented via official statements. This is a popular method for those who value research as a form of interrogation. For researchers of this persuasion, much can be gained by critically analysing the discourses that are at play in official papers, which makes sense because much of this form of documentation is a text-based version of an argument – for example, about the need for curriculum change, transformations in pedagogy, etc. As such, these arguments can be revealing as to the intentions (hidden or otherwise) behind the development of such policies (see the examples presented later in this chapter).

Advantages of documentary research

There are a range of advantages to documentary forms of research.

- Scope: Engaging in documentary research means that you can physically 'access' your database much more easily than in observational research, for example. Although researchers often need to visit libraries or archives to access such material, the scope of their documentary research is limited only by the availability of the documents themselves – as Cohen, Manion and Morrison state (2007: 201), documentary research 'can enable the researcher to reach inaccessible persons or subjects'.

- Lack of bias: As Ahmed points out (2010: 10), documentary records tend to be 'unbiased as the documents are collated usually for other purposes ... the researcher is not in a position to bias subjects and the authors of documents are unlikely to assume their future use in research fields'. While the documents can be interpreted in different ways by different researchers, whatever bias exists reflects the researcher/interpreter rather than the document itself. As such, the research subject is not an active part of the research process – more a passive entity, a fact that offers at least some form of 'objectivity' in the research.

- Ease of use: For most forms of document, there tends to be a finished product in existence that states the case for whatever is under discussion. This may be a biased and partial statement, but it is a statement that serves a particular purpose. The researcher can use this to his or her advantage and 'manipulate' the data in various ways until they are convinced that there is an appropriate fit between the documents, the research objective and the argument built on the available evidence. As the evidence comes mostly from static entities, this is for the most part doable, which is not the case with human subjects – the research site cannot be visited continually to gather more and more data and/or to view the research subject from other angles or interpretations. Of course, this is only true up to a point, since there is a limit to all forms of manipulation (regardless of form) but suffice it to say that such manipulation is much easier with documents than with humans.

- A window onto the past: While the memories of individual people can tell us a great deal about the past, documents extracted from historical situations are arguably a more effective way to take a longitudinal view of a research question. As Cohen, Manion and Morrison (2007: 201) argue, documents can show how situations have evolved over time:

Documents, many written 'live' and in situ, may catch the dynamic situation at the time of writing. Some documents, particularly if they are very personal (e.g. letters and diaries) may catch personal details and feelings that would not otherwise surface.

Disadvantages of documentary research

- Authenticity: It can sometimes be a challenge to gauge the authenticity of the documents themselves. Are they based on actual events, are they factually correct, or are they opinions masquerading as fact? There is always the danger that your interpretation of documents may be an interpretation of an interpretation, making the connection between the 'truth' and your research even more obscure – a case of Anthony Giddens' 'double hermeneutic' at its most damaging (Giddens, 1987).
- Context: Historical context is crucial. Cohen, Manion and Morrison (2007: 202) argue that documents should be understood 'within the context' in which they were written; otherwise, they tend to lose whatever meaning they had in the first place. For example, there's not much point in examining the discourse of education policy documents from the late nineteenth century without taking into account the nature of current social mores, increasing industrialisation and urbanisation and a national culture, which had only recently come to terms with the idea of a 'national' education system.
- Primary/secondary distinction: It is important to make a distinction between primary and secondary sources when it comes to documents. As Duffy points out (1999: 108):

Primary sources are those which came into existence in the period under research (e.g., the minutes of a school governor's meeting). Secondary sources are interpretations of events of that period based on primary sources (e.g., a history of that school which obtained evidence from the governor's minutes).

> **ACTIVITY**
>
> Think of a research topic that you would like to study.
> - Is the use of documents to gather evidence a viable research tool?
> - Make a list of the advantages and disadvantages of using documents in your chosen area.
> - Do the advantages outweigh the disadvantages?
> - Is it possible to mitigate for any limitations?

Document research case studies

Case study 1

White papers (WP) – a type of education policy document – were analysed in relation to Norwegian national educational reform (Larsen, Møller and Jensen, 2022). The focus of the analysis was on how teacher professionalism was constructed and legitimised in these policy documents. The findings identified an increasing focus on school leader accountability for fulfilling the rights of individual students:

> Our analysis further suggests that securing students' rights is given attention throughout all three policy documents. However, we find some indications that school leaders are held more explicitly responsible for the fulfilment of student rights in the recent policy documents from 2015 (WP 28 and 21) than in earlier policy documents (WP 30 and 31). In the earlier policy documents, the fulfilment of students' rights was placed on the shoulders of the local educational authority and the 'schools' (e.g., WP 31, 50, 76). WP 31 states that there is a need for increased state governance in order to 'adjust the balance between the local latitude and the governance by the state' (MoER 2008, 30). By contrast, WP 21 explicitly defines the fulfilment of students' rights as a responsibility of the principal: […] *the principal is the one who bears the practical responsibility for students' rights being fulfilled. At the same time, the principal shall be responsible for personnel, both for the administrative and the professional community* (WP 21, 35). So, there is a tendency toward decentralized responsibility for the local principal, but the principal is strongly held accountable for student outcomes. Both WP 31 and WP 21 argue for similar governing strategy, although in WP 31 governance and control by the state is combined with the need for distribution of authority to teachers.
>
> (Larsen, Møller and Jensen, 2022: 117)

Case study 2

School-level language policy documents (publicly accessible by school websites) from 264 English primary schools were analysed (Cushing, 2021). A number of language-related analytical approaches were applied to understanding these documents. The findings indicated an emphasis on teachers modelling 'Standard English' with an implied shared understanding of this term. Furthermore, some policy documents identified tensions between the use of 'Standard English' and regional dialects:

> Some policies revealed the tension that teachers experience in knowing how to ensure that their students gained awareness of standardised English in adhering to the demands of macro-level policies, whilst balancing a respect for non-standardised forms. This often resulted in somewhat contradictory policy statements, such as that of S103 which sought to:
>
> sensitively explore and celebrate the diversity of regional dialect' but also advocated for an assimilationist pedagogy whereby pupils' non-standardised features should be 'identified and converted into Standard English', and that teachers should use Standard English 'at all times, when interacting with children.
>
> (Cushing, 2021: 328)

These case studies are useful examples of projects using documents as research data.

Chapter summary

This chapter began by providing a brief historical overview of documentary research, pointing out that even before the advent of the internet, influential social theorists such as Karl Marx were busy using documentary records to develop their ideas. The chapter then detailed the different kinds of documents that can be used in this form of research (policy documents, archives, minutes of meetings and so on). The discussion outlined some of the advantages and disadvantages of this form of research, while also including two examples of research that have used documents to gather evidence.

Further reading

Grant, A. (2022) *Doing your research project with documents: A step by step guide to take you from start to finish*. Bristol: Policy Press.

- This book clearly explains what documentary research is, offers advice on finding documents, key types of analysis: content, thematic, discourse, in addition to addressing issues of bias in documents.

Tight, M. (2019) *Documentary research in the social sciences*. London: SAGE.

- A really helpful book which discusses the nature of documentary research, practicalities of using this approach and advice on analysing documents.

References

Ahmed, J.U. (2010) 'Documentary research method: New dimensions', *Indus Journal of Management and Social Sciences*, 4(1), pp. 1–14.

Altalhab, S., Alsuhaibani, Y. and Gillies, D. (2021) 'The reflective diary experiences of EFL pre-service teachers', *Reflective Practice*, 22(2), pp. 173–186. doi:10.1080/14623943.2020.1865903.

Cohen, L., Manion, L. and Morrison, K. (2007) *Research methods in education*. 6th edn. London: Routledge.

Cushing, I. (2021) "'Say it like the Queen': The standard language ideology and language policy making in English primary schools', *Language, Culture and Curriculum*, 34(3), pp. 321–336. doi:10.1080/07908318.2020.1840578.

Dolowitz, D., Buckler, S. and Sweeney, F. (2008) *Researching online*. Basingstoke: Palgrave Macmillan.

Duffy, B. (1999) 'The analysis of documentary evidence', in Bell, J. (ed.) *Doing your research project: A guide for first-time researchers in education and social science*. Buckingham: Open University Press, pp. 106–117.

Giddens, A. (1987) *Social theory and modern sociology*. Cambridge: Polity Press.

Larsen, E., Møller, J. and Jensen, R. (2022) 'Constructions of professionalism and the democratic mandate in education a discourse analysis of Norwegian public policy documents', *Journal of Education Policy*, 37(1), pp. 106–125. doi:10.1080/02680939.2020.1774807.

Mercieca, D. (2013) 'Engaging with students on reflective writing: Reclaiming writing', in Murphy, M. (ed.) *Social theory and education research: Understanding Foucault, Habermas, Bourdieu and Derrida*. London: Routledge, pp. 200–211.

Morgan, H. (2022) 'Conducting a qualitative document analysis', *The Qualitative Report*, 27(1), pp. 64–77. doi:10.46743/2160-3715/2022.5044.

Tight, M. (2019) *Documentary research in the social sciences*. London: SAGE.

CHAPTER

Creative and visual research methods

Introduction

This chapter discusses creative and visual research methods. Creative and visual research methods have become more mainstream as research 'with' participants is more widely undertaken. In addition, technological changes, such as the ubiquity of smartphones, have made taking photographs and videos increasingly feasible for participants. Firstly, an overview of creative and visual research methods is provided; secondly, the use of artefacts is discussed; and thirdly, the visual research methods of photography, drawing and collage are outlined. Fourthly, ethical issues are highlighted, and finally, data analysis is explained.

Overview

Creative research methods have gained increasing prominence in educational research, as they enable the researcher to work 'with' participants as a form of participatory research. The creation and use of artefacts by participants gives them ownership over the research process as well as acts as a stimulus for discussion. Visual research methods can be viewed as a subset of creative research methods and have origins in early anthropological studies. Visual research methods, such as photographs, drawings and video clips, also lend themselves effectively to participatory research, as well as have the key strength of powerfully conveying educational experiences and educational contexts. Visual and creative research methods can be used on their own or in combination with other methods, such as interviews (see Chapter 14).

Researchers need to make an important distinction in their study about if images or artefacts have been taken or made by the research team or the participants. Participants need

DOI: 10.4324/9781003569428-20

to give their consent for their images or artefacts to be used in a research study. There are three broad approaches to creative research methods:

1 Participants create images or artefacts and this can be likened to the Mosaic approach (Clark and Moss, 2001).
2 The researcher provides images or artefacts to facilitate a discussion with participants.
3 The participant provides images or artefacts and uses these as a starting point for a discussion with the researcher.

The relative advantages and drawbacks of each approach are discussed in the next section of this chapter.

Creative research methods – Using artefacts

Participants create artefacts

Participants create artefacts, and this can be likened to the Mosaic approach. A well-known approach to using creative methods with children is the 'Mosaic approach' (Clark and Moss, 2001), and this builds upon the principles of participatory research. However, not all education research focuses on children, and this chapter considers the use of creative research methods for teenagers, young adults and those adults involved in lifelong learning or training. A key factor to consider when using creative research methods with adults is that it is important that the approach does not make them feel patronized or infantilized. Therefore, whilst you may find that a group of children in an early year's setting might thoroughly enjoy using 'Play-Doh' or cereal boxes to create their ideal learning space, you may find a very different response from a group of undergraduates. If participants do not find the activity meaningful, the data that is generated will not be authentic to the experiences of the participants that you are hoping to explore and further understand. Therefore, it is important to think carefully about the suitability of the type of creative activity that you are asking participants to engage with. The background of the participants can be an important guide, for example a group of Fine Art students may be very comfortable with the idea of producing a sketch; a group of Engineers may be very happy to use Meccano and a group of Drama students may be happy to perform a 'flashback' or engage in 'hot-seating'.

However, it is of course important to not stereotype what may or may not work in the creation of artefacts by participants, and therefore, a range of choices can be an advantage, although this may make the analysis process trickier, as you may have a range of different artefact mediums to analyse. It may also be important to provide a set of prompts for participants and some time to prepare ahead of the interview/focus group/creative workshop for those amongst us that do not perceive ourselves to be creative. For some participants, the idea of telling a story about an experience based on object may fill them with dread and a fear of being judged, rather than any meaningful sense of a transformatory experience that we wish to share as part of a research project.

The researcher provides artefacts

Kara *et al.* (2021) report on a very successful creative activity undertaken by a researcher focusing on masculinity and ethnicity of male undergraduates, using cufflinks – with participants discussing these in a metaphorical manner. It would be equally possible to repurpose, for example: A set of buttons, a copious set of nail varnish colours or a range of Lego bricks for a similar approach. There are a number of advantages to creative approaches, for example it can enable participants to think differently about their experiences, which may lead to new analytical insights.

The participant provides artefacts

If participants have been asked to bring along their own artefacts, for example, object/s or photograph/s, then this can lead to rich data collection as emotional connections can be explored. In addition to stories about the significance of the object or photograph, it may yield 'richer' data that would not have emerged in the same way from a 'standard' interview format. The participant providing artefacts may mean it is possible to generate and extend conversations, and it may enable the participant to identify metaphors and analogies related to their experiences.

With the participant's permission – it is then possible to take a photograph of the object provided or a copy of the photograph shared, which can then be used as part of the data analysis. The key drawback of asking participants to bring an object is if they do not remember to do this. Therefore, it can be important to have a spare set of objects which you can ask the participants to pick from in relation to having a similar object themselves. It is also important to provide size, weight and value guidelines to the object as you do not want a very enthusiastic participant to inadvertently struggle to carry, for example a large musical instrument on a bus or train or equally bring something of great financial and/or emotional value that could be lost or stolen. In this case, if they are planning on bringing with them a musical instrument, such as a 'double bass' or a priceless heirloom necklace – then an alternative is to ask them to take a photograph of the article on a smartphone.

ACTIVITY

Thinking about an experience you might like to explore with your participants – how might you:

1. Ask your participants to create an artefact? What resources would you need? How would you ensure that this was something that they felt at ease with?
2. What type of artefacts could you provide for your participants? What sort of prompts might you provide to enable the participants to use these artefacts to discuss their experiences?
3. What guidelines would you provide to participants about bringing their own artefacts to the discussion? What 'back-up' artefacts might you provide?
4. What do you think are the pros and cons of each approach for your research?

Visual research methods

Visual research methods can be considered a subset of creative research methods. Visual research methods can include photos, paintings, film, drawings, graffiti, cartoons. Typically, there is an emphasis and preference for graphics, but 'an inclusive definition to visual sources, which incorporates anything we experience through the visual medium' (Pole, 2004: 4). One of the most popular approaches to using visual research methods is photo-elicitation. There are a number of different kinds of photo-elicitation that vary and overlap in relation to the purpose of the photographs, if the researcher or participant takes the photographs and how the photographs are then used (Cohen, Manion and Morrison, 2018). Photovoice is one approach to photo-elicitation, and this embodies participatory research principles as participants are documentarians and commentators in their own right (Sutton-Brown, 2014). Photovoice as a participatory research method helps to redress power imbalances and inequities participants may experience in other aspects of their lives related to their demographic characteristics. Participatory research builds upon the notion that participants have a voice, but that voice is seldom heard. The diary method can also ask participants to record short videos or audio clips if writing is not a preference of the participants.

> **ACTIVITY**
>
> - What does 'education' mean to you?
>
> Draw a picture of what 'education' means to you (stick people accepted!!), or create a collage from magazine/newspaper pictures, or take a photograph on a smartphone (*first read Ethical issue section below in this chapter). Now using your drawing, collage or photograph pair-up and ask a coursemate to explain:
>
> - Why did they take/draw/create/include these images?
> - Why does it represent 'education' to them?
> - What is omitted/significant?
> - How similar or different are the two representations of 'education'?
>
> Alternatively, draw a timeline of the highs and lows of your educational journey.
>
> - Explain your timeline to a coursemate and compare how similar or different your educational trajectories have been.

Practicalities of participants taking photographs

It is important to provide participants with a photo-elicitation protocol, such as do not include people in the photographs (including 'selfies') and ensure that if you take any photographs outside that you are in a safe place and you are not alone. The context for the research purpose of the photographs should also be provided, for example in a recent project we stated: 'Participants should only take photographs that represent their daily routine on the university campus and at home which are symbolic to them of the experience of studying in the UK context'. The number of photographs required and timeframe for collection should be designed so that it minimises the time commitment for participants. It may be that many participants have camera functionality on their mobile phones. Nevertheless, ensure that there are additional resources available such as digital cameras, which can be borrowed for the project to reduce any barriers to participation. In addition, participants should be provided with guidance on how to add words or captions to their photographs (part of standard smartphone functionality) or voice memos to enable participants to layer text onto their images to record feelings and additional contextual information. Alternatively, participants may be using their photographs as a starting point for an interview.

Drawings and collages

There is limited research on the effectiveness of drawing as a visual research method compared to video or photography. There are likely to be significant differences in drawing abilities of different individuals, and therefore, a consideration of the effectiveness of this approach should be considered. It may also depend on the quality of what is required to be produced, for example a simple timeline with a few notes and visuals may not feel daunting compared to being asked to provide a sketch. It may also depend on the role of the drawing – if it is being used as a starting point for a conversation, that may encourage more participants to engage rather than drawings which will be displayed or shared more widely. An alternative option might be to ask the participants to make a collage, as this may feel like less of a personal judgement of skill level. A collage could also be undertaken in pairs with rich conversation stemming from undertaking the activity. These types of creative activities tend to be less time-pressured than language-based research methods and give much greater opportunity for reflection. This may be particularly helpful for topics which may require a degree of introspection or for participants who may be less confident in sharing their thoughts and experiences verbally.

> **ACTIVITY**
>
> Reflect with a partner on the following challenges of using creative research methods:
> - What could you do to limit feelings of discomfort with participants who are engaging with creative techniques?
> - Which research issues might be more pertinent when using creative research methods?

Ethical issues

Participants should only choose to upload/send photographs that they are happy to share with the researchers. It is important to check that participants consent to their photographs being used in the public domain (e.g. dissertations, conference PowerPoint slides and academic publications). No penalty or detriment should be attached to participants who choose to withdraw from the photo-elicitation research. It is important to ensure photographs are labelled in such a way as to ensure anonymity in the data management process, for example:

- '[location initials]_participant [number]_photovoice_[number] (e.g. UK_participant_1_photovoice_1)'.

Information about the length of time the images will be stored is also required, for example 'all photographs will be deleted upon successful completion of the dissertation and graduation from the degree programme'.

Data analysis

A challenge associated with visual research methods is data analysis, as the representativeness of an image can be questioned. Nevertheless, despite the potential limitations of analysis with creative and visual research methods, they have a great deal to offer to educational researchers. Goldstein (2007: 64) proposes: 'That we treat photographic images in the same way as a scientist treats data. No experimentalist assumes that data are perfect. Indeed, all data are assumed to have a variety of types of error'. Photographs are a 'snapshot' in time, and in that sense, the moment that it has been taken is chosen and can be understood as 'manipulated' (Goldstein, 2007: 75). A good starting point for analysing photographs can be returning to consider the extent to which they help to address the research questions that frame the study. Other factors to consider are:

- Who took the photograph?
- What is the purpose of the image?
- What emotional response does the image elicit?
- Are there multiple meanings in the image?
- What is present in the image?
- What is absent in the image?
- What is at the centre of the image?
- What is on the periphery of the image?

The chapter on data analysis in this book also provides further information about how to analyse data (see Chapter 5).

Chapter summary

This chapter has outlined the potential benefits of using creative research methods with participants, such as artefacts and photography. The popularity of creative research methods in participatory approaches to research has been highlighted. The potential limitations of participants feeling confident to participate with more creative approaches to research have been raised. Further, the practicalities and ethical issues of visual research have been emphasized. The chapter also provided some prompts to help the researcher start the process of analysing the data.

Further reading

Kara, H. *et al.* (2021) *Creative research methods in education: Principles and practices*. Bristol: Policy Press.

- The introductory chapter provides a detailed account of creative research methods. The book also provides a useful account of different research designs that can utilise creative research methods. Chapters highlighting different case studies applying creative research approaches to gathering data with children and adults are included, as is information about data analysis.

Spencer, S. (2022) *Visual research methods in the social sciences: Awakening visions*. 2nd edn. Abingdon: Routledge.

- Part one of this book considers some of the challenges and benefits of using photographs in research. The chapter links visual research methods to different methodological approaches, such as ethnography, case study and narrative research. Issues of 'space' and 'identity' are explored within the book. A wide range of data analysis techniques are explained. A range of interesting case studies illuminate the issues raised in earlier parts of the book.

References

Clark, A. and Moss, P. (2001) *Listening to young children: The mosaic approach*. London: National Children's Bureau.

Cohen, L., Manion, L. and Morrison, K. (2018) *Research methods in education*. 8th edn. Abingdon: Routledge.

Goldstein, B.M. (2007) 'All photos lie: Images as data', in Stanczak, G.C. (ed.) *Visual research methods: Image, society and representation*. Los Angeles, CA: Sage.

Kara, H. *et al.* (2021) *Creative research methods in education: Principles and practices*. Bristol: Policy Press

Pole, C. (ed.) (2004) *Seeing is believing approaches to visual research*. Oxford: Elsevier.

Stanczak, G.C. (ed.) (2007) *Visual research methods: Image, society and representation*. Los Angeles, CA: Sage.

Sutton-Brown, C.A. (2014) Photovoice: A methodological guide. *Photography and Culture*, 7(2), pp. 169–185.

PART

Theorising research

CHAPTER 18

Using theories and concepts in educational research

Introduction

In planning a research project, it is vital that key concepts associated with the topic of the research are adequately explored in the literature and defined by the researcher undertaking the project. Concepts are slippery and do not have clear or fixed meanings, and often researchers and others understand things in different ways. Therefore, it is critically important that key concepts are clarified. This also makes it more straightforward to plan the research. In addition to clarifying key concepts, it is important to draw on theories that have already been established and to relate these to your own research in order to ground the study in what is 'already known'. This chapter considers what 'theory' is and explains why it is important to explore theories that are relevant to one's research. As the field is so vast, this chapter concentrates on the use of *social* theory in educational research.

The place of theory in education research

It is often the case that books on educational research emphasise the correct approaches to using specific types of research tool, such as interviews and questionnaires, or focus on the construction of a dissertation and set out how the constituent parts are assembled to construct the finished product. Of course, this is invaluable guidance, and it is an essential aspect of any text that aims to educate those undertaking research in educational settings. It is a form of knowledge that is well catered-for in the literature, which has expanded to keep up with the increasing demand for applied research.

Nevertheless, there is a tendency to pay less attention to the role of theory in the construction of such projects, and the various ways in which theories generated in the social sciences, in particular, can be used to extract *meaning* from the research site under examination. As attested by the variety of publications that link social theory and educational research (Murphy, 2022), it is a tremendously worthwhile activity to engage the two concepts, so long as the researchers themselves come armed with an understanding of the challenges that await them.

What the published research illustrates is not just the complexity of concepts in social theory but also the varied sets of issues that may be faced when applying such ideas in educational research contexts, which is a field of complex interwoven imperatives and practices in its own right. These challenges – epistemological, operational, analytical – can be seen to impact on researchers and their attempts to make sense of educational questions, whether of, for example governance and management, inclusion, teaching and learning or professional identities. Previously published research indicates that the application of a challenging set of ideas onto a challenging set of practices should be treated with care and a strong consideration for intellectual arguments as well as the concerns of the professional researcher.

There is much to be gained for the educational research community generally from taking advantage of the originality, rigour and intellectual insight of ideas from the social sciences. The work of theory – about power and control, democracy, social organisation, language and communication, selfhood and subjectivities, the state and the economy, offers an excellent source of ideas, and can, when implemented effectively, contribute to the delivery of higher quality educational research.

What is social theory?

Broadly speaking, social theories are analytical frameworks or paradigms used to examine social phenomena. The term 'social theory' encompasses ideas about 'how societies change and develop, about methods of explaining social behaviour, about power and social structure, gender and ethnicity, modernity and "civilization", revolutions and utopias' (Harrington, 2005: 1). In contemporary social theory, certain core themes take precedence over others, such as the nature of social life, the relationship between self and society, the structure of social institutions, the role and possibility of social transformation, and themes such as gender, ethnicity and social class (Elliott, 2022). Alongside the existence of this broad range of issues, there is also a large number of what could be termed social theories – feminist theories of various persuasions could be labelled as such, likewise critical race theories. Space precludes a more detailed examination of the field of social theory – there are other sources that offer such an overview (e.g. Benzecry, Krause and Reed, 2017; Elliott, 2022).

ACTIVITY

- Pick a concept to read about, for example feminism, critical race theory, globalisation or power.
- In what ways does this concept help you to understand an aspect of education? Would another social theory help to illuminate this issue further or in a different way?

Issues to consider in theoretical application

- Moving from practice to theory: The application of concepts from social theory brings its own set of challenges. Some of these reflect issues of design, including the development of tools such as data measurement and analytical criteria. Just as significant are the difficulties faced when grappling with the core concepts of social theory, which themselves already come with a range of contradictory meanings. Notions of 'power', 'culture' and 'practice' are challenging at the best of times, but such challenges are compounded when they are aligned with the core educational concepts of teaching, learning, assessment and curriculum. All forms of research, regardless of subject, come with a set of issues that need addressing in practical settings. Educational research is no different, and the fact that it is most often embedded in forms of professional practice merely adds further challenges. As a result, it should be emphasised from the outset that the movement from practice to theory is as challenging an intellectual journey, if not more so, than the journey from theory to practice. While the latter can often confound researchers who face difficulties in applying theoretical models and principles in other contexts, the former can often compound the situation for the educational researcher. Many of those engaged in educational research tend to arrive at this research topic via the linked but distinct field of professional practice. While this can have certain advantages in terms of insight, providing a level of insider knowledge that is unavailable to the non-professional, it can also mean that intellectual judgement may be clouded by immersion in the hothouse of educational politics.

- (Inter)disciplinarity: This scenario is also compounded by the nature of professional training. Educators may be well versed in the application of educational theory to educational practice, but rarely are they required to apply theories from other disciplines in any meaningful way. This is both a blessing and a curse of being an educational researcher – an *un*disciplined approach to the field of research can have drawbacks as well as benefits, providing professionals with a multidisciplinary grounding while also bringing a disinclination to belong to and work within the parameters of any specific disciplinary paradigm.

- Theoretical 'authenticity': When applying theory to research, it is often tempting to try to stay true to the 'authentic' version of the theory being applied. However, nowhere is it written that researchers may not choose how and in what contexts they apply the work of theory. While the overzealous might demand the 'pure' use of someone's work, regardless of context, it should not be forgotten that all theorists have at various stages in their careers, cherry-picked from the work of those who have influenced them. To suggest that there is a 'right' and a 'wrong' way to understand and apply educational or social theorists is to misinterpret the role of theory in research – the latter should never be made to bow down to the former. If anything, cherry-picking and cross-pollination should be positively encouraged, for how else do we arrive at original and innovative forms of knowledge, which can help us progress through the world of often stale and moribund arguments and paradigms in educational policy and practice?

- The concept of power: Another issue in educational research relates to the special status assigned to the concept of power in social theory and also in educational research. However, given this close relationship between power and educational research, one needs to be even more careful in the pursuit of research objectives. One does not need to be a Foucauldian to understand that power is omnipresent, and that power and knowledge have a tight bond that is not easily broken. Nevertheless, the workings of power in educational settings should never be taken lightly or over-simplified, given that educational institutions and their assorted sets of practices provide ideal environments for the interplay of multiple forms of power – cultural, social, structural – which in many cases are irreducible to each other. Power is a notoriously difficult concept to pin down, and the researcher can all too easily fall into the trap of looking for power in the wrong places – or worse still, misrecognising their own capacity as power brokers in educational research settings. It is important for the researcher to recognise their own powerful presence in educational settings, while also accepting the fallibility of one theory of power in the face of complex and highly differentiated institutionalised arrangements. Erring on the side of intellectual caution does not do the educational researcher any harm, especially when combined with a recognition of the unfinished debates in social theory that form the backdrop to such forms of research in the first place (Murphy, 2022).

- Inductive or deductive: Using theory inductively means that after empirical data has been collected, theory may be applied to understand and analyse the data. Using theory deductively would mean starting with the theory and then testing its relevance when collecting empirical data. There is no 'correct' way to approach using social theory in research, but it is important to be clear about if the theory was 'a priori' – that is the reasoning proceeds from theoretical deduction rather than observation. The inductive approach begins with a set of empirical observations, seeking patterns in those observations, and then applying theory to those patterns. The deductive approach begins with a theory, developing hypotheses from that theory, and then collecting and analysing data to test those hypotheses.

The application of theory in research: Four examples

Theories are flexible enough to be applied in a diversity of educational contexts. Alongside this diversity of context, there is also an evident diversity of research *design* at work in the field of theoretical application. Theories are applied for a variety of reasons, which can only impact on the application itself and the ways in which theories are used both to examine the findings of the research and to draw out implications and recommendations for future studies.

EXAMPLE 1

ClassDojo is a gamified behaviour tool that is popular in school classrooms (Manolev, Sullivan and Slee, 2018). ClassDojo enables teachers to collect data on pupil behaviour. This article argues that this online tool normalises and increases the surveillance of pupils. Foucault's concepts of 'power' and 'discipline' are applied effectively to analyse the impact of this approach to classroom behaviour management.

EXAMPLE 2

Thirteen White working-class men aged between 16 and 24 years from an estate in North-East England participated in a research study in relation to 'Not being in Education, Employment or Training' (NEET). Bourdieu's theory of social, cultural and economic capital, alongside his theoretical concepts of 'field' and 'habitus', was used to understand why education and employment were not seen to be relevant to this group of young men, although sometimes engaging in illicit activities for material gain were relevant (Simmons, Connelly and Thompson, 2020). The study involved participant observation and interviews.

EXAMPLE 3

This study explored teachers' perceptions on the role of dialogue in Greek primary schools (Vavitsas, 2024). Fifteen teachers participated in interviews about dialogue in the classroom. The teachers emphasised the importance of dialogue for understanding different cultures. The findings were theorised through Habermas' work on 'communicative action'.

EXAMPLE 4

This article discusses an autoethnographic study by two teachers. The two teachers conceptualise language and culture in relation to intercultural pedagogies. The article draws on both 'Bakhtin's (1981) *The dialogic imagination: Four essays* notion of dialogism and Derrida's (1997) *Of grammatology* notion of translation' (O'Neill and Viljoen, 2021: 572) for the teachers to 'describe and explain how our reflexive practice enables us to deepen our focus both on language, culture, and knowing as integral in creating and interpreting meaning, and the self' (O'Neill & Viljoen, 2021: 572).

ACTIVITY

Read the work of a social theorists and consider how it could be applied to an educational topic that you are interested in.

Chapter summary

This chapter has explored the place of theory in educational research, especially that branch known as 'social theory'. It defined what this is, before considering some of the issues faced in applying such a theory in research (including moving from practice to theory, interdisciplinarity, the nature of theoretical authenticity and the challenges of using power as a concept in educational research). The chapter also provided a range of published examples of research that have applied social theory in their design.

Further reading

Elliott, A. (2022) *Contemporary social theory: An introduction*. 3rd edn. Abingdon: Routledge.

- This is a very comprehensive text on social theory and social theorists. Classic social theorists: Marx, Weber and Durkheim are discussed. The work of Structuralists, such as Barthes and Foucault, is highlighted. Poststructuralism is explained. The work of Bourdieu is explored. Feminism and Globalisation are examined. Useful critiques of theories are included, as are questions for the reader and further reading recommendations.

Murphy, M. (ed.) (2022) *Social theory and education research: Understanding foucault, habermas, bourdieu and derrida*. 2nd edn. Oxon: Routledge.

- Mark Murphy's edited collection *Social theory and education research* (2022) brings together a set of case studies that have applied either Foucault, Derrida, Bourdieu or Habermas in educational research contexts. These contexts include academy schools, school surveillance, the geography curriculum and school regulation. An introductory chapter provides a useful context within which the ideas of these four social theorists are situated.

References

Benzecry, C.E, Krause, M. and Reed, I.A. (2017) *Social theory now*. Chicago: Chicago University Press.

Elliott, A. (2022) *Contemporary social theory: An introduction*. 3rd edn. Abingdon: Routledge.

Harrington, A. (2005) 'Introduction: What is social theory?' in Harrington, A. (ed.) *Modern social theory: An introduction*. Oxford: Oxford University Press.

Manolev, J., Sullivan, A. and Slee, R. (2018) The datafication of discipline: ClassDojo, surveillance and a performative classroom culture. *Learning, Media and Technology*. doi: 10.1080/17439884.2018.1558237.

Murphy, M. (ed.) (2022) *Social theory and education research: Understanding foucault, habermas, bourdieu and derrida*. 2nd edn. Oxon: Routledge.

O'Neill, F. and Viljoen, J.-M. (2021) Expanding 'conceptual horizons': A reflexive approach to intercultural pedagogies in higher education. *Language and Intercultural Communication*, 21(5), pp. 572–587. doi:10.1080/14708477.2021.1888965.

Simmons, R., Connelly, D. and Thompson, R. (2020) 'Education ain't for us': using Bourdieu to understand the lives of young White working-class men classified as not in education, employment or training', *Research in Post-Compulsory Education*, 25(2), pp. 193–213. doi:10.1080/13596748.2020.1742992.

Vavitsas, T. (2024) 'Dialogue as a tool for intercultural coexistence in the multicultural classroom: Teachers' views', *European Journal of Social Sciences Studies*, 9(4). doi:10.46827/ejsss.v9i4.1629.

CHAPTER 19

Evaluating methods

Introduction

All research requires that the methods and conclusions are justifiable. Denscombe (2017: 362) highlights: 'This account of the methods is vital in order for the reader to make some informed evaluation of the study. Basically, if the reader is *not* told how and why the data were collected, he or she cannot make any judgement about how good the research is and whether any credibility should be given to its findings or conclusions'. To ensure that your research findings are viewed as credible – that is, 'true' and worth taking notice of – a series of evaluative measures must underpin your design. The types of evaluation will depend on whether your research aligns itself most closely with the interpretivist or positivist paradigm. The reader requires several pieces of information before they can evaluate whether research findings are credible. This chapter discusses the approaches for evaluating both positivist and interpretivist research (alternatively see Chapter 8 on mixed-methods research). First, however, key factors that enable the evaluation of *all* research are discussed.

Evaluating *all* research

Regardless of which paradigm your research fits into, there are elements that should be included so that your results can be evaluated by others. These are:

- Inclusion of your research questions or hypothesis
- Inclusion of your research design
- Explanation of the reasons for your choice of design
- Explanation of how you analysed your findings
- Sufficient evidence from your findings to demonstrate that this is an accurate representation of your analysis

Contextual information is useful in all types of educational research and generally includes:

- The number of participants
- Data collection methods employed
- Number and length of data collection sessions
- Time period over which the data was collected

ACTIVITY

- Make a list of the contextual information provided in the extract below.
- How does this information enable you to evaluate the credibility of the study?

This chapter is part of a larger exploratory, qualitative study that focused on the university experiences of working-class women students' (and included working-class men and middle-class women as comparator groups). This chapter focuses specifically on the 'experiences of belonging at university' in relation to the 'formation of friendships' of the 14 working-class students who participated in the research (12 women; 2 men). The focus of this chapter is on aspects of the two sub-research questions in relation to social factors influencing their experience of university and the extent to which they perceived their experiences of learning as positive.

The interview call for the study requested participants who identified as 'working-class' and/or as 'female'. A semi-structured interview was deemed an appropriate research tool due to the possible complexity of perceptions and experiences of each research participant. The interview schedule was informed by research literature on students' experiences of university with particular emphasis on social class, gender and journeys into higher education. The questions were evaluated for being open and neutral and enabling participants to provide detailed responses. The interview schedule was supplemented by follow-up questions, such as 'could you tell me a bit more about this?' The interview schedule was piloted internally through the researcher adopting the position of a participant. The interview themes are presented to help researchers develop an interview schedule on the same subject. The interviewer asked the participants to self-identify their social class background like a number of other studies (for example, see [8]). The participants discussed their self-identification of socio-economic status in relation to factors such as parental occupation, familial experiences of financial hardship, and the level of education of their parents and if they were one of the first members of their family to go to university. Social class can be considered a 'British' concept and may not always translate effectively into other cultures and countries. This chapter has used terms such as low socio-economic status (SES) to accurately convey the measures used by other researchers in different contexts but refers to the participants in this study as 'working-class' as a term meaningful to them and based on the information provided about their familial backgrounds. However, information such as parental occupation often indicates the level of education achieved and financial position, with many countries using occupational scales to indicate socio-economic status regardless of exact terminology and the parameters of definitions.

(Shields, 2023: Section 3 - Methodology)

TABLE 19.1 Evaluating validity and reliability in positivist research

Internal validity	Demonstrating validity is about showing how 'truthful' your research findings are. In positivist research, this means seeking to ensure that the study measures or tests what is actually intended.
External validity	Merriam (1998) suggests that external validity is concerned with the extent to which the findings of one study can be applied to other situations. In positivist research, the concern often lies in demonstrating that the research findings can be applied to a wider population.
Reliability	Positivists use techniques to show that if the work was repeated, in the same context with the same methods and using the same type of participants, similar results would be obtained.
Objectivity	The basic issue here can be framed as one of relative neutrality and reasonable freedom from the unacknowledged researcher biases (Miles and Huberman, 1994).

Evaluating positivist research

Evaluation of positivist research is based on the extent to which the methods used can be seen as an objective way of understanding the laws of human behaviour. This is because positivism tries to replicate the natural sciences. Therefore, the way in which this type of research is evaluated reflects this premise. According to Denzin and Lincoln (2011: 108–109), positivists focus on 'rigorous data produced through scientific research ... Value is found in the scientific method. Gold standard is scientific rigour'. This enables researchers to verify 'hypotheses established as facts or laws' (Denzin and Lincoln, 2011: 101). Table 19.1 gives some key terms and definitions for evaluating positivist research:

Positivist research evaluation

In a positivist research project testing the hypothesis that the fitness level of an average ten-year-old boy is higher than that of a ten-year-old girl, you would need to ensure that the variables are carefully controlled. For example, the variables may be when and how heart rate is measured, and the type and duration of the exercise. The researcher would be neutral and objective and would give exactly the same instructions to each participant. If a different researcher repeated this experiment the findings should be largely replicated based on children of the same age, gender and height/weight ratio. To demonstrate the reliability of this experiment, you would have to explain how all the conditions were kept constant so that it would be possible for another researcher to conduct exactly the same experiment with a different class of children.

If you consider the information required to repeat the research, it will help you think about the level of detail you need to convey to the reader. The results of the experiment are discussed in relation to your hypothesis. The results are likely to be in the form of a statistical analysis. Appropriate statistical tests can be conducted, such as a chi-square test, to compare the average fitness levels of boys and girls. The checklist in the following section recaps on the information you need to include indicating the validity and reliability of your positivist research project.

Checklist for indicating the validity and reliability of positivist research

- ✓ State the hypothesis clearly
- ✓ Explain the variables in the study
- ✓ Describe the characteristics of the population
- ✓ Explain how the sample was selected
- ✓ Include the research design and justification of research instruments
- ✓ State the criteria for dealing with identified missing data
- ✓ Use appropriate statistical techniques
- ✓ Discuss results in relation to the original hypothesis
- ✓ Acknowledge the limitations of the study

Evaluating interpretivist research

'Qualitative research involves an interpretive naturalistic approach to the world. This means that qualitative researchers study things in their natural settings, attempting to make sense of, or interpret phenomena in terms of the meanings people bring to them' (Denzin and Lincoln, 2011: 3). Interpretivist researchers want to ensure that they can demonstrate the validity and reliability of their research, but they acknowledge that they are not neutral and objective researchers and that research with humans is not the same as a scientific experiment with chemical compounds. The language and processes used in interpretive research are different from the evaluation of positivist research. This can be confusing because different words can refer to the same concepts and sometimes the same approaches can overlap when being used to indicate validity and reliability. Generally, validity is about 'truth', and the terms *credibility*, *trustworthiness* and *transferability* are associated with this concept. Reliability is about how carefully the research was carried out and the likelihood of the same findings emerging if the study was to be replicated. Words associated with reliability in interpretivist research are *dependability* and *confirmability*. Table 19.2 summarises the definitions.

Credibility and transferability

The notion of validity, literally meaning truth, identifies how accurately an account represents participants' realities of social phenomena (Cresswell and Miller, 2000). Interpretivist researchers often acknowledge that all knowledge is relative to the context in which it is situated, and because of this, there can be no 'truth' because reality is socially produced knowledge. So, while researchers may believe that no individual participant's account can represent reality as other people see it, they nevertheless believe they have a duty to provide 'truthful' representations of the participants' voices. There are several strategies you can use to increase the credibility of your findings, such as member checking and reflexivity.

TABLE 19.2 Validity and reliability in interpretivist research

Credibility	Credibility refers to sufficient illustration of the social reality being studied. Lincoln and Guba (1985) recommend a set of activities that help to improve the credibility of research results: Prolonged engagement in the field, persistent observation, triangulation, negative case analysis, checking interpretations against raw data, peer debriefing and member checking.
Transferability	Lincoln and Guba's (1985) notion of 'transferability' is a useful technique to support the trustworthiness of the data. They suggest that a rich enough depiction of the data should be presented so that the reader can make comparisons to an other setting.
Dependability	Lincoln and Guba suggest that in order to assess the dependability of a study, the researcher should consider the question – 'How can an inquiry persuade his or her audience that the research findings of an inquiry are worth paying attention to?' (1985: 290).
Confirmability	Confirmability means that steps must be taken to help ensure that as far as possible the findings of the study are the result of the experiences and ideas of the participants, rather than the subjectivity of the researcher. Reflexivity and the triangulation of methods can promote confirmability since these indicate how researcher bias in the analysis has been addressed.

Member checking

- Give each participant a copy of their own transcript for 'member checking', to ensure that participants agree that the transcript is an accurate record of what they said. Give participants the opportunity to add to or amend any of their comments.

- Additionally, it is worth sharing your analysis with participants to see if this resonates with them. They may be able to shed additional light on your interpretations. By asking participants to discuss the extent to which your analysis resonates with their perceptions you are increasing the validity of your research (Lather, 1986). They may also be able to explain any quirks or discrepancies in your data.

Reflexivity

- Interpretivist researchers often explain their own personal beliefs and biases to ensure the validity of their work (Cresswell and Miller, 2000).

- Lather (1993) uses the term 'construct validity' to indicate reflexivity. This approach suggests that the researcher should consistently explain all the steps taken in the research process and evaluate how she has influenced the process of the research.

- Following Oakley (2005: 226), it is worth commenting on 'The social/personal characteristics of yourself as the interviewer, the quality of the interviewer- interviewee interaction, hospitality offered, attempts by interviewees to use interviewers as sources of information, and the extension of interviewer- interviewee encounters into more broadly based social relationships'. By doing this, the reader can judge the research in light of your position and any circumstances influencing your research.

> **ACTIVITY**
>
> - What does this abstract tell us about reflexivity?
> - What issues does the researcher have to negotiate when reflecting on their own positionality?
> - Why are reflexive accounts important?
>
> This paper is a critical reflection of a critical ethnography', a study focused on how 'healthy lifestyle education' programmes were implemented and experienced in two primary schools. In an attempt to disrupt the *status quo* I employed a range of ethnographic methods: 'hanging out' with children and adults; building trusting relationships; having research conversations with participants; observing children and adults; and, journaling. However, the messy assemblage of diverse organisations, people, relations of power, discourses, truths, and practices, resulted in the emergence of ethical and methodological conundrums, including how to represent children's voices, whether (or not) to 'intervene' during problematic pedagogical moments, and how to 'act' as a critical ethnographic researcher in schools. Applying a critical lens to my own methodology helped to ensure that I embarked on a continuous, reflexive process; one that enabled a critique of research methods and a negotiation of issues of power, positionality, and privilege.
>
> (Powell, 2022: 18)

Transferability

Your analysis needs to be credible, and this means that enough of the data needs to be present in order for the reader to be satisfied with the trustworthiness of the analysis being claimed. Lincoln and Guba's (1985) notion of 'transferability' is a useful technique to support the trustworthiness of the data. They suggest that a rich enough depiction of the data should be presented so that the reader can make comparisons in another setting. Geertz (1973) also argues that the validity in your research comes from context-rich, meaningful and 'thick' descriptions. The interview quote below is an example of 'thick' description:

> I do not have time to do social activities. The timetable does not permit it. Most of the activities are at night so I cannot really join. I'm only free Thursdays. They do not have activities I'm interested in on Thursdays. I know like my friends who are doing the same degree but I do not really have much time to spend with them and socialise with them. I just have to get on with my own thing which is taking all of my time. And yeah that's one of the big things for me. I know I have to socialise and get a bit of experience, a full experience from university and get the most out of it. But it's kind of hard to move on to that if you have got loads of responsibilities in your personal life. Yeah it's not easy but I'm trying. You want to get all of them and sometimes you miss them.
>
> (Thuta, Modern University, in Shields, 2023: Section 4.1)

The data you use should be rich examples of the points that you wish to convey. When writing up your findings, you may choose to use one or two excerpts for each point and then explain the significance of these. In the interpretivist paradigm, one of the best ways to consider how to write up your findings so that the reader can evaluate your research is by looking at journal articles which have used qualitative data analysis in educational research. Good examples will be found in journal articles written by Stephen Ball and Diane Reay. Like other qualitative researchers, you are not claiming that your research design will allow for generalisable findings. Rather, you hope that aspects of the narrative or 'story' (Tesch, 1990: 2) that emerge will resonate with others.

Dependability and confirmability

The term 'dependability' is often used by interpretivist researchers, rather than 'reliability', which has more positivistic associations (Lincoln and Guba, 1985). Dependability requires the researcher to take into account any issues of instability, as well as changes that may be induced by the research design. Dependability is often described as a consideration of the extent to which the process of the study, including the research methods and researcher, are consistent over time (Miles and Huberman, 1994). You can address the issue of dependability through consistency in the research process – for instance, using the same interview questions, digitally recording all interviews and transcribing all the interviews yourself. Reporting an audit trail is perhaps one of the best ways to indicate dependability, for example by providing the reader with copies of questionnaire designs and interview transcripts. Including copies of this information in your appendices, so that the reader can 'audit' the dependability of your research, is also helpful.

- An audit trail (Lincoln and Guba, 1985) is a map for the reader detailing the key decisions taken from the conception of the research question through to the findings derived from the research. 'An inquiry audit cannot be conducted without a residue of records stemming from the inquiry, just as a fiscal audit cannot be conducted without a residue of records from the business transactions involved' (Lincoln and Guba, 1985: 319).
- Diachronic reliability is the stability of an observation over time. Collecting your data over a period of time ensures the findings are consistent over a prolonged period.
- Triangulation is the use of a variety of research methods to enhance the validity and dependability of the findings, since the same findings may be identified regardless of the method.
- Synchronic reliability is the similarity of observations within the same time period, for example through the triangulation of research methods.

Checklist for indicating the validity and reliability of interpretivist research

- State your research questions clearly
- Explain and justify your choice of research design

- Describe the characteristics and selection of your participants
- Explain how the research was conducted
- Explain how you developed the validity of your findings
- Justify the dependability of your research
- State your analytical processes
- Include sufficient original data to support your interpretation
- State how your own subjectivity and identity influenced the research
- Include copies of interview schedules, transcripts etc.
- State discrepancies in the data
- Discuss findings in relation to similar research
- Acknowledge limitations of the research and areas for future research

Chapter summary

In summary then, providing the reader with enough information about your research is important to enable them to evaluate your findings. This means incorporating sufficient information about the research design, the research questions and how the findings have been analysed. It is also important to include information about the context, such as participant numbers, participant demographics, the length of data collection sessions and the time period in which the whole data collection phase took place. The way in which your research is evaluated will depend on whether your research aligns itself with the positivist or interpretivist paradigm. The language used for evaluating research also depends on the research paradigm. Essentially, research needs to be evaluated on the extent to which the findings can be deemed accurate and truthful. The terms often used for this are validity and reliability. However, it is not unusual within interpretivist research to see the terms dependability and confirmability.

Further reading

Denzin, N.K. (2023) 'The elephant in the living room, or extending the conversation about the politics of evidence, part 2', in Denzin, N.K., Lincoln, Y.S., Giardina, M.P. and Cannella, G. (eds.) *The sage handbook of qualitative research*. 6th edn. Thousand Oaks, CA: SAGE, pp. 549–566.
- This is a thought-provoking chapter that explores the tensions between positivist and interpretivist research. Suggestions are made for how interpretivist research can be evaluated in its own right.

McGregor, S.L.T. (2017) *Understanding and evaluating research: A critical guide*. London: SAGE
- A very comprehensive book with in-depth guidance on how to evaluate qualitative and quantitative research in relation to findings. The book also helpfully explores different kinds of statistics in addition to providing information about different philosophical and theoretical positions that may underpin research.

References

Cresswell, J.W. and Miller, D.L. (2000) 'Determining validity in qualitative inquiry', *Theory into Practice*, 39(3), pp. 124–130.

Denscombe, M. (2017) *The good research guide for small-scale research projects*. 6th edn. Buckingham: Open University Press.

Denzin, N.K. and Lincoln, Y.S. (eds.) (2011) *The SAGE handbook of qualitative research*. 4th edn. Thousand Oaks, California: SAGE.

Geertz, C. (1973) *The interpretation of cultures: Selected essays*. New York Basic Books.

Lather, P. (1986) 'Issues of validity in open ideological research: Between a rock and a soft place', *Interchange*, 17 (4), pp. 63–84.

Lather, P. (1993) 'Fertile obsession: Validity after poststructuralism', *The Sociological Quarterly*, 34(2), pp. 637–673.

Lincoln, Y.S. and Guba, E.G. (1985) *Naturalistic inquiry*. Beverly Hills, CA: SAGE.

Merriam, S.B. (1998) *Qualitative research and case study applications in education*. San Francisco: Jossey-Bass.

Miles, M. and Huberman, M. (1994) *An expanded sourcebook: Qualitative data analysis*. 2nd edn. London: SAGE.

Oakley, A. (2005) *The Ann Oakley reader*. Bristol: The Policy Press.

Powell, D. (2022) Critical ethnography in schools: Reflections on power, positionality, and privilege. *International Journal of Qualitative Studies in Education*, 35(1), pp. 18–31, doi:10.1080/09518398.2021.1888160.

Shields, S. (2023) '"I've found Friends": Experiences of persistence and shared academic identities in Friendship formation for working-class university students', in Da Silva Dias, D. and Ribeiro Candeias, M.T. (eds.) *Education and human development*. London: IntechOpen. doi:10.5772/intechopen.113775.

Tesch, R. (1990) *Qualitative research*. New York: Falmer.

CHAPTER 20

Ethical issues in educational research

Introduction

Sometimes in our everyday lives we have to make difficult decisions. When there is no definitive 'right' or 'wrong' answer we use our individual morals and principles to guide our choices. Carrying out research can also be fraught with ethical dilemmas. Ethical research guidelines are codes of conduct which outline a system of moral principles which researchers are expected to follow. For ethical guidance, refer to the documents provided by your institution and the educational association you are most closely aligned to; for instance, this might be the British Educational Research Association (BERA), the American Educational Research Association (AERA) or the European Educational Research Association (EERA). The ethical guidelines outlined by BERA can be downloaded from their website: www.bera. ac.uk. The BERA ethical guidelines are underpinned by:

> The Association believes that all educational research should be conducted within an ethic of respect for: people; knowledge; the quality of educational research; the environment; and academic freedom. We believe there should be an ethic of care for all involved in educational research by and for researchers. Trust is a further essential element within the relationship between researcher and researched, as is the expectation that researchers will accept responsibility for their actions.
>
> (BERA, 2024: 9)

Therefore, an overriding concern when thinking about ethics is one of respect (BERA, 2024). Respect and trust are important principles which you should keep at the forefront of your mind during the entire research process. Ethical guidelines are put in place to protect the researcher and the researched. We have a duty of care to the participants in our research, and we also need to make sure that we do not put ourselves in dangerous situations. Research ethics help us to remember why it is unacceptable to report our findings inaccurately, and why covert research is generally not appropriate. In addition, ethical guidelines help us to respond to difficult situations such as finding out that your research participants are involved in illegal activities. Overall, we need to remember that educational research brings ethical responsibilities to a number of stakeholders: Participants, sponsors of the research, the community of educational researchers, educational professionals, policymakers and the general public (BERA, 2024). This chapter discusses the most likely ethical considerations you will need to think about as you prepare to undertake a piece of education research: Anonymity, confidentiality, informed consent, potential harm to participants, gaining ethical approval for your research from an ethics committee and writing up your research.

Anonymity

Anonymity is important for participants in research – after all, they are unlikely to disclose the information if it will be possible to identify them in later reports or publications. Consequently, a guarantee of anonymity will allow participants to feel confident in providing their perspectives or experiences. Generally, when you carry out research you change the names of the participants. This is known as providing each participant with a pseudonym – for example, 'Mrs Smith, a Year 3 teacher' may be referred to throughout the reporting stage as 'Ms Jones, a Key Stage 2 teacher'. If you have a very small number of participants, you may need to go further still in ensuring their anonymity by actively obscuring any features which may identify them. For example, if your participants are teachers from a small village school with only one male member of staff, any readers of your research who are familiar with the school may be able to guess his identity. The names of locations in your research should also be changed – for example, 'Borrow Wood Primary School in Walsall' could become 'Greenfields Primary School in the West Midlands'. By changing any distinguishing features of your research participants and their location, you should be able to ensure their anonymity.

Confidentiality

Maintaining the confidentiality of your research participants implies that you do not disclose information that was given to you during the data collection. This means that you cannot repeat any 'juicy gossip' given to you by a participant in an interview. If you are going to share a recording of an interview with your dissertation supervisor, or if someone else is transcribing your data, participants should be made aware of this. Additionally, you should remind any third parties sharing your data that it is important that they keep this information confidential. However, at the same time you should be aware that there may be limitations to the level of confidentiality you can provide participants – and you should be honest with them about this. A good example of this is police officers who undertake educational research as part of their qualifications to support them in training newly appointed officers. If police officers are made aware of illegal activities, they have a duty to report them, and therefore they make this clear to potential research participants at the outset. You could find yourself in a similar situation in your own research, for instance if your teenage participants tell you about their drug-taking habits. Ethical guidelines suggest that you must not keep this information confidential.

With regard to disclosure, the BERA guidelines state:

> There are circumstances in which confidentiality may need to be broken, and information sheets and consent forms should state this. Researchers who judge that adherence to agreements they have made with participants about confidentiality is likely to result in illegal or harmful actions should carefully consider making disclosure to the appropriate authorities. In some cases, such as revelations of abuse or proposed acts of terrorism, researchers may be under statutory duty to disclose confidential information to relevant authorities. Researchers should seek advice from a relevant responsible person before proceeding to disclosure if and when appropriate (for example, a student undertaking research should seek advice from their supervisor[s]). Insofar as it does not undermine or obviate the disclosure, or jeopardise researcher safety, researchers should inform the participants, or their guardians or responsible others, of their intentions and reasons for disclosure.
>
> (BERA, 2024: 24)

At times it will be ethically impossible to maintain confidentiality. For example, an interview with a child could cause you real concern if they disclose that they may be suffering from abuse in the home, and in this instance, you must make your unease known to the relevant professionals. Other incidents may also cause you more of an ethical dilemma in terms of maintaining confidentiality, as the 'Activity' below indicates.

ACTIVITY

Andrew Barbour's description of observations in the classroom highlighted some challenging ethical dilemmas for him (Barbour, 2010). His observations were allowed by 'gatekeepers' who were also his colleagues – other Further Education Lecturers – so from this perspective he felt loyal towards them. However, the teaching practices he observed were of poor quality and his interviews with students reinforced this point. Additionally, when lecturers were peer observed by senior colleagues there was a distinct change in their teaching approaches, suggesting that they were aware of their teaching approaches.

> If my interpretations of data were accurate, to avoid confrontation yet identify this unprofessionalism in my research, however anonymously, could become tantamount to a betrayal of trust to my colleagues. After all, without their permissions the research would not have been able to take place. I was caught in a dilemma of being torn between disloyalty to colleagues and a moral obligation to those students receiving a less than ideal education.
>
> (Barbour, 2010: 167)

- How does this situation challenge the principles of anonymity and confidentiality?
- To what extent should Barbour have remained loyal to the gatekeepers?
- How would you write up findings that are potentially controversial or damaging?

Informed consent

Homan and Bulmer (1982) describe the principle of informed consent as meaning that in all circumstances participants should be completely aware of factors that affect them, and based on this information they choose freely to take part (or not) in the research. You should also be aware that consent is an ongoing process – just because participants have signed a consent form does not mean that they have to continue with the research. Participants can change their minds about their involvement in your project at any time. Should participants decide not to continue their involvement in your research (for whatever reason), this should be respected and their decision should not have any negative consequences for them.

Making decisions about whether to participate in research assumes that participants understand what the research involves. It can be difficult to know whether some participants are truly able to give 'informed consent'. A variety of ways have been developed to ensure that more vulnerable participants can give consent, for example by the use of participatory research methods (Hart, 1992) in which children carry out the research themselves if they want to. The mosaic approach (Clark and Moss, 2001) is a good example of a research method that allows participants to give 'informed consent'. There are examples within education research in which participants have not been in full possession of all the facts when making a decision to take part or that not all potential participants have given their consent.

ACTIVITY

Read the two extracts below:

Extract 1

I found that the most difficult issue regarding the non-participating pupils had to do with the categories those pupils represented, and I faced this challenge in both schools. At Lakeside, the main problem was that some minority girls, defined by many pupils as belonging to the same collective, were not participating in the study because, according to the teachers, their parents had not consented. At Woodside, many of the non-participants were boys who were referred to as "problem kids" by teachers and some of the other pupils, part of the reason for their non-participation I explained above. In both schools, the categories that these pupils represented were, in my experience, critically important for understanding the social dynamics among the pupils. If I left the categories they represented out of my analyses, I would not be able to represent the social dynamics of the respective schools accurately. Yet the dilemma was that if I included them in my analyses, would I be guilty of not respecting their (and their parents') decision not to participate? My way of tackling this problem in the text was to describe and use the category labels assigned to these pupils by their peers, but to abstain from providing any information whatsoever about the individual pupils to whom the labels referred. While this way out of the dilemma may not be perfect, I regarded it as a compromise between representing the collectives accurately and respecting pupils' and parents' decisions not to participate in the research.

(Smette, 2019: 58)

Extract 2

As it became evident that understandings based on such research could only be partial, the research gradually moved towards the home environment. Meanwhile, it also became clear that to understand the experiences of children, it was necessary to explore the perspectives of older members of the communities. From my perspective, this seemed to significantly enrich the data that were being gathered. This view was not necessarily shared by participants:

Ethan (30s): I thought your research was about our kids' education.

Me: It is.

Ethan: So why are you asking me now about how I feel about moving from my trailer to a house?

Me: Well, as I've been talking to people, I've come to realise that there are all sorts of things involved that affect attitudes, and I think it's important to find out what parents are feeling if I'm going to understand where their children are coming from.

Ethan: So, what you said the first time was just bollocks, and what you're doing now is trying to find out about lots of new things.

Me: OK. If you want to put it like that, but it's not as if I ever set out to deceive you.

Ethan: 'Course, if I'd known that from the start, I might never have agreed to talk to you.

Me: Fair enough - course you can still tell me to get lost.

Ethan: I can and I might but all this time you've been talking to Jack and Crystal (Ethan's children), and I don't know what sort of things they've been telling you.

(Levinson, 2010: 198–199)

■ In what ways has the principle of informed consent been challenging in these two examples?

The general consensus within education research is that it is important to be honest about your identity and the aims of your research so that participants can make an informed decision, in possession of all the facts, about whether they wish to participate. This information can be incorporated into your participant consent form.

SAMPLE PARTICIPANT CONSENT FORM

1. You are invited to take part in a research study entitled 'A case study of female, working-class students' experiences of learning at university'.

2. Please read this document carefully and ask any questions you may have before agreeing to take part in the study.

3. The study is conducted by Samantha Shields from the School of Education, Communication & Language Sciences at Newcastle University.

4. The purpose of this study is to examine female, working-class undergraduates' experiences of learning at university. The more limited opportunities of working-class students (in comparison to students from more advantaged socio-economic backgrounds) have been documented, but

previous research has not considered how these experiences are understood through the lens of achievement. The principal researcher will conduct one-to-one semi-structured interviews with female students. Female undergraduates will be self-selecting, voluntary participants who self-identify as 'female' or 'working-class'. The findings from this research project will enable more nuanced understandings of the intersection between gender and socio-economic background to understand the aspirations and experiences of female, working-class undergraduates.

5 You have been invited to take part in this study because you self-identify as 'female' or 'working-class'. Your experiences of learning at university are therefore valuable in offering insight into the research topic of how your gender and socio-economic background impacts upon your experiences of learning.

6 If you agree to take part in this study, you will be asked to participate in a one-to-one interview with the researcher. Each participant can choose how this interview is conducted. It can be face-to-face at a pre-booked room at your university. Alternatively, the interview can take place over the telephone or via Zoom. The interview will not last longer than one hour. A copy of the interview questions will be available ahead of the interview so that you can decide which questions you would like to discuss.

7 Your participation in this study will take approximately 30 minutes to one hour.

8 The researcher will be only the person listening to the audio recordings for the purpose of interview transcription.

9 The personal data that is required for this study is your name and email address. This is to arrange a mutually convenient time for the interview and to send electronic copies of the published journal article and book chapters which result from the study (if you would like copies of these). If you choose to have a telephone interview you will be asked to provide a contact number (this will be deleted from the call history of the researcher after completion of the interview).

10 Participants will be provided with a peer debriefing sheet. They will also have the option of choosing to be sent electronic copies of the peer reviewed article or book chapters that result from the findings of the project.

11 You are free to decide whether or not to participate. If you decide to participate, you are free to withdraw at any time without any negative consequences for you.

12 All responses you give or other data collected will be kept anonymous and confidential. The records of this study will be kept secure and private (in a password-protected desktop PC at a lockable office at Newcastle University and a password-protected laptop). All files containing any information you give will be password protected and/or locked (office at Newcastle University). In any research report that may be published, no information will be included that will make it possible to identify you individually. There will be no way to connect your name to your responses at any time during or after the study. The interview data will be retained for a period of 5 years to allow suitable time for publication. Names and email addresses will also be retained if the participant has requested copies of the publications for the same time period.

13 If you have any questions, requests or concerns regarding this research, please contact me via email at xxxx or by telephone at xxxx.

This study has been reviewed and approved by the School of Education, Communication & Language Sciences Ethics Committee at Newcastle University, UK.

Faithfully yours
A. Person
(Adapted from ECLS Ethics Committee paperwork, Newcastle University, UK).

Potential harm to participants

The Hippocratic Oath taken by doctors requires them to 'do no harm' – and this is a good starting point for thinking about the way in which we conduct all research, not just research in medicine! A questionnaire about how children would like to improve the playground facilities at their school is unlikely to cause any distress to participants. Nevertheless, you should always be mindful of the potential for research to harm participants. For example, if you are using a narrative life history approach when asking participants to reflect on their school days, this could dredge up memories of being bullied. Providing potential participants with a research statement about your research (see the exemplar participant consent form above) means that they can make an informed decision about whether they are likely to be harmed in any way by taking part in your research.

Gaining ethical approval

The likelihood of gaining ethical approval often depends on what you are trying to find out and the research methods you wish to use. For example, if you are interested in researching the teaching and learning strategies teachers use in the classroom and you wish to carry out non-participant observation, this is unlikely to be problematic. Anonymity and confidentiality are probably the biggest ethical concerns, and you will need to reassure the ethics committee and your participants that you can guarantee this. On the other hand, if you want to interview children (vulnerable participants who may not be able to give 'informed' consent) about their experiences of being bullied (with potential for emotional distress), this may be much more difficult to gain ethical approval for. In this case, you may need to think of alternative strategies or a different research focus.

Writing up your research

When writing up your research you may wish to include a discussion of any ethical issues you encountered as an indicator of your reflexivity. Reflexivity means that we acknowledge we are part of the social world that we are studying (Hammersley and Atkinson, 1989) and as such our identity can influence the research process. Cicourel (1964) argues the importance of explaining the set of circumstances and conditions that favourably or unfavourably influence data collection. For example, you may be concerned that you were 'exploiting' participants during the interview process, if you felt your identity could be seen as one of 'authority' and 'dominance' because you were asking the interview questions and probing for further explanation. Also, as the researcher you are in a more powerful position because you have control over writing up the findings. If you have spent time gaining the trust of your participants, what happens if your findings cast the participants in a negative light? Do you try to 'skew' your findings to avoid the participants being shown in a negative way? Issues regarding bias may also occur if your research is funded. The funding body may anticipate certain outcomes, and you may be under pressure to write up your research in a certain way to satisfy the funding body.

Chapter summary

Hopefully the ethical dilemmas that you face in your research will not be too challenging. In general, ethical concerns such as anonymity, confidentiality and informed consent should be fairly straightforward to address. Nevertheless, this chapter will have given you an insight into educational scenarios where this is not always the case, and how it can be difficult to resolve these concerns. As Ferdinand et al. (2007: 540) argue, 'how researchers deal with ethical dilemmas ultimately comes down to personal choice and the responsibility that goes with this'. However, the BERA ethical guidelines (2024) are an excellent reference source and it is important to remember the key principle of respect when carrying out your research.

Further reading

Brooks, R., te Riele, K. and Maguire, M. (eds.) (2014) *Ethics and education research*. London: SAGE.
- This book begins with vignettes posing a range of ethical dilemmas. The book incorporates examples from both the Global North and Global South. The book considers ethics in terms of research design and issues such as reciprocity, positionality and power.

Miller, T., Birch, M., Mauthner, M. and Jessop, J. (eds.) (2012) *Ethics in qualitative research*. London: Sage.
- This book explores ethical issues in a theoretical and practical way. It is particularly useful for understanding the concept of 'informed' consent.

References

Barbour, A. (2010) 'Exploring some ethical dilemmas and obligations of the ethnographer', *Ethnography and Education*, 5(2), pp. 159–173.

BERA (2024) *Ethical Guidelines for Educational Research*, 5th edn. Available at: https://www.bera.ac.uk/publication/ethical-guidelines-for-educational-research-fifth-edition-2024 (Accessed: 19 June 2024).

Cicourel, A. (1964) *Method and measurement in sociology*. New York: Collier-Macmillan.

Clark, A. and Moss, P. (2001) *Listening to young children: The mosaic approach*. London: National Children's Bureau.

Ferdinand, J., Pearson, G., Rowe, M. and Worthington, F. (2007) 'A different kind of ethics', *Ethnography*, 8(4), pp. 519–543.

Hammersley, M. and Atkinson, P. (1989) *Ethnography: Principles in practice*. London: Routledge.

Hart, R. (1992) *Children's participation: From tokenism to citizenship*. Florence: UNICEF Innocenti.

Homan, R. and Bulmer, M. (1982) 'On the merits of covert methods: A dialogue', in Bulmer, M. (ed.) *Social research ethics*. London: Macmillan Press.

Levinson, M.P. (2010) 'Accountability to research participants: Unresolved dilemmas and unravelling ethics', *Ethnography and Education*, 5(2), pp. 193–207.

Smette, I. (2019) 'Ethics and access when consent must come first: Consequences of formalised research ethics for ethnographic research in schools', in Busher, H. and Fox, A. (eds.) *Implementing ethics in educational ethnography*. London: Routledge, pp. 51–63.

CHAPTER 21

Research with children and vulnerable groups

Introduction

By its very nature, the majority of educational research involves children and young people. Some research may also involve other vulnerable people or hard-to-reach individuals. This chapter considers the kinds of strategies that are most effective for working alongside younger people and other vulnerable groups. It asks questions about how one might gather data from very young children, and other vulnerable people, and considers how schools, colleges and universities elicit 'data' from their students. It distinguishes between the various levels of participation – for instance, research conducted: 'About', 'on', 'for', 'with' and 'by' children or vulnerable groups. Approaches involving students as researchers and co-researchers are also outlined and discussed. The chapter concludes by outlining key issues for these approaches to research – most notably, issues of power in terms of differences and equity in adult-child and researcher-vulnerable participant research relations.

Constructions of childhood and young personhood

Since Phillipe Aries wrote his landmark book 'Centuries of Childhood' in 1960 (translated 1962) the idea that 'childhood' is a social construction has prevailed. This notion suggests that what it means to be a child is shaped and defined by the cultural, environmental, economic, political and social contexts of a given time and place. 'Childhood' changes over time and means different things in different places. In recent years, debates about the changing nature of childhood have been dominated by moral panics – a decline in children's safety and innocence, a 'commodification' of childhood, a potential 'end of childhood', or, as Palmer (2006) famously suggested, the emergence of 'toxic childhood'.

However, a more positive reading of childhood in Global North societies today would point to a growth in children's prominence, status and 'voice'. Advances in technology, mass media, education and the leisure industries provide children with far more access to products and information, and many more opportunities to express their viewpoints. Children are no longer 'seen but not heard'. Arguably, they are listened to far more and their rights, needs and interests are taken far more seriously than in the past. The United Nations Convention on the Rights of the Child (UNCRC) was enshrined in international law in 1990 and ratified in the UK in 1991. In theory, the convention provides all young people under the age of eighteen with specific protections, entitlements and services. It also affords children rights to be informed and to participate. Consider the following activity:

ACTIVITY

- Read the following extracts from two articles in the UNCRC:

Article 12:
States Parties shall assure to the child who is capable of forming his or her own views the right to express those views freely in all matters affecting the child, the views of the child being given due weight in accordance with the age and maturity of the child.

Article 13:
The child shall have the right to freedom of expression; this right shall include freedom to seek, receive and impart information and ideas of all kinds, regardless of frontiers, either orally, in writing or in print, in the form of art, or through any other media of the child's choice.

- How do you think these two articles might inform an educational researcher's methods of studying school children?
- What approaches to data collection might enable children to utilise these rights in educational research?
- How might research approaches differ when conducted in: Pre-school? Primary school? Secondary school? Further education? Higher education?

Levels of participation

As you would expect, the majority of educational research is concerned with children and young people. This research takes various forms and has many different purposes – from a teacher's research to inform and improve her own practice, to large-scale longitudinal and international projects. Hart's highly influential 'ladder of participation' (1992) has had a considerable impact upon conceptualisations of children's participation.

Hart's ladder encourages educational researchers to rethink the relationship between children and their research. There are various ways that children and young people might engage with educational research, including:

- About but without children: Research might be concerned with the experiences of children, but not include them in data collection or analysis. For instance, a researcher might choose to interview teachers or parents rather than children because the children of interest are too young. Alternatively, depending on the topic, there might be ethical concerns regarding the children's involvement in terms of adverse effects on their social or emotional wellbeing or their academic achievement.

- For children: Adult researchers might conduct research on behalf of children. The purpose of the project might be to make recommendations that will improve the conditions that children and young people live and learn within, whether or not they take part in the research itself.
- On children: Educational research today frequently involves children participating as respondents/sources of data. For example, Piaget famously conducted research on children to identify different stages of development (see Voyat, 1982), and his observations have had tremendously positive impacts on learning and teaching ever since. Depending on ethical constraints and the children's age, communication and skill levels, different modes of involvement may be possible and/or desirable. Data collection can involve children in many different activities, including:
- Keeping diaries
- Drawing pictures
- Making models
- Completing questionnaires
- Being interviewed
- Taking photographs
- Making films
- Participating in discussion
- Telling stories
- Developing spider diagrams or mind maps
- Completing worksheets
- Being the focus of observations

Methods are frequently combined – most influentially in Clark and Moss's 'mosaic approach' to understanding young children's perspectives on early years' settings (2001).

- With children: Increasingly, children and young people participate in the collection and analysis of the data – especially in research intended to evaluate and enhance existing educational provision. Working alongside more experienced researchers, children and young people become active participants in the research process.
- By children: While still relatively uncommon, some educational research is conducted by children, who might take responsibility for all or particular stages of enquiry (developing aims and objectives, gathering and analysing data, presenting findings).

Students as researchers and co-researchers

Recent years have witnessed considerable interest in strategies that encourage students to take an active role in research, in particularly as a means of enhancing educational provision. In the UK, Michael Fielding (e.g. Fielding and Bragg, 2003) has been the most influential advocate for both 'students as researchers' and 'students as co-researchers' – that is, as partners in research with teachers or academics. Projects that involve students as 'co-researchers' generally take the form of collaborative enquiry, whereby the different experiences, skills and knowledge of young people and adults are brought together to generate new knowledge and to improve current practice. Projects are generally instigated by academics or practitioners, and interested students are invited to join and form a research team. Conversely, 'student as researcher' projects are initiated and shaped by student interests. With the support of teachers and academics, individual (or groups of) students embark on their own research projects. Participatory action research (PAR) (see Chapter 11) is a model commonly used in projects where students are involved as researchers and co-researchers. This entails participants theorising their own lives and using collaboration and reflection to improve current circumstances (see Bland and Atweh, 2007 for a discussion of students as researchers and PAR).

Students as (co-)researcher projects are designed to empower students and to enable them to participate in the evaluation and development of their own learning environments. They are also intended to impact positively on educational practice. Reviewing the literature on 'students as researchers', Bahou (2011: 7) identifies five common aims:

- 'Address issues that matter to students
- Create new knowledge about education for critical evaluation and action
- Set an agenda for students to make a difference
- Enable students to develop a kind of professionalism whereby student voices can be taken seriously by adults
- Enhance the conditions and processes of learning and teaching'.

Advantages of children and young people as researchers

There are many advantages of employing 'students as researchers'. In this section, these are grouped around three headings: Improving the quality of research, benefitting the children who participate and enhancing democracy, citizenship and social relations.

Improving the quality of research

The quality of research can be improved in the following ways:

- Collecting data: Young people are experts in their own lives. When gathering data, they are likely to be more able to relate to other young people, making interview settings less formal and putting interviewees at ease. They are more likely to be able to recognise when young respondents are exaggerating or messing about.

- 'Agents of change': The idea that children and young people are effective 'agents of change' (Kay, Dunne and Hutchinson, 2010) has gained increasing currency in recent years. Many educational institutions encourage their students to play an active role in the research, evaluation and development of new assessments, curriculums and resources. Young people might be more able to articulate change because they are less constrained by existing assumptions and practices.
- Multiple voices: 'Researcher triangulation' entails increasing validity by employing a number of different researchers in research design, data collection and analysis. Validity is likely to be further increased if these researchers come from groups that are generally marginalised or excluded from such processes. Despite changes in society noted above, the voices of children and young people remain relatively unheard (UNICEF, 2015).

Benefitting the children who participate

Children and young people can also benefit in the following ways:

- Sense of ownership and involvement: As Hart (1992) argues, young people can demonstrate great competence if they feel some sense of ownership and are involved in the design and management of the project. Participation encourages young people to feel they can make a meaningful contribution.
- Improved academic performance: There is compelling evidence that engagement in research impacts positively on the attainment of those who take part. As Fielding and Bragg (2003) argue, student researchers are likely to develop in confidence and motivation, become more engaged and develop academic skills.
- Personal and social development: Students will also develop wider skills, associated with relating to other people and working effectively as a member of a team. They develop a greater understanding of their learning contexts and are likely to play a more active role in their school and their wider environment.

Enhancing democracy, citizenship and social relations

Benefits to wider democratic society include:

- Democratic engagement: Active participation in the development and evaluation of knowledge and practice will foster the kinds of qualities and skills ideally suited to active citizenship and democratic engagement. If young people are able to participate and shape the settings they study within, they are far more likely to take part in the wider world in adulthood.
- Promoting 'intergenerational learning': These strategies enable people from different generations to work together. This creates opportunities for children and adults to

collaborate on projects and learn from one another. For Fielding, such 'intergenerational learning' fosters a sense of collegiality and develops a shared sense of 'mutual responsibility' and 'energising adventure' (2012: 53).

Eliciting student voices

Since the beginning of the twenty-first century, legislation in England has dictated that schools must consult with their students about provision. There is considerable evidence that schools, colleges and universities engage with their students in a variety of ways. Most have a 'school council' or something similar, which discusses and informs institutional policy. Some schools and universities ensure they have student representation on interview panels, boards of governors and other institutional committees. Most educational establishments survey their learners to evaluate modules, curriculums and student experience. For universities, the National Student Survey has become a vital instrument in measuring student satisfaction in various aspects of provision. As these examples indicate, student voices are sought to evaluate existing practice as well as to inform future developments.

While enabling the student voice is valuable in and of itself, there is a big difference between providing opportunities to speak and ensuring that such contributions are meaningful and have impact. There is a danger that such activities are tokenistic – that critical student perspectives are ignored, or that consultation is only offered on relatively insignificant issues. Moreover, it is relatively straightforward to elicit the opinions of confident and articulate young people. It may be more difficult to do so with students who are reticent, disengaged or students with special educational needs. Effective strategies should always seek to promote dialogue with more marginalised or 'silent' students.

Evaluating educational research with children

There are many issues to consider when conducting research with child participants. Among the questions to reflect on are:

Levels of participation

- What stages of research might children be involved in?
- What are the advantages and disadvantages of children participating in or being excluded from developing research design and research questions, data collection, data analysis and writing up and presenting work?

Power relations

- How do you avoid exploitation of child researchers?
- Can research participation be empowering? If so, how can this be ensured/maximised?

- To what extent is the relationship between adult and child equal?
- How can you facilitate shared decision-making?
- How do roles differ?

Avoiding tokenism

- How can you ensure the process is meaningful and worthwhile?
- Are the children who participate listened to seriously?
- Does the research have real outcomes and impact?
- Representing divergent voices
- How are child participants recruited/selected?
- Do participants share the same characteristics as the whole (student) population?
- How do you ensure that quieter and/or marginalised voices are heard?

Developing appropriate research skills

- How are 'novice' researchers supported in the fieldwork site?
- How will child participants be trained and supervised to develop the relevant skills?
- Who provides this support?

The impact of participation

- Are children safe and protected?
- Are child researchers likely to be exposed to distressing situations and/or feelings?
- How is participation likely to impact on children's wider relationships?

ACTIVITY

Using the prompts above, develop a 'student as co-researcher' strategy for each of the following topics of study:

- To compare differences in boys' and girls' numeracy development
- To evaluate the impact of new special educational needs provision in a secondary school
- To identify effective strategies for supporting school leavers' choices
- To investigate school gang cultures

Research with migrants, refugees and other vulnerable populations

It is not merely children under the age of eighteen that are considered 'vulnerable' in research. There are other individuals and groups who also fall into this category. This includes 'hard-to-reach' groups such as sexual and ethnic minorities, or certain types of migrants such as refugees and asylum seekers. Researchers often find it difficult to access these groups due to their physical location or 'hidden nature' (Ellard-Gray et al., 2015). For example, refugees are often marginalised in their host countries (O'Neill et al., 2019) and may thus be culturally or socially disadvantaged. Challenges of researching marginalised groups affect all aspects of the research process, including participant recruitment and sampling, data collection and analysis, and write-up and dissemination of research findings. Below, we illustrate some of these complexities by using asylum seekers as a case in point. This group is especially vulnerable due to their uncertain legal status and the sensitive nature of their experiences (Van Eggermont Arwidson et al., 2022).

Asylum seekers need special protection in research given their 'relative powerlessness associated with the challenges experienced pre and post arrival in a resettlement country' (Davidson, Hammarberg and Fisher, 2023). We offer possible solutions and strategies for overcoming barriers by drawing on recent example studies.

Access and recruitment

Researchers may find it difficult to get access to asylum seekers, as they may be dispersed across many different locations, including refugee camps, detention centres or community housing in the host country (International Centre for Migration Policy Development (ICMPD), 2023). Establishing contact likely requires the cooperation of a gatekeeper such as a charity, government agency or a local council. Even when access is successfully granted, asylum seekers may be reluctant to participate in research, especially if it involves disclosing sensitive information about their immigration journey, due to concerns around privacy or distrust of authorities (Abbas et al., 2021; Essex et al., 2022). For example, asylum seekers may be fearful that disclosing personal information could have negative repercussions for their asylum claims (Karadag et al., 2021).

The forced displacement that asylum seekers experience likely includes experience of persecution, violence or other distressing situations, and may mean that they arrive in their host countries with considerable trauma (Liebling et al., 2014). It is therefore crucial that researchers prioritise the safety and wellbeing of their participants, and ensure confidentiality is maintained throughout the research process. Before researchers embark on studies that involve asylum seekers, it is advisable that they equip themselves with information regarding organisations that can offer appropriate support and mental health services (see, e.g., the UK Refugee Council; Mental Health Foundation). When obtaining informed consent, researchers need to be aware of social, cultural, economic and linguistic barriers (see Deps et al., 2022 for guidelines on ethical research with refugee populations). It is recommended that a 'cultural insider' is present when seeking informed consent (European Commission, n.d.). This could be a familiar person with knowledge of the participant's cultural background and, ideally, their native language. Finally, researchers need to be aware that logistical constraints may limit the scope of research involving asylum seekers and could affect sampling. Given the hard-to-access nature of asylum seekers, it may be that researchers need to compromise on sample size.

EXAMPLE: ETHICAL CONSIDERATIONS

In an interview-based study of asylum seekers in Sweden, the researchers (Van Eggermont Arwidson *et al.*, 2022) maintained ethical standards in the following ways:

- Before the interviews, written information was provided to literate participants in Arabic and Persian.
- All participants were informed about the purpose of the study verbally in a language they were proficient in.
- All participants were informed that that their participation in the research would not have any impact on their asylum claim.
- All participants were informed that they had the right to withdraw their consent at any time, without repercussions for their asylum claim.
- Written or verbal informed consent was obtained from all participants. Verbal consent was obtained from participants who had low levels of literacy or were illiterate.
- The researchers used a pre-planned distress protocol to safeguard participants' mental well-being. In the event of distress, the protocol could be used to provide support during the interview and, if needed, to refer participants to support services.
- To preserve the participants' confidentiality, the interview transcripts were anonymised and coded by number.
- In the write-up of the findings, pseudonyms were used for all quotes.

Data collection and analysis

Collecting data from asylum seekers brings unique challenges that researchers must navigate with sensitivity, flexibility and, at times, creativity. Firstly, when conducting research involving asylum seekers, researchers need to be aware of their own biases and power dynamics inherent in their relationship with participants (Block *et al.*, 2013; Pincock and Bakunzi, 2021; UKRI, 2024). In order to obtain meaningful data, researchers need to establish rapport and build trust (Ahmed *et al.*, 2022). This can be difficult given that asylum seekers are often marginalised in their host societies and broader discourses around immigration mean that research with asylum seekers is likely politically charged (Georgiou, 2022). Thus, researchers need to think carefully about their methodological choices when conducting research with asylum seekers, or other vulnerable migrant populations. There are several research approaches that can help researchers to empower their participants. This includes, for example, PAR, community-based participatory research, culturally responsive approaches and co-design methodologies (Mertens, 2021).

Secondly, given that forced displacement likely involves trauma, researchers must recognise the impact of trauma on the perspectives of participants. This can influence how data are interpreted but may also mean that there is potential for re-traumatisation or 'secondary traumatization' (Karadag et al., 2021) in the data collection process. For example, asking asylum seekers to recall past experiences can trigger painful memories or emotions (Stewart and Shaffer, 2021).

Researchers should set out protocols of how to manage situations that may trigger distress in their participants. 'Trauma-informed' research approaches (Isobel, 2021) may be appropriate here. In an interview-based study, this could include, for example, adopting a conversational style, using open questions and paying particular attention to non-verbal cues (see a toolkit on trauma-informed interview techniques here: https://digitalmedic.stanford.edu/trauma-informed-interviewing-techniques). It is recommended that researchers familiarise themselves with trauma-informed research approaches which are gaining momentum.

Thirdly, logistical constraints in the data collection process include language and communication issues. Asylum seekers likely come from diverse cultural and linguistic backgrounds and may not speak the dominant language of the host country. Unless the researchers are able to draw on their own linguistic repertoire, they may need to rely on interpreters and translators to facilitate data collection. For example, if they conduct interviews, they may need an interpreter present who speaks the native language of the participants. They may then also need a translator who can translate interview transcripts into English for analysis purposes. The use of multiple languages in research with asylum seekers means that power relations and language hierarchies require careful consideration (Holmes, Reynolds and Ganassin, 2022). Researchers need to deal with 'linguistic messiness' (Ganassin and Holmes, 2013) and need to consider carefully how participants' voices can be included authentically without misinterpreting meaning.

In addition, data collection is shaped by the cultural context in which it takes place and may affect how participants behave in interactions with the researcher (Bayeck, 2021). Cultural differences in communication styles and cultural norms may affect how asylum seekers engage with the research process. For example, participants may be reluctant to disclose information on certain sensitive topics if these are considered a cultural taboo. Researchers should familiarise themselves with culturally sensitive approaches (see Au, 2019 for cross-cultural differences in qualitative interviewing). Different expectations of gender roles may also mean that female participants may not feel comfortable speaking to a male interviewer (Karadag et al., 2021), or vice versa, researchers must thus be flexible and open to adapting their approach throughout the research process. It is also recommended that researchers educate themselves about how to deal with problematic incidental findings, that is information that they may discover unintentionally as part of the research process (e.g. human trafficking, female genital mutilation, domestic violence) (European Commission, n.d.). Finally, longitudinal research and follow-up studies may be difficult given the high mobility of asylum seekers (Karadag et al., 2021), as they may be resettled without much notice as well as their changing legal status.

Write-up

In the final stages of the research process, researchers may encounter challenges when writing up their research findings due to the sensitivity of the topics discussed and other ethical considerations. When reporting research data, it is paramount that researchers protect the identity of asylum seekers and ensure anonymity. This is important given that identifying information could be detrimental to the legal status of the participants. It can be a balancing act for researchers to, on the one hand, report data accurately, comprehensively and transparently and, on the other hand, to responsibly protect the identity of participants. Researchers must consider carefully how to anonymise data and do their utmost to ensure that any information reported does not lead to the identification of participants. This should include, at the very least, using pseudonyms but can also mean changing or omitting certain details where possible, as illustrated in the example below.

EXAMPLE: MAINTAINING ANONYMITY IN WRITE-UP

Stewart and Shaffer (2021) undertook the following steps to protect the identities of their participants in their research with asylum seekers:

- Major identifying details were removed from interview transcripts. This included names of cities, schools, addresses, streets, neighbourhoods, names of places of worships, places of employment and support services accesses by the asylum seekers.
- For a small sample that was geographically limited, the researchers were aware that nationality could identify an individual and thus decided to change 'country of origin' to 'region of origin' (e.g. East, West, Southern Africa, Middle East).
- They were mindful that while single details were likely unproblematic, cross-referencing of data (e.g. nationality AND occupation) may expose participants' identity.
- This led to the redaction of some data where appropriately vague labelling was not possible. This meant that they used descriptors such as 'sensitive details removed', 'personal details removed' or 'location details removed'.

Research with asylum seekers typically involves complex political, social and legal issues. Researchers must thus ensure that they communicate this complexity in an effective and accessible way ensuring that their findings reach multiple audiences. To achieve this, researchers should consider disseminating their findings in multiple languages and beyond the written medium to include oral and visual formats (Clark-Kazak, 2017).

Researchers also need to ensure accuracy in their representation of asylum seekers' experiences. It is recommended that researchers closely involve relevant stakeholders, including asylum seekers themselves, to ensure that the voices of their participants are heard and represented accurately and sensitively in the writing-up process. This can help researchers to avoid generalisations or stereotyping and allows them to ensure that the nuances of asylum seekers' experiences are captured. This could be achieved by involving community researchers in the process (Hearn et al., 2022).

Finally, researchers may also need to rely more on 'grey literature' (i.e. literature that is not peer reviewed) in their writing. This may, for example, include non-academic sources such as government reports, newsletters and websites. Governments often have easier access to 'hard to find' or 'hidden' groups like refugees and asylum seekers (Enticott, Buck and Shawyer, 2018).

Chapter summary

Changing conceptions of childhood, especially as ratified in the UNCRC, promote greater involvement of children and young people. This chapter has outlined some of the different ways that children and young people might be involved in educational research, identifying a number of 'levels of participation'. Evidence suggests that the participation of children and young people in educational research improves the depth and validity of the findings. It also appears to benefit the children and young people who take part, increasing engagement as well as social and academic development. The chapter has also outlined some of the challenges of researching other vulnerable groups and discussed the case in point of asylum seekers. It showcases examples of how research with vulnerable migrant groups can be conducted ethically and discusses the complexities of research involving marginalised groups.

Further reading

Fielding, M. and Bragg, S. (2003) *Students as researchers: Making a difference*. London: Pearson.

- Michael Fielding's work on 'students as researchers' has been especially influential. This book, written with Sara Bragg, provides an excellent introduction to this work.

Fox, A. et al. (2020) Ethics-in-practice in fragile contexts: Research in education for displaced persons, refugees and asylum seekers. *British Educational Research Journal*, 46(4), pp. 829–847.

- An informative article in which researchers reflect on their work in the field with vulnerable groups and the ethical implications in practice.

References

Abbas, P. et al. (2021) 'The texture of narrative dilemmas: Qualitative study in front-line professionals working with asylum seekers in the UK', *BJPsych Bulletin*, 45(1), pp. 8–14.

Alessi, E. J. and Kahn, S. (2023) 'Toward a trauma-informed qualitative research approach: Guidelines for ensuring the safety and promoting the resilience of research participants', *Qualitative Research in Psychology*, 20(1), pp. 121–154.

Ahmed, A. et al. (2022) 'An examination of how to engage migrants in the research process: Building trust through an 'insider' perspective', *Ethnicity & Health*, 27(2), pp. 463–482.

Aries, P. (1962) *Centuries of childhood: A social history family life*. Trans. Robert Baldwin. New York: Vintage Books.

Au, A. (2019) 'Thinking about cross-cultural differences in qualitative interviewing: Practices for more responsive and trusting encounters', *The Qualitative Report*, 24(1), pp. 58–77.

Bahou, L. (2011) 'Rethinking the challenges and possibilities of student voice and agency', *Educate*, pp. 2–14.

Bayeck, R.Y. (2021) 'The intersection of cultural context and research encounter: Focus on interviewing in qualitative research', *International Journal of Qualitative Methods*, 20, doi:1609406921995696.

Bland, D. and Atweh, B. (2007) 'Students as researchers: Engaging students' voices in PAR', *Educational Action Research*, 15(3), pp. 337–349.

Block, K, et al. (2013) 'Addressing ethical and methodological challenges in research with refugee-background young people: Reflections from the field', *Journal of Refugee Studies*, 26(1), pp. 69–87.

Clark-Kazak, C. (2017) 'Ethical considerations: Research with people in situations of forced migration', *Refuge*, 33(2), pp. 11–17.

Davidson, N., Hammarberg, K. and Fisher, J. (2023) 'Ethical considerations in research with people from refugee and asylum seeker backgrounds: A systematic review of national and international ethics guidelines', *Journal of Bioethical Inquiry*, 21, pp. 1–24.

Clark, A. and Moss, P. (2001) *Listening to young children: The mosaic approach*. London: National Children's Bureau.

Deps, P. D. et al. (2022) 'Ethical issues in research with refugees', *Ethics, Medicine and Public Health*, 24, p. 100813.

Ellard-Gray, A. et al. (2015) 'Finding the hidden participant: Solutions for recruiting hidden, hard-to-reach, and vulnerable populations', *International Journal of Qualitative Methods*, 14(5). doi:10.1177/1609406915621420.

Enticott, J., Buck, K. and Shawyer, F. (2018) 'Finding "hard to find" literature on hard to find groups: A novel technique to search grey literature on refugees and asylum seekers', *International Journal of Methods in Psychiatric Research*, 27(1), p. e1580.

Essex, R. et al. (2022) 'Trust amongst refugees in resettlement settings: A systematic scoping review and thematic analysis of the literature', *Journal of International Migration and Integration*, 23(2), pp. 543–568.

European Commission (n.d.) Guidance note — Research on refugees, asylum seekers & migrants. guide_research-refugees-migrants_en.pdf (europa.eu). Available at: https://ec.europa.eu/research/participants/data/ref/h2020/other/hi/guide_research-refugees-migrants_en.pdf (Accessed: 21 June 2024)

Fielding, M. (2012) 'Beyond student voice: Patterns of partnership and the demands of deep democracy', *Revista de Educación*, 359, September-December 2012, pp. 45–65.

Fielding, M. and Bragg, S. (2003) *Students as researchers: Making a difference. Consulting pupils about teaching and learning*. Cambridge: Pearson Publishing.

Ganassin, S. and Holmes, P. (2013) 'Multilingual research practices in community research: The case of migrant/refugee women in North East England', *International Journal of Applied Linguistics*, 23(3), pp. 342–356.

Georgiou, A. (2022) 'Conducting multilingual classroom research with refugee children in Cyprus: Critically reflecting on methodological decisions', in Holmes, P., Reynolds, J. and Ganassin, S. (eds.) *The politics of researching multilingually*. Bristol, Jackson: Multilingual Matters, pp. 111–130.

Hart, R. (1992) *Children's participation: From tokenism to citizenship*. Florence: UNICEF Innocenti. Available at: https://www.cph.co.nz/wp-content/uploads/RogerHartLadderOfParticipation.pdf (Accessed: 24 June 2024).

Hearn, F. et al. (2022) 'Having a say in research directions: The role of community researchers in participatory research with communities of refugee and migrant background', *International Journal of Environmental Research and Public Health*, 19(8). https://www.mdpi.com/1660-4601/19/8/4844

Holmes, P., Reynolds, J. and Ganassin, S. (2022) 'Introduction: The imperative for the politics of 'Researching Multilingually'', in Holmes, P., Reynolds, J. and Ganassin, S. (eds.) *The politics of researching multilingually*. Bristol & Blue Ridge Summit: Multilingual Matters, pp. 1–27.

International Centre for Migration Policy Development (ICMPD) (2023) 'Asylum seeker dispersal policies – Setting the stage for successful integration?' Asylum seeker dispersal policies – Setting the stage for successful integration? – ICMPD.

Isobel, S. (2021) 'Trauma-informed qualitative research: Some methodological and practical considerations', *International Journal of Mental Health Nursing*, 30, pp. 1456–1469.

Karadag, O. et al. (2021) 'Challenges and lessons learned in mental health research among refugees: A community-based study in Turkey', *BMC Public Health*, 21, pp. 1–8.

Kay, J., Dunne, E. and Hutchinson, J. (2010) 'Rethinking the values of higher education – Students as change agents?' *The quality assurance agency for higher education*. Gloucester: QAA.

Liebling, H. et al. (2014) 'Understanding the experiences of asylum seekers', *International Journal of Migration, Health and Social Care*, 10(4), pp. 207–219.

Mertens, D.M. (2021) 'Transformative research methods to increase social impact for vulnerable groups and cultural minorities', *International Journal of Qualitative Methods*, 20. doi:10.1177/16094069211051563.

O'Neill, M. et al. (2019) 'Borders, risk and belonging: Challenges for arts-based research in understanding the lives of women asylum seekers and migrants 'at the borders of humanity'', *Crossings: Journal of Migration & Culture*, 10(1), pp. 129–147.

Palmer, S. (2006) *Toxic childhood: How the modern world is damaging our children and what we can do about it*. London: Orion Books.

Pincock, K. and Bakunzi, W. (2021) 'Power, participation, and 'peer researchers': Addressing gaps in refugee research ethics guidance', *Journal of Refugee Studies*, 34(2), pp. 2333–2348.

Stewart, E. and Shaffer, M. (2021) 'The ethical and practical challenges of archiving refugee accounts: Reflections from two research projects in the UK', *Bulletin of Sociological Methodology/Bulletin de Méthodologie Sociologique*, 150 (1), pp. 51–69.

Van Eggermont Arwidson, C. et al. (2022) 'Living A frozen life: A qualitative study on asylum seekers' experiences and care practices at accommodation centers in Sweden', *Conflict and Health*, 16(47), pp. 1–14

UKRI (2024) *Research with potentially vulnerable people*. Available at: https://www.ukri.org/councils/esrc/guidance-for-applicants/research-ethics-guidance/research-with-potentially-vulnerable-people/ (Accessed: 24 June 2024).

UNICEF (2015) *UNICEF procedure for ethical standards in research, evaluation, data collection and analysis*. Available at: https://www.unicef.org/media/54796/file (Accessed: 24 June 2024).

Voyat, G. (1982) *Piaget systematized*. Hillsdale: Lawrence Erlbaum Associates.

Glossary

Action research a cyclical research process of reflection, research and action intended to solve practical problems.

Case study aims to explore a specific 'case' that can help illuminate whatever research question is under investigation.

Coding putting labels on data to categorise it into themes and patterns.

Descriptive statistics Typically, descriptive statistics may take the form of percentages, frequency counts or fractions.

Documentary research a form of research that analyses documents as a primary research tool, and can encompass the study of official records, government publications and diaries.

Epistemology a framework or theory for specifying the constitution and generation of knowledge about the social world.

Ethnography an in-depth study of the culture(s) of a particular group of people.

Experiment researchers manipulate specific variables within controlled conditions.

Focus group interviews a way of collecting qualitative data from a group of people in order to explore their perceptions, opinions, beliefs or attitudes. They differ from one-to-one discussions as the researcher asks questions in an interactive group setting where participants respond by entering into group discussion with one another.

Grounded theory a systematic approach to generating a theory typically from qualitative empirical data originally developed by Glaser and Strauss (1967) in 'The Discovery of Grounded Theory'. This methodology uses a specific type of comparative analysis which includes 'open', 'axial' and 'selective' coding.

Interpretivism a theoretical approach that views research as an interpretive rather than scientific act and is usually described as an opposing view to positivism in research contexts.

Member-checking asking participants to check their contribution to data collection for accuracy, such as an interview transcript.

Memos notes about any thoughts, ideas or questions that are emerging from the concepts in the data.

Methodology a specific framework (e.g., Case Study or Survey) for guiding a research study which includes its philosophical underpinning (e.g., positivism vs. interpretivism) and how the piece of research is designed. It is likely to include a discussion of the principles and values that underpin the research and explain the decisions taken, such as how research methods are selected.

Mixed-methods research a combination of research methods that produces both qualitative and quantitative data in a study – providing both in-depth accounts and broad statistical patterns. This approach tends to draw upon a pragmatic philosophical framework – with a focus on 'how best' to answer a research question.

Naturalism studying people and activities as they ordinarily take place (often via observations).

Paradigm a set of beliefs which have particular epistemological and ontological values.

Positionality the notion that the 'position' or 'stance' a researcher takes (either knowingly or unknowingly) can impact on the research design and also on the ethical nature of the research process.

Positivism an approach to research that assumes the neutrality and objectivity of a detached researcher, believed to be free from any bias related to social, political or cultural context.

Qualitative research qualitative research places emphasis on meaning and is more popular in smaller-scale research projects.

Quantitative research quantitative research is an approach to research that places emphasis on the analysis of numbers and is popular in large-scale studies.

Reflexivity when the researcher reflects honestly about all the steps taken in the research and how she has influenced the process of the research.

Reliability the consistency and dependability of research processes and measurements.

Research bias research bias is the existence of subjective assumptions that negatively affect the veracity of the research findings.

Respondent validation asking participants to consider your data analysis and the extent to which it relates to their own interpretation of their experiences and perceptions. Respondent validation may be woven into the write-up of the study to demonstrate validity.

Social theories social theories are analytical frameworks or concepts used to examine social phenomena, and are commonly used in educational research to explore how education connects to issues of power and structural inequalities such as gender, ethnicity and social class.

Subjectivity a belief that a researcher's views are not neutral, but are mediated by their experiences of life, and these experiences are (consciously or unconsciously) influenced by social class, gender, ethnicity and age as well as other factors. Researchers who accept their subjectivity in the research process will consider the impact that their own identity can have on participants when conducting research.

Triangulation commonly the use of a variety of research methods to enhance the validity of the findings (method triangulation). Other approaches to triangulation include investigator triangulation (more than one researcher), data triangulation (using different groups of participants/different settings/different times) and theory triangulation – explaining phenomena with more than one theory. The concept was originally developed by Denzin (1978) 'The research act: A theoretical introduction to sociological methods'.

Validity literally meaning 'truth', validity identifies how truthfully an account represents participants' realities of social phenomena.

Variable an attribute that describes a person, place, thing or idea. Qualitative variables take on values that are names or labels. Quantitative variables are numeric, which means they can be measured in a more numerically complex manner.

References

Denzin, N.K. (1978) *The research act in sociology: A theoretical introduction.* 2nd edn. New York: McGraw-Hill.

Glaser, B.G. and Strauss, A.L. (1967) *The discovery of grounded theory.* Chicago: Aldane.

Index

abstract 21–22, 51, 116, 174
action research, cycle of, types of, 92, 97–103
adult learning 5, 22, 86, 154
Aggleton, Peter 88, 95
AI, ChatGPT 55
aims 9, 11–12, 15, 19
anonymity 49, 54, 83, 108
artefacts, using, creating 87, 153–155, 158
audio recording 131, 139, 156, 183
audit trail 175
authenticity 91, 149, 165, 167
autobiography 94
autoethnography 87, 92, 94–96
averages, measures of central tendency 43–44, 74, 143, 171

Ball, Stephen 24, 27, 88, 95, 135, 144
BERA (British Educational Research Association) 54, 57, 178–180, 185
bias 21, 23, 28, 32–35, 65–66, 73, 84–85, 93, 119, 121–122, 128, 141, 143, 148, 171, 173, 184, 194, 201
biographical research 104, 106, 109, 147
Bourdieu, Pierre 152, 167, 168

case studies, advantages of, design, disadvantages 25, 80–86, 150–151, 159, 168
category questions 119
causality 66, 119
'cherry-picking' 165
children, informed consent, participatory research 64, 99, 127, 128–129, 131, 134, 136, 142–143, 154, 181, 192, 197

chi-square test 37, 45, 171
closed question 117, 119
cluster sampling 30–31
coding 37–39, 74, 75, 108, 122, 140, 200
cohort surveys 3, 6, 31, 35, 36, 63
computer assisted data analysis *see* NVivo; SPSS
comparative, comparative research design 2, 5, 6, 10, 20, 62, 99, 200
concepts 4, 18, 19, 23, 25, 50, 52, 163–167, 172, 200, 201
conceptual names 39
conclusion, writing of 25, 50, 52, 54, 56, 169
confidentiality 54, 108, 121, 123, 131, 179, 180, 183–185, 193–194
confirmability 172, 173, 175, 176
consent, informed 52, 108, 121, 138, 142, 179, 181, 182, 184, 185, 193, 194
consent form 52, 121, 180, 184
contents page 51, 52
contrastive rhetoric 40, 41
convenience sampling 28, 32, 33
convergent mixed-methods design 72, 74, 75
covert research 135, 138, 142, 179, 185
creative research methods, using 153–159
credibility 21, 94, 169, 170, 172, 173
cross-sectional design 3, 62, 67, 114, 115

data analysis, anomalies, case studies, interviews, questionnaires 1, 4, 33, 37–43, 45–47, 49, 50, 52, 67, 72, 74, 75, 82, 83, 84, 93, 108, 109, 114, 116, 118–119, 122–124, 158–159, 171, 173, 174–175, 194, 198
databases 22, 25, 26, 55, 75, 88, 116

data collection, documents, ethnography, evaluating methods, interviews, involving children, observations, questionnaires 3, 4, 13, 70, 72, 73, 83, 90, 113, 119, 135–136, 184, 188, 195
deadlines 15, 52
decisions, justifying 29, 35, 76, 136, 137, 175, 178, 181
deductive 166
demographic data 2, 3, 28, 114, 119, 156, 176
dependability 172, 173, 175, 176
design, of questionnaires, of research 11–13, 64, 70, 75, 76, 84, 113–117, 120–123
desk-based research 145, 146
detachment from observations 139
diary research 49, 137, 138, 139, 140, 141, 156
disclosure 137, 180
discrete data 42
discussion, writing up 26, 50, 51, 74, 151, 184
documentary research, advantages of, disadvantages of, 145, 146, 147, 148, 151
documents 21, 83, 106, 145–149, 151, 200
drawing 153, 156, 157, 188

early years 2, 5, 128, 188
ecological validity 136, 143
educational research, defining 1–2, 4–5, 6, 9, 33, 49
educational research themes, social justice, curriculum, assessment and pedagogy, comparative education, educational selves and identities 9–11
empirical 25, 49, 50, 56, 77, 166
epistemology 133, 200
ethical approval 139, 142, 179, 184
ethical considerations, BERA ethical guidelines, in observations, researcher position, 142, 179, 194; *see also* anonymity; confidentiality
ethnography, 'going native', participant observation 142, 83, 84, 90, 91, 135, 137, 138, 141
evaluating methods 98, 105, 169, 171–172
event sampling 140
experimental design 6
explanatory sequential design 72–74, 76
exploratory sequential design 73, 75
external validity 171; *see also* validity
extremist talk 40, 41

familiarity 93, 95, 142
feasibility 15, 29, 48, 53, 114, 115, 153
feminist researchers 164, 106, 128
Fielding, Michael 189, 197
fieldwork diary 137, 138, 139, 141

focus group interviews 73, 81, 125, 132, 133
Foucault, Michel 145, 166, 168
frequency table 43

generalisability 23, 32, 85
grounded theory 37, 38, 39, 90, 126, 136, 200
group interview 73, 81, 125, 132, 133; *see also* focus group interview

Hargreaves, David 40, 47, 88, 96
harm to participants, ethical issues 179, 180, 184
Hawthorne effect 142
headings 51, 54
higher education 2, 5, 9, 20, 23, 71, 94, 170, 187
hypothesis 49, 90, 169, 171, 172

identities 5, 10, 101, 106, 164, 196
illegal activities 142, 179, 180
images, photographs, drawings, cartoons 90, 105, 153, 156–158, 188
independent variables 3
inductive 166
informed consent 52, 108, 121, 138, 142, 179, 181, 182, 185, 193, 194
'insider' status 89, 93, 101, 127, 136, 137, 143, 165, 194
internal validity 171; *see also* validity
interpretivist research 1, 5, 32, 37, 50, 169, 172, 173, 175, 176
interval data 42
interval sampling 140
interviews, semi-structured, structured, unstructured 34, 125–126, 170, 183
interview schedule, interview questions 130, 170, 176
interview technique 126, 130, 195
introduction, writing up 25, 49, 51

Journal of Mixed Methods Research 77
Journal of Mixed Methods Studies 77

keywords 21, 22
knowledge, types 12, 13, 18, 90, 93, 114, 128, 163, 165, 166, 178, 189, 194

Lewin, Kurt 97, 98, 103
library-based project 51
life history research 105, 106, 184
Likert scale questions 42, 63, 64, 118, 119, 123
literature review, accessing literature, critically engaging with, writing up, 18, 19, 20, 22, 23, 24, 25

location, interviews 133, 193
longitudinal design 3, 114, 115
longitudinal survey 62

Mac an Ghaill, Mairtin 88, 96, 35, 144
Manageability 13, 53, 146
Marx, Karl 88, 146, 151, 168
mean 43, 44
meanings 87, 89, 91, 93, 94, 104, 142, 158, 164, 165, 172
median 43, 44
memos 40, 147, 148, 157, 200
metaphors 40, 41, 155
methodology, writing up 9, 12, 13, 48, 50, 51, 201
Mirza, Heidi 88, 96, 135, 144
missing data 172
mixed-methods, opportunities, challenges, analysis 69, 77, 78
mode 43, 44
mosaic approach 154, 159, 181, 185, 188, 198
multiple-choice questions 118, 121, 123

narrative inquiry, defining 104, 105
National Student Survey 191
naturalistic observation 90, 138
Newly Qualified Teachers (NQTs) 32, 42, 117
nominal data 42
non-probability sampling 28, 32, 34, 35
non-response rate 66
non-verbal responses 139, 195
NVivo, qualitative data analysis software 38, 46

Oakley, Ann 126, 127, 128, 134, 173, 177
objectives and aims 9, 11–12, 19, 24, 49, 50, 51, 53, 56, 92, 188
objectivity 101, 126, 139, 148, 171
observations 90, 94, 99, 123, 135–144, 166, 175, 180, 188
observer effect 135, 142
ontology 133
oral history 105
ordinal data 42, 45, 46
overt observation 138

panel survey 62, 63
paradigms 1, 4, 6, 13, 50, 71, 164, 165
paraphrasing 55
participation, children, member-checking, vulnerable groups 142, 157, 181, 185, 186, 187, 190, 191, 196, 197, 200
participatory research 99, 100, 153, 154, 156, 159, 181, 189, 195

photography 153, 157, 158
pilot study 98
plagiarism 25, 54, 55, 56, 146
planning, research, writing-up 9, 13, 80, 98, 155, 163
policy documents 21, 148, 149, 150, 151
population, sampling 61, 67, 74, 76, 82, 114, 115, 172, 194
positionality 4, 95, 127, 174, 185, 201
positivist research 1, 4, 5, 32, 50, 91, 169, 171–175, 176
postal survey 65
power dynamics 125, 127, 128, 132, 133, 194
pragmatism 69, 71
privacy 54, 142, 143, 193
probability sampling 28, 30, 35
professional learning 5, 165
proposal, research 9, 10, 15, 16
psychology 5, 13
purposive sampling 32

qualitative data 37–38, 46, 70, 72, 73, 74, 83, 118, 138, 175
quantitative data 37, 42, 45, 46, 50, 69, 70, 72, 73, 74, 76, 138, 140
quasi-experimental design 3, 6
questionnaires, advantages of, data collection, difference to survey, disadvantages, layout of, question types, response rates 12, 52, 64, 66, 67, 113–124
quota sampling 30, 31, 33

random sampling 30
rapport 126, 128, 133, 194
rating scales 140, 141
ratio data 42
recording, audio, video 139, 183
reference list 20, 52, 55
reflexivity 23, 50, 90, 91, 173, 174, 184, 201
relationships, in ethnography, practitioners 91, 93, 102, 128, 173, 192
reliability 13, 23, 29, 33, 50, 67, 72, 91, 99, 141, 171–172, 173, 175, 176
repurpose, items as artefacts 155
response rates 61, 65, 66, 67
results, writing up 11, 12, 22, 30, 33, 42, 45, 50, 61, 62, 65, 66, 83, 119, 122, 169, 171, 172, 173
retrospective study 63, 66, 83, 105
review of literature 18, 19, 20, 22, 23, 24, 25; *see also* literature review
routine, writing advice 53

sampling, non-probability sampling, probability sampling 28–35, 76, 140, 193
sampling bias 33–34
scope, research 148, 194
secondary research 51
semi-structured interviews 70, 72, 74, 76, 125, 170
sensitive topics 31, 102, 116, 127, 132, 193, 194, 195, 196
significance, of study 2, 10, 12, 15, 35, 45, 62, 89, 102, 139, 155, 175
Skeggs, Beverley 88, 96
small-scale research 6, 23, 32, 98, 124, 132
'snowball' sampling 26, 32
social theory 152, 163–168
sociology 2, 5, 13, 20, 26, 27, 35, 88, 95, 96, 28, 152, 185, 202
SPSS 45, 46, 75
standard deviation 44, 45
statistical tests 46, 61, 62, 76, 122, 171
statistics, descriptive 37, 42, 43, 46, 74, 75, 200
Stenhouse, Lawrence 92, 96, 97, 103
stories, 'telling', 'big', 'small' 104–109
stratified sampling 30
structure, of project 25, 49, 50, 51
structured interviews 115, 122, 126
sub-headings 53, 54
surveys, definition, different approaches, structured interviews 61, 62, 63, 64, 65–68, 136
systematic sampling 30

tally charts 138, 140
targets, writing up 11, 12, 53
'thick description' 89
'third' research paradigm 71

timeline, in proposal 12, 15
title page 51
topic selection 2, 9, 10, 11, 13, 15, 18, 19, 25, 26, 32, 48, 49, 53, 55, 66, 83, 116, 128, 143, 147, 150, 163, 165, 167
transcription 131, 132
transferability 172, 173, 174
trend surveys 62
triangulation 13, 15, 173, 175, 190, 201–202
Turnitin 55

UNCRC (United Nations Convention on the Rights of the Child) 128, 134, 187, 197

validity, in interpretivist research, in positivist research 13, 23, 66, 67, 85, 91, 95, 99, 136, 143, 171–172, 173, 174, 175, 176, 190, 197, 202
variables, dependent, independent 3, 4, 42, 43, 45, 46, 74, 84, 171, 172, 202
variance 44–45, 75
video recording 137, 139, 157
visual research methods, defining 2, 153, 157, 158, 159
voice, of participants 132, 156, 172, 174, 187
vulnerable groups, research with 121, 181, 184, 186, 193, 194, 197

Willis, Paul 88, 96, 135, 144
writing plan 52
writing-up 38, 48, 52, 57, 196

young people, research 'with' 28, 186, 187, 189, 190, 191, 197

For Product Safety Concerns and Information please contact our EU
representative GPSR@taylorandfrancis.com
Taylor & Francis Verlag GmbH, Kaufingerstraße 24, 80331 München, Germany